PRAISE FOR *INNOVATION ON TAP*

"One of the most unique and useful books on entrepreneurship I've ever read. Eric deftly guides us through a journey with history's greatest entrepreneurs— their innovations, incredible obstacles, and the drama that fueled their historic impact. Every chapter and page offer modern entrepreneurs unique lessons and insights to succeed in their own ventures."

—CJ CORNELL, serial entrepreneur and author, *The Age of Metapreneurship* and *The Startup Brain Trust*

"Imagine the ability to eavesdrop on the banter of entrepreneurs across three centuries of American innovation as they chat at the bar, comparing notes of their successes and challenges. *Innovation on Tap* puts that opportunity at your fingertips with a well-researched, accessible, and fun read that makes these undervalued histories highly relevant to today's entrepreneurs and innovators."

—GREG GALER, Ph.D., Executive Director, Boston Preservation Alliance and former Curator, Industrial History Center, Stonehill College

"Schultz tells the sweeping story of American ingenuity over the centuries through the decisions and decisive actions of some of our greatest entrepreneurs. From razor blades to musicals, fiber bars to automobiles, national parks to cybersecurity, he skillfully blends history with an understanding of business and innovation to craft a must-read book."

—MATTHEW MOEN, Ph.D., President, Gettysburg Foundation and Distinguished Professor Emeritus, University of South Dakota

"In *Innovation on Tap* Eric Schultz paints an informative and inspiring panorama of the history of entrepreneurial achievement in America. The unique perspective provided in this book will be an invaluable guide forward for entrepreneurs and leaders of all kinds in navigating the busy intersection of entrepreneurship and innovation."

—DANIEL ISENBERG, former entrepreneur and professor at the Harvard Business School; author, *Worthless, Impossible and Stupid: How Contrarian Entrepreneurs Create and Capture Extraordinary Value*

"Eric Schultz—accomplished innovator turned penetrating historian—deftly links foundational moments in business history to today's challenges, while making legendary entrepreneurs feel as familiar as the folks at the corner bar. Open a cold one and enjoy these stories—you'll want to start applying them right away."

—JON KLEIN, former President, CNN/US

"By emphasizing sustainability as a theme of modern entrepreneurship, Eric Schultz has hit on one of the drivers of the global economy. From ensuring clean water and preserving public lands, to developing new renewable energy models and launching urban gardens, Eric tells powerful stories of entrepreneurs that will educate and inspire."

—JOHN MANDYCK, CEO, Urban Green Council; visiting scientist, T.H. Chan School of Public Health, Harvard University

"Eric Schultz is a talented CEO and entrepreneur who guided the growth and sale of Sensitech, an Ascent portfolio company. Whether you are a serial entrepreneur or just launching your first start-up, you will find important lessons and wisdom in the entertaining stories of innovation and community that Eric shares in *Innovation on Tap*."

—MATT FATES, General Partner, Ascent Venture Partners

"When Eric Schultz writes about the birth of jazz and *Hamilton*'s rise on Broadway, he reminds us that social and cultural innovation can transform the world every bit as much as the latest technological breakthrough."

—CRAIGIE ZILDJIAN, CEO, Avedis Zildjian Company, Cymbal makers since 1623

INNOVATION

on TAP

INNOVATION
on TAP

STORIES OF ENTREPRENEURSHIP

FROM THE COTTON GIN

TO BROADWAY'S *HAMILTON*

ERIC B. SCHULTZ

GREENLEAF
BOOK GROUP PRESS

Published by Greenleaf Book Group Press
Austin, Texas
www.gbgpress.com

Distributed by Greenleaf Book Group

For ordering information or special discounts for bulk purchases, please contact Greenleaf Book Group at PO Box 91869, Austin, TX 78709, 512.891.6100.

Design and composition by Greenleaf Book Group
Cover design by Greenleaf Book Group

Publisher's Cataloging-in-Publication data is available.

Print ISBN: 978-1-62634-663-5

eBook ISBN: 978-1-62634-664-2

Audiobook ISBN: 978-1-62634-699-4

Part of the Tree Neutral® program, which offsets the number of trees consumed in the production and printing of this book by taking proactive steps, such as planting trees in direct proportion to the number of trees used: www.treeneutral.com

TreeNeutral

Printed in the United States of America on acid-free paper

19 20 21 22 23 24   10 9 8 7 6 5 4 3 2 1

First Edition

To Steve Dodge (1945–2019)
Entrepreneur, Inspiration, Friend

CONTENTS

PART THREE—CONSUMERISM

PART FOUR—SUSTAINABILITY

PART FIVE—DIGITIZATION

IT ALL STARTED IN A BAR

It all started in a bar, like many good stories do. Or rather, a makeshift bar in the lobby of a venture capital firm in Boston, just as an after-work presentation by a group of start-up CEOs had concluded. Asked to profile their companies, these leaders stood before investors and peers and gave glowing accounts of their progress. Revenue growth would soon resemble a hockey stick. Product development was on schedule. The competition was a year behind. Prospects had never been rosier. Now, however, with the pressure off, standing in a circle and sipping drinks as the day wound down, their stories took on a different tone.

Several CEOs were racing the clock for new financing. One was threatened by a competitor who had appeared from nowhere three months earlier. Another had lost two of her star software developers to a rival, and a third feared he was about to lose his largest customer.

Around that time, I happened to be reading a biography of Eli Whitney (1765–1825), learning about some of the challenges he had faced launching a start-up two hundred years earlier to market his revolutionary cotton gin. Whitney had barely survived a shipwreck, smallpox, malaria, a devastating factory fire, the untimely death of his partner, the theft of his core technology, years of patent litigation, and a near nervous breakdown. Later, as he launched a second enterprise to manufacture muskets, he had weathered the embargo of 1807, the War of 1812, the Panic of 1819, and, throughout, a nation being fractured by slavery.

Wouldn't it be interesting, I thought, if Eli Whitney could have joined us at the bar that evening, just so we might all compare notes? And maybe we could have invited someone like Alfred Sloan (1875–1966), the fabled CEO of General Motors, who lived midway in time between Whitney and today's entrepreneurs. How had Sloan managed through World War I, the 1918 influenza pandemic, the Great Depression, and World War II? In what ways would entrepreneurs of different eras have framed the opportunities and obstacles encountered during their careers? Is there a consistent set of qualities that has contributed to entrepreneurial success in America? And most interesting of all, are these qualities still relevant to today's entrepreneurs?

To answer these questions, I began to assemble just such a virtual barroom conversation between the living and the dead. The idea was to survey America's entrepreneurs from the Revolution to the present, trying to determine if history might "rhyme" in a way that would be meaningful to modern entrepreneurs. As I accumulated these fascinating stories—some gathered from historical archives and some from interviews over coffee—I was able to assemble a framework of six interrelated and roughly chronological themes that helped to shape entrepreneurial activity throughout America's history. I was also able to identify a handful of strengths that seemed "uncommonly common" among successful entrepreneurs, regardless of their backgrounds, personalities, industries, or eras.

The fun part, then, was "introducing" these remarkable people to one another and watching what would happen as they met around our virtual bar. To be honest, I wasn't sure myself. What developed, however, was an evening full of surprises, more than a few rounds of beverages consumed, and above all, the telling of some of the most extraordinary stories of entrepreneurship the world has ever known.

Introduction

INNOVATION ON TAP

Atalented and colorful collection of entrepreneurs drifted into the bar that evening. From top hats and corsets to hoodies and yoga pants, the crowd quickly grew in size and diversity. People welcomed one another, filled their glasses, and settled in for a night of talking shop and storytelling.

Someone mentioned an outbreak of yellow fever that had stalled the growth of his business. Another lamented the disruption and loss experienced during the Panic of 1893. Several complained about patent disputes. "My first company barely survived the recession of 2008," one of the younger entrepreneurs said, taking a long draught of his beer. "I'm not sure how my current start-up would handle another downturn like that."

There was agreement around the room that innovation and competition were not for the faint of heart.

"True, economic panics are bad," a voice called out from across the tavern. Heads turned. The speaker, handsome and six feet tall, was all the more distinguished by his knee-length breeches and tailcoat. "But having your invention stolen is worse, and losing your only factory to fire a curse." The speaker, Eli Whitney, saw that he had caught the attention of his audience. "Then there was getting infected with smallpox," he added, "and malaria, and that time I barely survived a shipwreck." The entrepreneur paused momentarily, thinking just how "green" he always felt on the open seas. All eyes were on him. "Care to hear my story?" he asked.

There were nods as the room grew quiet with expectation. Fire, smallpox, shipwreck? If this first story lived up to its billing, it was going to be quite an evening.

* * *

If you could share a drink and stories with the most fascinating entrepreneurs in American history, who would you invite to your table? Eli Whitney would undoubtedly be welcome, and Alfred Sloan, too. Both were extraordinary entrepreneurs and among the most famous Americans of their time. But fame would not be the only criterion, and perhaps not an important factor at all. Guests might include other, less familiar individuals whose impact was more limited but whose success helped to solve a particular problem of their time or demonstrated a key aspect of entrepreneurship.

In fact, we might call on a bouncer to help narrow the huge field of successful entrepreneurs from American history, someone to check IDs at the door. He or she would need a discriminating eye and a clear definition to reliably spot a genuine entrepreneur. Given these requirements, one unusually capable person comes to mind.

In 1911, the Austrian economist Joseph Schumpeter (1883–1950) presented a revolutionary work in which he defined an entrepreneur as someone who brings to market a new combination that disrupts an economic flow. These "new combinations" are what we today call innovations, and Schumpeter said they might be a new product, process, or method of production; the development of a new market or source of supply; or a new form of organization. Whatever their shape, innovations could generate a "perennial gale of creative destruction" in which new products and processes replace old ones.

If we accept this definition, then the only measure of entrepreneurship—and the only way to get through our barroom door—is by delivering an innovation that disrupts an economic flow. And the fundamental sign of entrepreneurial success is the creation of new customers, an act that revitalizes the engine of capitalism. Just when a product's growth begins to slow or a market becomes saturated, an entrepreneur can combine two or more ideas into something never before available and unleash a new wave of customer demand. These waves can form repeatedly and endlessly. "Capitalism's belief in perpetual economic growth," the anthropologist Yuval Noah Harari writes, "flies in the face of almost everything we know about the universe." Yet, thanks to this profound insight from Schumpeter, the growth of a capitalist economy need never stop, so long as entrepreneurs keep it continuously fueled.

Schumpeter's definition is especially helpful in separating entrepreneurship from the act of starting a business, which often says nothing about innovation. There have been countless enterprising individuals in America, from blacksmiths to dry cleaners to app makers, who have launched businesses designed to steal existing market share, perhaps through lower prices or more aggressive marketing, but failed to deliver any new combination. To paraphrase a famous Schumpeter quote, "Launch as many new taxi companies as you want, but you will never create an Uber."

When we study entrepreneurs through the lens of their economic impact, our barroom conversation expands to include all sorts of interesting characters who don't otherwise conform to the image of the fearless, dashing figure that dominates business narratives. Some of the entrepreneurs profiled in this book are accidental, for example; they were going about the business of making a living when they stumbled upon a new combination. Others are reluctant or unsure, requiring encouragement to engage in "creative destruction." Some are rich, some poor; some honest and some not so much; some well-educated and others unschooled. As long as their innovation disrupts an economic flow and creates new demand, they are welcome to join the conversation at the bar.

THE SIX THEMES OF
ENTREPRENEURSHIP IN AMERICA

The stories that will unfold over the course of the evening reveal five distinct themes that intersect and build upon one another over time, and a sixth that runs alongside and throughout. The oldest of these themes is *mechanization*, the ability to automate processes that had been performed traditionally by hand. Next in time came *mass production*, a system of manufacture that enabled factories to produce thousands of the same item quickly and efficiently. *Consumerism* emerged in the early twentieth century to focus America's business leaders away from *what* they were making to *whom* they were making it for. *Sustainability*, the concept of maintaining ecological balance, became a pressing concern in a twentieth-century culture where overconsumption and fossil fuels threatened the environment. *Digitization* also arose at mid-century, allowing for the capture and exchange of information in ways that improved the production of physical goods and created new virtual products and services. Running side by side with these five dominant themes, *social and cultural entrepreneurship* has inspired new business models designed to reshape our concept of community and the ways in which Americans live and work together.

 MECHANIZATION

Mechanization gained momentum in the late eighteenth century and became a defining feature of America's Industrial Revolution. The nation's craftsmen became so good at producing uniform parts on specialized machinery—the underlying magic of mechanization—that the process became known globally as the "American System of Manufacturing."

The ability to work with cams, pistons, ratchets, and escapements in 1800 was much like the ability today to write software, providing an ambitious young man of the nineteenth century an opportunity for wealth and fame. "There is not a working boy of average ability in the New England States," politician John K. Kane told the Franklin Institute in Philadelphia, "who has not an idea of some mechanical invention or improvement . . ., by which, in good time, he hopes to better his position, or rise to fortune and social distinction." The language of mechanization, like today's common programming languages, provided a *lingua franca* by which America's mechanics could communicate and collaborate across industries.

Two entrepreneurs in our virtual barroom epitomize the theme of mechanization. Eli Whitney, famous as the inventor of the cotton gin and later as a manufacturer of muskets, was known for more than a century after his death as the "father of interchangeable parts." He became expert at leveraging his personal network, weathered hard lessons along the way about how to match innovation to a profitable business model, and emerged as one of America's first successful serial entrepreneurs. Whitney's contemporary, Oliver Ames (1779–1863), rode America's "transportation revolution" in turnpikes, canals, and railroads to develop a business that would one day produce two-thirds of the world's shovels. Ames might have become a prosperous village smithy like his father, but thanks to a formative experience in the renowned Springfield Armory working alongside some of the country's finest craftsmen, he founded instead a mechanized business that achieved success on a global scale.

 MASS PRODUCTION

Mechanization spread throughout the nineteenth century, prompting household-based activities such as textile manufacture to migrate to factories. With the adoption of coal and steam, the telegraph, and the railroad, America's factory system expanded in the 1840s and 1850s, and even more dramatically after the Civil War. As the population grew and the American frontier spread westward, farms, towns, and cities became interconnected in a national transportation and communications network that formed the world's first extensive mass market. By 1900, seventy-six million Americans occupied forty-five states and territories, the country stretching from sea to shining sea. This vast nation, the third most populous in the world, was stitched together by two hundred thousand miles of railroad, two hundred thousand miles of telegraph, and more than a million miles of telephone wires. To supply America's growing demand, managers leveraged their skills in mechanization to create goods using mass production, the second important theme in America's entrepreneurial history.

"Increases in the speed of output," writes business historian Alfred D. Chandler Jr. about this period in the nation's development, "were spectacular." A skilled American clock maker might have been able to produce four wooden clock movements a year in 1800, and some 1,500 annually by 1820 in a small, mechanized factory. By the Civil War, however, a single factory, replacing wooden components with brass, could mass-produce 130,000 clocks per year. Likewise, a cigarette-making machine patented in 1881 could produce more than seventy thousand cigarettes every ten hours compared to three thousand per day for a highly skilled worker. Photographic negatives, soap, candy and foodstuffs, shoes, clothing, wooden products, musical instruments, wagons, and rubber goods came to be mass-produced in enormous quantities.

Boxing and canning also became automated so that laborers might load raw material into one end of a factory and not touch it again until a finished product was ready for transport at the other end. Mass production also touched America's service industries, requiring them to organize people and processes to rapidly scale services for an expanding national audience.

The barroom entrepreneurs who exemplify this embrace of mass production and scale include King Camp Gillette (1855–1932), a traveling salesman for Crown Cork & Seal, a company that specialized in disposable bottle stoppers. "Why don't you try to think of something like the Crown cork, which, when once used, is thrown away, and the customer keeps coming back for more," the firm's president, William Painter, once challenged Gillette. In response, the entrepreneur founded a company designed to mass-produce razor blades from thin sheet steel, resulting in a game-changing business model.

Seated nearby in this virtual barroom is Mary Elizabeth Evans (1884–1985), who adopted mechanization in her home-based candy company and scaled it into a national brand so successful that competitors believed she was fronting a giant business "trust." Also present is African-American entrepreneur John Merrick (1859–1919), who built a personal network across racial lines, enabling him to launch and scale insurance products for a large, vulnerable, and underserved segment of the American population.

Another critical figure in the adoption of mass production was Willis Carrier (1876–1950), the force behind the development of modern air-conditioning. As industry after industry sought to leverage mechanization into high-speed mass production, managers required a standardized environment to produce standardized goods. It was impossible, for example, to consistently print magazines, bake bread, weave cloth, build furniture, or mold ceramics if the temperature and humidity in an automated factory fluctuated from hour to hour. Carrier's air-conditioning company, built on the strength of his personal network and grown through an innovative business model that sold results, not hardware, became a pervasive innovation in a nation committed to high-speed, standardized manufacture. And, once managers and workers came to enjoy the benefits of working in air-conditioned factories and offices, they began to seek "comfort air" in department stores, movie theaters, and their own homes. Carrier and his cofounders were happy to oblige, adapting their product and business model for an emerging consumer world.

CONSUMERISM

As America became expert at mass production, business leaders faced an entirely new problem. The dilemma of the nineteenth century had been how to create enough goods and services to meet a growing population. The crisis at the turn of the twentieth century became how to keep giant, automated factories from oversaturating their market with goods. The solution to this problem defines the third entrepreneurial theme, consumerism, a fundamental change in America from a land of sober and frugal *citizens* defined by what they *produced*, to a land of ravenous *consumers* defined by what they *purchased*.

This transition began in the closing decades of the nineteenth century and was solidly in place by the 1920s. The journalist Samuel Strauss captured this cultural revolution in an influential 1924 article, saying that "the problem before us today is not how to produce the goods, but how to produce the customers." Entrepreneurs in America who had become expert at mechanization and mass-producing goods and services now had to become expert at mass-producing demand.

Three of our "barroom" entrepreneurs tell the story of the nation's consumer revolution. Elizabeth Arden (1884–1966), a Canadian immigrant who moved to New York City in 1908, built a billion-dollar empire that redefined beauty for American women in such a fundamental way that she was described as a "sociological and historical" phenomenon. Joseph Knowles Milliken (1875–1961) was interested in a different kind of beauty when he founded the country's largest textile bleaching factory under one roof. Milliken's successful business model involved the creation of new technologies, new consumer fashions, and a storybook worker's village that provided fifty years of employee goodwill before his workforce revolted under stifling paternalism.

The giant of American consumerism is Alfred Sloan, credited with being a marketing genius so effective that Schumpeter considered General Motors' innovations to be as significant to consumption as Ford's assembly line had been in production. A GM executive believed Sloan's leadership had turned the question "Can I afford an automobile?" into "Can I afford to be without an automobile?" By 1929, Sloan had integrated mechanization, mass production, and consumerism into a company that nearly bankrupted Henry Ford. When Sloan retired as chairman in 1956, GM had 52 percent of the US market and was one of the world's most profitable, admired, and best-run companies, its annual revenues surpassing the GNP of half the world's countries.

SUSTAINABILITY

The fourth entrepreneurial theme emerging from the stories of our barroom crowd is *sustainability*, the application of entrepreneurial tools to launch innovations that maintain ecological balance and help shift from carbon-intensive industries to renewable ones. By the 1930s, economists had begun building models that emphasized nonrenewable resource management, and in 1935 a British scientist coined the term "ecosystem" to express the important relationship between living creatures and their environment.

For many Americans, however, the moment of awakening came in 1962 with the publishing of Rachel Carson's book *Silent Spring*, which described the environmental damage resulting from pesticides. Others remember the creation of the Clean Air Act in 1963 and the first Earth Day, in 1970. For some, sustainability first became visible in Spokane, Washington, when Expo '74 was staged; this smaller, "pocket" world's fair was the first in America to focus on the environment, with its mission "to stimulate greater understanding of our environmental problems and their solutions." Maurice Strong, executive director of the United Nations Environment Programme, spoke at the fair on United Nations Earth Day, saying, "For the first time in history, man has the potential to usher in a new golden era for all of his species—or the potential to bring the human experiment to a miserable end."

Modern entrepreneurs face a world of global warming and regular warnings of a "miserable end" while working to build business models that create sustainable growth. For example, Kate Cincotta (b. 1984) runs a US–based nonprofit that provides clean water and solar power for villages in Ghana while exporting a model for creating new female entrepreneurs. Emily Rochon (b. 1979) is an environmental advocate who helps to pave the way for sustainable business models focused on renewable energy. Viraj Puri (b. 1981) is the CEO of Gotham Greens, a pioneer in the urban agriculture movement. And the story of Stephen Tyng Mather (1867–1930), the founder of America's National Park Service, is one of national transformation that spans two centuries. Mather viewed natural resources as something to be protected and preserved for future generations, not exploited for profit—work that goes on every day in the country's national parks and remains a beacon to today's sustainability entrepreneurs.

DIGITIZATION

By the mid-1950s, America's fifth entrepreneurial theme, *digitization*, had begun to subtly shape the world. Defined as the conversion of text and other analog signals into a digital format that can be understood by computers and electronic devices, digitization became a headline in 1954 when General Electric installed the first business computer to process payroll and control manufacturing programs. In 1960, American Airlines digitized its flight reservation system, and later that decade US libraries began using Machine-Readable Cataloging records.

In 1976, the digital revolution leapt from business to home when Steve Jobs and Steve Wozniak incorporated Apple Computer. Four years later, Apple and its competitors had sold 724,000 personal computers, and in 1982, *Time* magazine named the PC its "Person of the Year." Today, digitization is pervasive, with global commerce dependent on digital information, nearly 80 percent of Americans owning a smartphone, and more than twenty billion items of all kinds connected to the Web.

The entrepreneurs in our virtual barroom who are focused on digitization reflect a rich set of experiences. Brenna Berman (b. 1976), former chief information officer for the City of Chicago, uses analytics to drive innovation and improve service delivery in a large urban setting. Jean Brownhill (b. 1977), the CEO of Sweeten, has networked skillfully to form a company that offers a trusted Web community in a residential- and commercial-renovation industry traditionally filled with distrust. Brent Grinna (b. 1981), the CEO of EverTrue, volunteered to help his alma mater solicit alumni donations and discovered an industry ripe for disruption. Much like Whitney two centuries earlier, Grinna has leveraged his college network at critical moments to create a successful fund-raising automation platform.

Jason Jacobs (b. 1976) turned his passion for running into one of the iPhone's earliest apps, Runkeeper, forming a booming online community. Guy Filippelli (b. 1975) adapted machine learning tools designed to reduce casualties on the battlefield to create new business models that mitigate risk in the corporate world. And Meghan Winegrad's (b. 1978) experience as an "intrapreneur" emphasizes the power of community within large companies to inspire entrepreneurial thinking, spark digital innovation, and serve as a springboard to more traditional start-up initiatives.

SOCIAL AND CULTURAL ENTREPRENEURSHIP

Those five themes—mechanization, mass production, consumerism, sustainability, and digitization—have driven the dominant entrepreneurial narrative over three centuries in America. But there is an important missing piece to this story of national innovation, and not to include it would do a disservice to our barroom conversation. *Social and cultural entrepreneurship* has had a staggering impact on the country, running alongside and touching upon the other five themes. Here, we find stories that illustrate disruptive business models focused on social change, often representing opportunities for individuals who have been excluded from the pursuit of mainstream entrepreneurial activities. Social and cultural entrepreneurship is a reminder that the opportunity in America to bring "new combinations" to market is pervasive and unbounded.

In the earliest period, when Eli Whitney was developing the art of mechanization, African-American entrepreneur Thomas Downing (1791–1866) founded an oyster restaurant in New York City that gained special status as "the only oyster house to attract the aristocracy as well as ladies in the company of their husbands or chaperones." Downing used his profits and fame to support the abolitionist movement, the cellar of his establishment becoming a safe haven for escaped slaves along the Underground Railroad. One such escaped slave, William Grimes (1784–1865), worked courageously to build a career in the North. Grimes published his life story in 1825, a tribute to his persistence but a lesson in how difficult entrepreneurial success can be without a welcoming and supportive community. A third entrepreneur of color in the early republic, James Forten (1766–1842), relied on assistance from the local Quaker community, employed a mixed-race workforce in his sail-making business, and became a leading spokesperson for African-American rights and one of the richest businessmen in Philadelphia.

Nearly a century later, as entrepreneurs developed mass production and began addressing the consumer revolution, Buddy Bolden (1877–1931) had a short but brilliant career, buoyed by a vibrant New Orleans music community and his own unmatched creativity, to help create American jazz. A half-century after Bolden, as American consumers assembled in huge parks to enjoy another iconic American creation, Wesley Branch Rickey (1881–1965) and a courageous Jackie Robinson (1919–1972) changed the face of baseball and, in the process, the face of America.

The final social and cultural entrepreneur in our virtual barroom is Lin-Manuel Miranda (b. 1980), whose creation of *Hamilton* provides a living example of how entrepreneurs leverage community to amplify their own talents and create brilliant innovations—not to mention some unforgettable music.

THREE ENTREPRENEURIAL LESSONS

Twenty-five entrepreneurs, three centuries, six major themes. From the cotton gin to *Hamilton*, entrepreneurs have adapted and prospered. Each of the stories told around our virtual barroom is different, shaped by time and circumstance. But taken together, these narratives offer three compelling lessons for modern entrepreneurs.

NURTURE AND LEVERAGE COMMUNITY

The one quality that successful entrepreneurs in America have shared over three centuries is the ability to access, nurture, and leverage community. No entrepreneur has all the tools necessary for success. Few entrepreneurs avoid a period in their careers when they are overwhelmed or a moment when they feel defeated. None of our barroom entrepreneurs was successful without the collaboration of friends, partners, and the wider community. Winners are those who become skillful at situating themselves in a supportive network. Education, intelligence, courage, grit—all are secondary factors. The entrepreneurial experience in America, no matter the period, is built on this cornerstone: The stronger the community, the greater the chances for success. From Eli Whitney to Mary Elizabeth Evans to Lin-Manuel Miranda, a strong personal network is the most striking attribute and powerful resource of a successful entrepreneur.

FOCUS FIRST ON A PROFITABLE, SCALABLE BUSINESS MODEL

There is no substitute for a profitable, scalable business model. Before entrepreneurs can worry about leadership, team building, technology deployment, or customer growth, they need to get the business model right and reassess it continually. A blockbuster innovation matched with a flawed business model results in frustration and failure; entrepreneurial grit powering a defective business model can drive a company into the ground.

A supportive network and a winning business model have absolved countless entrepreneurs of their sins and weaknesses, helping to explain why successful individuals often do not meet the brilliant, courageous, committed, and extroverted stereotype.

THINK BROADLY: ENTREPRENEURSHIP IS PERVASIVE AND UNBOUNDED

While the five dominant themes of mechanization, mass production, consumerism, sustainability, and digitization have driven entrepreneurship in America over the past three centuries, brilliant social and cultural entrepreneurship outside of these themes is a constant. No aspiring entrepreneur in America should be discouraged if he doesn't "look like" one of the day's heroic successes or if his interests differ from that moment's dominant narrative. There were successful entrepreneurs in 1800 who had no mechanical skills and successful entrepreneurs today who cannot write software code. America is a nation of entrepreneurs because it is filled with talented individuals who excel at innovating *along* the major themes, as well as those who excel at innovating *around* the major themes.

* * *

The formation of a sophisticated entrepreneurial ecosystem that supports both traditional and social entrepreneurship, community building, and the design of successful business models has emerged in America as a national competitive advantage. Beginning after World War II and accelerating at the turn of the twenty-first century, a great virtual network has been constructed in the form of incubators, accelerators, innovation labs, meet-ups, business-plan contests, microlending, angel investment, venture capital, private equity, and investment banking.

The government has contributed in countless ways, including the Defense Advanced Research Projects Agency, the Small Business Innovation Research program, the Orphan Drug Act, the National Nanotechnology Initiative, technology licensing, and trickle-down R&D from government agencies such as NASA. This ecosystem is a supercharged national community, capable today of taking the raw materials of people, ideas, and capital, and producing entrepreneurial success.

In short, despite the problems faced by the CEOs in that makeshift Boston bar, there has never been a better time to be an entrepreneur in America. The stories "on tap" in our virtual barroom will illustrate, reinforce, and celebrate this conclusion.

BACK AT THE BAR

Whitney looked out across his attentive audience and could suddenly see the faces of the many juries he had faced trying to defend the patent rights to the cotton gin. He shuddered, hoping nobody noticed. But that part of his story was jumping ahead, and it had all turned out well. If he wanted his audience to understand his career, he'd have to begin at the beginning.

He took a sip of ale, cleared his throat, and thought back to that farm of long ago when he'd first discovered the power—and magic—of mechanization.

Part One

MECHANIZATION

Chapter 1

ELI WHITNEY: ACCIDENTAL ENTREPRENEUR

Born in December 1765 on a farm thirty miles west of Boston, Eli Whitney demonstrated early signs of mechanical genius. At twelve years old he fashioned a violin that made "tolerably good music" and was, many said, "a remarkable piece of work for such a boy to perform." Later, Whitney dismantled and reassembled his father's watch, the most sophisticated piece of machinery on an eighteenth-century American farm. As a teenager, he designed machines in his father's workshop that mechanized the manufacture of nails, stickpins, and walking canes.

While Whitney was unsure what he wanted to do with his life, he was certain he wanted to escape the drudgery of family farming. With funds provided by his father, he entered Yale University in 1789 to secure a "liberal education" of Latin and Greek, ancient history, geometry, ethics, and rhetoric. Friends were perplexed by the decision, one admirer informing Whitney that "there was one good mechanic spoiled when you went to college." Indeed, it's likely that nothing Whitney learned at Yale enhanced his innate mechanical skills. However, it is also likely that had he not attended Yale, he would have failed as an entrepreneur and been lost to history. Despite his mechanical genius, it would be the support of the greater Yale community at critical moments in his career that enabled Whitney to succeed.

Graduating in 1792, Eli accepted a tutoring position on a plantation in South Carolina, providing a way to repay the tuition advanced by his father and plot his career. He was grateful for the job but distressed by the location, which—compared to New England—featured a humid, subtropical climate. "In four days I shall set out for South Carolina," he wrote to his brother. "The climate is unhealthy and perhaps I shall lose my health *and perhaps my life.*"

This fear was well founded. Whitney and his contemporaries lived at a time when medicine was powerless against regular outbreaks of tuberculosis, typhoid, scarlet fever, yellow fever, and diphtheria. While attending Yale, Whitney himself nearly died of some unspecified disease—what his sister called "Hypo." In 1792 he contracted smallpox, and in 1794 malaria, a sickness whose fever and chills would visit him periodically throughout his career. It's possible that Whitney lost months and perhaps years of productivity due to personal illness and the ravages of disease on his workforce, an element of "business risk" with which all entrepreneurs in America's early republic had to contend.

THE YALE TUTOR MEETS COTTON

Whitney had been recommended for his tutoring position by fellow Yale alumnus Phineas Miller (1764–1803), the first act in a partnership essential to Whitney's success. Miller had been hired to tutor the children of General Nathanael Greene (1742–1786) at the general's Mulberry Grove plantation, situated along the Savannah River. When Greene died suddenly, Miller became manager of the plantation on behalf of the general's widow, Catharine (1755–1814). Catharine and Phineas eventually married, their union bringing sound management and profitability to Mulberry Grove.

Whitney set out for Savannah, sailing from New Haven and barely escaping disaster when his ship slammed into rocks off Manhattan. Stepping ashore in New York City, he encountered a friend on the street, shook hands, and contracted a case of smallpox, adding two weeks of convalescence to his journey. Whitney then spent six miserable, seasick days sailing to Savannah before arriving at Greene's Mulberry Grove, just across the river from his new job. That's when he was informed that the wages for his tutoring engagement had been halved, making the position untenable. Catharine extended her home and hospitality to Whitney while he regrouped. In turn, he made himself useful through odd jobs, including the redesign of a tambour embroidery frame that Catharine had found difficult to use. This inconsequential act would soon have historic implications.

When friends of the late general stopped by the plantation to pay their respects to Catharine, the group's discussion turned to agriculture. One of the visitors expressed regret that the South lacked a reliable cash crop. Cotton seemed promising, but nobody had been able to design a mechanized cotton engine, or "gin," that could efficiently separate the sticky green seed from the white cotton boll. A series of textile inventions in Great Britain, including the flying shuttle (1733), the spinning jenny (1764), and the spinning mule (1779), had powered spectacular global growth in the textile industry. The visitors to Mulberry Grove agreed that the market for cotton was insatiable but impractical for American farmers to supply in quantity without substantial improvements to the speed with which raw cotton could be processed.

There had been some limited success. Planters along Georgia's coast had been able to grow Sea Island cotton, a *long-staple* variety whose fiber was up to 2½ inches in length. Long-staple varieties such as Sea Island were prized by the British textile industry. The cotton's shiny black seeds could be easily separated from the boll by a roller gin, a device that forcibly squeezed the seeds from the fiber, preserving its long staple for spinning. A roller gin could remove seeds from long-staple cotton about five times faster than by hand.

Unfortunately for Southern planters, Sea Island cotton required sandy soil and protection from upland insects. A crop some had hoped would revitalize the Southern economy turned out to be profitable for a few well-situated planters but a dead end for most others.

On the other hand, short-staple cotton had been grown ornamentally in the South for years, but traditional textile mills spurned its shorter, ¾-to 1½-inch fibers, making it appropriate only for the coarse, handwoven cloth known as homespun. Short-staple cotton was also cursed for its fuzzy green seeds, which, as the guests at Mulberry Grove knew, adhered to the lint so tenaciously that traditional roller gins proved ineffective. Common wisdom held that separating a single pound of clean staple was an entire day's work for a single person.

What short-staple cotton lacked in manufacturing appeal, however, it more than made up for in hardiness. It flourished almost anywhere with fertile soil and a two-hundred-day growing season. In the United States, those requirements were met by a colossal swath of rich land that stretched from Virginia to eastern Texas.

American mechanics had been unable to solve the ginning problem of short-staple cotton. "The colonial records are filled with claims that a successful gin had at last been 'invented,'" historian Carroll Pursell writes, "but no one made the claim stick." The state of Georgia had gone so far as to appoint its own commission to address the issue. With few good crop options available, some Southern farmers began to plant short-staple cotton in the 1790s, hoping a process would be developed to make it salable in quantity. In 1792, two to three million pounds had been picked "but for the want of a suitable Gin but a small part of it had been prepared for Market." Raising a crop destined to rot in the field or warehouse was an act of agricultural desperation.

In the midst of this worried conversation, Catharine Greene introduced the group to Eli Whitney, telling the story of her new tambour frame. Whitney denied any claim of mechanical genius and further admitted that he had never seen cotton or a cotton seed in his life. However, he also sensed opportunity, soon writing to his father about "a number of very respectable Gentlemen at Mrs. Greene's who all agreed that if a machine could be invented which would clean the Cotton with expedition, it would be a great thing both to the Country and to the inventor." No such machine existed in September 1792, a fact important to the defense of Whitney's future patent claim. Otherwise, these well-connected, well-traveled gentlemen planters would have been in hot pursuit. Even the *rumor* of a solution would have set the countryside in a frenzy. What Whitney found before him, suddenly and unexpectedly, was a problem that had stumped a nation, in a region facing economic collapse for lack of a profitable crop.

A FLASH OF GENIUS?

Just days after his conversation with Greene's guests, Whitney wrote his father to say that he had struck upon the idea for a machine to clean short-staple cotton. This revelation comes as close to a "flash of genius" as exists in the annals of invention. Within a few weeks of his arrival at Mulberry Grove, Whitney had designed a cotton gin prototype that could clean ten times as much cotton as a single person working by hand. Sensing great opportunity, Miller and Greene agreed to underwrite further development of the gin.

The heart of Whitney's new machine was a cylinder studded with rows of stiff iron wire. When the cylinder was turned by hand, horse, or water power, the wire teeth grabbed the cotton fiber and forced it through an iron breastwork (a grille so tightly spaced that green cotton seeds were unable to pass through), literally tearing the fiber from the seed, which then fell into its own compartment for removal. A set of spinning brushes would then sweep the cotton off the iron teeth and into a hopper. Once in motion, a clattering cotton gin tossed clean, seedless cotton into its hopper like exploding popcorn.

Though more complex than the traditional roller gin, Whitney's device could be duplicated from memory by a talented mechanic. Whitney and Miller recognized this weakness and, from the start, sought to keep prying eyes from viewing the inner workings of their invention.

Contemporaries wrestled with the question of how Whitney could instantly solve a problem that had puzzled others for decades. Some modern historians remain incredulous. Charles Morris concluded, for example, that "it is hardly credible that Whitney, with no experience in the cotton industry, more or less immediately conceived such a complex solution upon a chance overhearing of a conversation." Is there some way, then, to plausibly explain the nature of Whitney's "flash of genius"?

Invention often involves the ability to apply models across industries. Samuel Colt (1814–1862) conceived his idea for the revolver aboard a sailing ship when he observed how the spokes of the ship's wheel aligned with its clutch. Henry Ford's moving assembly line was inspired in part by the visit of one of his managers to a Chicago meatpacker's line created for *dis*assembling animal carcasses. Perhaps Whitney had been exposed to some device that would lead to his design of the cotton gin?

There is one tantalizing clue. In 1852, Judge Garrett Andrews (1798–1873) of Washington, Georgia, published a letter in the *Southern Cultivator* reporting on a conversation with his friend, eighty-three-year-old Thomas Talbot. Talbot had lived on the plantation adjoining Mulberry Grove in 1792, the year of Whitney's arrival. He remembered Whitney and Miller's first ginning house, which was "gated, so that visitors might look through and see the cotton flying from, without seeing the gin." Talbot also offered a fascinating observation, saying that Whitney had conceived the idea for his invention "from a gin used to prepare rags for making paper, . . . which he saw on a wrecked vessel."

A wrecked vessel? Whitney had survived a shipwreck off Manhattan. A gin used to prepare rags for paper? Could there have been such a machine on board Whitney's ship from New Haven, perhaps being shipped to a paper mill in New York? And what exactly would this machine have been?

In 1792, paper was manufactured by hand except for a single automated device introduced by the Dutch around 1750. The Hollander beater was an oblong tub used for washing rag scraps, tearing apart the fibers, and reducing them to a pulp. Power was applied to a beater roll, which turned and pulled the rags through a grate, slicing them into smaller scraps. The Hollander was a marvel of mechanization, producing pulp about eight times faster than by traditional hand methods.

The similarities of the inner workings of the Hollander and Whitney's cotton gin are striking. Is it possible that Whitney's "flash of genius" was based on the application of an existing mechanical concept, which he examined by chance aboard a ship heading from New Haven to New York? Whitney's "flash of genius" may also have been inspired by one other advantage: a total ignorance of the needs of the textile industry. Only a Yale-trained farm boy from New England with a Dutch paper-making apparatus as his model would have designed a gin that violently tore cotton from the seeds rather than attempting to gently remove the seeds. The resulting product was sure to be inferior to long-staple cotton.

And it was, but it turned out to make little difference. The speed and efficiency of Whitney's new cotton gin, along with the dire economic straits of Southern agriculture, forced the textile industry to adapt. End users traded unlimited quantity for inferior quality and adjusted their practices accordingly.

Today, open sourcing of research and development is common. Inside experts bring deep knowledge but their own set of biases, sometimes being too quick to see why something should not be done. In one study of open-sourced R&D, 30 percent of cases that could not be solved by an experienced corporate research staff were solved by nonemployees. In another modern open-source environment, observers found that "'ninety to ninety-five percent of the time, the individual who comes up with the awarded solution does not have the background and résumé' of someone you would hire to solve the problem." Eli Whitney was apparently just such a case.

AN ACCIDENTAL ENTREPRENEUR

At twenty-six years old, Eli Whitney was the astonished inventor of the cotton gin. "'Tis generally said by those who know anything about it," Whitney wrote his father, "that I shall make a Fortune by it." After searching for direction and purpose, Whitney had stumbled into a future that satisfied him on all counts: a brilliant innovation, potential wealth, and possibly fame. He had become an accidental entrepreneur.

Unplanned, unintended, unexpected—this new opportunity was

suddenly the compelling force in Whitney's life. He confided to a friend that "I hear of wars and rumors of wars; but very little of the news of the Day. I have not seen a News Paper these three months." The challenge before him was to move from surprised inventor to focused entrepreneur by mechanizing manufacture of the gin and choosing a business model that matched the brilliance of his invention.

Events moved quickly. In May 1793, Miller and Whitney formed their partnership. Whitney's role was to patent and build the gins while Miller secured financing and marketed the business. In June 1794 the two signed a document sharing half interest in the patent, with profits to be split.

Throughout this period and until his untimely death from fever at age thirty-nine in December 1803—just the terrible fate Whitney had feared for himself—Phineas Miller exerted a steadying influence on his younger friend. Miller brought to the partnership not just capital, but also confidence, energy, resourcefulness, loyalty, and optimism. As the most important player in Whitney's professional network, he propped up the inventor through periods of despair while continually promoting their cotton gin business. There could have been few better partners or friends, and it is difficult to envision Whitney having anything like the success and acclaim he eventually enjoyed without this support early in his career.

Whitney's patent was enthusiastically received in March 1794 by the recently retired secretary of state, Thomas Jefferson, endorsed by his successor, Edmund Randolph, and ultimately issued by President George Washington. With three members of the Constitutional Convention in his corner—the very men who had introduced the intellectual property clause of the Constitution—Whitney seemed to have the protection he required to support his new ginning machine. The happy inventor wrote his father, "I had the satisfaction to hear it declared by a number of the first men in America that my machine is the most perfect & the most valuable invention that has ever appeared in this Country."

While visiting Philadelphia that year, Whitney was also introduced to Oliver Wolcott Jr. (1760–1833), comptroller (and soon to be secretary) of the Treasury Department—and yet another Yale alumnus. Wolcott would prove, like Miller, to be an indispensable member of the community that would ensure Whitney's ultimate success.

Eli Whitney was triumphant and ready to conquer the world. Ironically, however, the young entrepreneur had just latched on to the most contentious and costly issue of his career. His patent submission, promising a "new and useful improvement in the mode of spinning cotton," would not only be Eli Whitney's first and most famous patent, it would also be his last and most bitter.

TOO MANY WORTHLESS PATENTS

Like many hopeful entrepreneurs, the Founding Fathers were sometimes long on vision but short on implementation. They recognized in Article I of the Constitution that patents could "promote the Progress of Science and useful Arts, by securing for limited Times to Authors and Inventors the exclusive Right to their respective Writings and Discoveries." The willingness to extend this benefit to anyone—rich or poor, male or female, black or white—was itself an innovation, the world's first modern patent system. It reflected a forward-looking nation of abundant natural resources and educated citizens.

The patent process was inexpensive, another important difference from a British system that featured high costs and favored the elite. The Founding Fathers believed, if inventors were rewarded for risk-taking with a fourteen-year monopoly, creativity would flourish. And it did. From 1790 to 1846, patents grew nearly 500 percent per capita.

However, execution remained flawed. The first patent bill sought "any useful art, manufacture, engine, machine, or device, or any instrument thereon not before known or used." The shorthand for this definition became *novelty* and *usefulness*, ideas simple in concept but sometimes difficult to judge in practice. The bill also required the secretary of state, the secretary of war, and the attorney general to read and assess all patent applications, along with completing their constitutional tasks. It was a system that proved impractical.

The first tribunal awarded three patents in the first year, thirty-three in the second, and eleven in the third before crying uncle. In 1793, the patent law was amended, allowing the secretary of state to issue a patent to anyone who presented drawings, a model of their invention, and the requisite application fee. This new process now required federal judges to determine the novelty and usefulness of an invention, solve disputes, and build a body of law to guide the patent process forward.

Jefferson was the author of the 1793 Patent Act and intended high standards for patentability, more than obvious or frivolous ideas, so that the public award of a monopoly was ultimately an advantage to society. "Change of material, like making a comb from iron instead of ivory, or . . . making a square bucket instead of a round one," did not meet Jefferson's standards.

This byzantine process forced federal judges to rule on topics beyond their education and interests. Short on time and faced with demanding schedules, they tended to invalidate patents. It was into this confusing world that young, optimistic Eli Whitney arrived in 1794, ready to profit from his game-changing invention.

A CARDINAL SIN:
CHOOSING THE WRONG BUSINESS MODEL

In the same month the patent for the cotton gin was granted, Phineas Miller placed an advertisement in the *Gazette of the State of Georgia* letting the public know that the firm of Miller and Whitney was open for business. This announcement provided the confidence that planters needed to sow short-staple cotton that spring and created the implicit promise that ginning would be available at harvest. The firm chose a business model that was simple, compelling, and leveraged their innovative gin's newly estimated, fiftyfold improvement over hand processing: Bring any quantity of cotton to one of its ginning stations, and Miller and Whitney promised to return one pound of clean cotton for every five pounds of raw cotton delivered.

The benefits of this outsourced model to Georgia's depressed planting community seemed persuasive. It meant no capital or additional labor was required for processing the season's crop, and no need to purchase machines that would lie idle in the off-season. Planters need not secure hard currency in a nation that had little available. This model also ensured that the inner workings of the cotton gin would remain beyond the reach of Southern mechanics who might wish to copy the invention.

The stage was set. In 1794, Phineas Miller and Eli Whitney were two accidental but passionate entrepreneurs with a transformative product in hand. They believed they had a business model perfectly in sync with their market. That's when things began to unravel.

"ALMOST RUNNING MAD"

Whitney traveled north to establish a workshop in New Haven, Connecticut, back within the comfort of his Yale and New Haven communities. Here, he could access skilled labor, raw materials, and, if need be, friends capable of providing additional financing. Whitney struggled with the cracking of wooden cylinders as his workers attempted to set hundreds of iron teeth in each, but his factory eventually turned out six large machines designed to handle the fall 1794 cotton crop being grown by the planters around Mulberry Grove.

By late spring, Miller understood that he and his partner had placed themselves at ground zero of an agricultural revolution. Whitney had struggled to build six machines; Miller forecast the need for at least fifty and perhaps a hundred new gins simply to meet known demand. "Do not let a deficiency of money, do not let anything hinder the speedy construction of the gins," Miller wrote Whitney. "The people of the country are almost running mad for them."

This included the planters around Mulberry Grove, though the potential market for the cotton gin was several states high and would soon be half-a-continent wide. Miller and Whitney were in no position to meet the enormous demands of Southern agriculture, and Southern agriculture was in no position to wait. Had the entrepreneurial pair done a sober assessment in the late spring of 1794, they might have elected to license the design of the gin to plantations throughout the South, and perhaps manufacture in whatever volume they could to support outright purchases. The outsourced model they had created was thoughtful, but it was clear almost immediately that it would fall far short of meeting the needs of local planters in 1794, much less those clamoring across several states.

The market responded in predictable fashion. By the fall, Miller and Whitney were receiving reports that Southern mechanic Edward Lyon was selling a bootleg cotton gin, their original design probably having been stolen and shared by an unreliable business associate with whom Miller had worked that spring. Lyon's gins even appeared to be an improvement over Whitney's design, swapping the wire-tooth roller with "twenty circles of sheet iron, formed in the manner of ragwheels." Not only was this "saw gin" design easier to manufacture, but it was gentler on cotton fiber.

As cash ran low and bootleg gins multiplied, Miller and Whitney suffered yet another setback. A fire in New Haven in the spring of 1795 destroyed Whitney's shop, tools, and the makings for twenty gins, leaving him with no income or assets and substantial debt. Over the next twenty-four months, Miller and Whitney's business came to a virtual standstill while copycat gins transformed Southern agriculture.

At thirty-two years old, Whitney seemed beaten. "Toil anxiety and disappointment have broken me down," he wrote to Miller from New Haven. "My situation makes me perfectly miserable." Miller's response demonstrated his essential role in the partnership, and the power of community. "I think with you, that we ought to meet such events with equanimity," he wrote his friend. "We have been pursuing a valuable object by honorable means; . . . I trust that all our measures have been such as reason and virtue must justify. It has pleased Providence to postpone the attainment of this object." He then implored Whitney, "I feel a secret joy and satisfaction, that you possess a mind in this respect similar to my own—that you are not disheartened—that you do not relinquish the pursuit—and that you will persevere, and endeavor at all events to attain the main object. This is exactly consonant to my own determinations." Miller was demonstrating the kind of persistence required by successful entrepreneurs, adding that he would devote all his time, energy, and money to make the business successful. Never, he told Whitney, should they let this extraordinary opportunity slip away.

By the fall, Whitney was back on his feet, reenergized and ready to ship two dozen new gins. Miller's encouragement would last a lifetime. From that point on Whitney worked tirelessly, aggressively defended his invention, and sought to diversify his business ventures. This timely encouragement from Miller was the turning point of Whitney's career.

In 1799, Miller and Whitney finally adjusted their business model, offering to sell the patent-right to their product. It was far too little, far too late, however. Southern planters had little inclination to buy Whitney's design when purchasing an improved saw gin could be done with impunity. The pair of entrepreneurs soldiered on together and, after Miller's tragic death in 1803, Whitney proceeded to defend his invention alone. Twenty-seven times, the firm of Miller and Whitney attempted to enforce their patent claim in court, and twenty-seven times they failed. That is, until December 1806, when Whitney brought suit against planters John Powell and Arthur Fort in the Louisville, Georgia, courtroom of the Honorable William Johnson (1771–1834) of the Federal Circuit Court.

"Has Any Man Not Experienced the Cotton Gin's Usefulness?"

Fort had been among the first planters to make use of a saw gin. His defense before Judge Johnson was logical and spirited. Machines in Europe used the same principles as Whitney's cotton gin, he said, proof that there was nothing "novel" about the invention. Worse, the original gin damaged cotton staple, so it could hardly be "useful." Regardless, Fort noted, he had never in his life seen one of Whitney's cotton gins and therefore could not possibly have used one.

Armed with years of litigation experience, Whitney came prepared to meet these arguments, but it was his closing demonstration that was most impressive: Whitney ran his own gin and a saw gin side by side. Court observers could not tell the difference in operation or output between the two.

Judge Johnson watched intently and then laid out a legal decision that cemented Eli Whitney's fame for the ages. Before Johnson's verdict, the birth of the cotton gin was in dispute; afterward, every American would come to learn (if nothing else in history class) that Eli Whitney was its inventor.

The green seed species of cotton, Johnson began his ruling, was more productive than the black and able to be grown successfully under a greater variety of conditions. However, the fiber adhered to the seed in a way that required a different and more powerful machine than the traditional roller gin. Thanks to Whitney, the judge wrote, "The cultivation of it has suddenly become an object of infinitely greater national importance than that of the other species ever can be." Further, the novelty was clear; it had been years since Whitney had secured his patent, and nobody had proved the preexistence of a similar machine.

As for utility, the judge asked if there was any person who had not experienced the cotton gin's usefulness. "The whole interior of the Southern States was languishing, and its inhabitants emigrating for want of some object to engage their attention and employ their industry, when the invention of this machine at once opened views to them, which set the whole country in active motion." Cotton was overtaking wool, flax, and silk in manufacturing, Johnson noted, and the entire country benefited from its cultivation and manufacture.

Finally, the judge hit on the real issue: Did the improvement made by replacing the wires with the saw amount to something novel and different? When a mechanic "cut teeth in plates of iron, and passed them over the cylinder," Judge Johnson wrote, it was a "meritorious improvement" but, he concluded, nothing more than a "more convenient mode of making the same thing." The basic characteristics of Whitney's invention remained unchanged, and any small improvement did nothing to damage his rights. With that, Johnson entered a decree for perpetual injunction.

The verdict was already a complete vindication for Whitney, but the judge went on to place the inventor's star in the entrepreneurial heavens. "We cannot express the weight of the obligation which the country owes to this invention. The extent of it cannot now be seen."

It took thirteen years and dozens of patent suits before Whitney's claims were upheld in court, and victory was bittersweet. Miller never lived to see it. Whitney never grew rich on his invention. When the patent expired in November 1807, Congress, with staunch opposition from Southern politician-planters, refused to renew it.

Whitney would never again submit a patent. The lesson from his experience with the cotton gin was that all the mechanical genius in the world was of little value if he could not deliver on the promise of his business model.

AMERICA'S FIRST SERIAL ENTREPRENEUR

In 1798, Americans were expecting war with France. Napoleon had become a threat to all of Europe, international trade was disrupted, and the flow of imported muskets to America had dried to a trickle. George Washington had authorized the establishment of an armory in Springfield, Massachusetts, during the Revolution, but, in the four years leading up to 1798, it had produced less than a thousand muskets. A second armory established at Harper's Ferry in Virginia three years earlier was still nascent. Fearing for the country's defense, federal officials now encouraged private contractors to bid for contracts to produce muskets for the government.

By far the most infamous of the contractors to answer his country's call was Whitney. His cotton gin business had ground to a halt, mired in courtroom drama. He was in debt and running out of options. Placing quill to paper in May 1798, Whitney addressed a letter to Oliver Wolcott Jr., the fellow Yale alumnus he had met in Philadelphia four years earlier who was now secretary of the treasury. Whitney was worried that falling demand in his cotton gin business would idle his workforce in New Haven. "I have a number of workmen and apprentices," he wrote, "whom I have instructed in working wood and metals, and whom I wish to keep employed." He proposed building ten thousand stands of arms, or complete sets of muskets including bayonets, ramrods, wipers, and screwdrivers. Wolcott received the letter just as Congress fretted about war, having voted $800,000 for the purchase of cannons and small arms.

Three weeks later Whitney had in hand a contract to build ten thousand stands of arms at $13.40 each, with four thousand due a year from September and the other six thousand a year after that. This enormous, $134,000 contract included a $5,000 advance, the first ever paid to a private citizen by the United States government, and the only advance given of the twenty-six private contracts awarded for arms manufacture. Whitney later admitted that Wolcott's willingness to bet on his fellow alumnus—and the $5,000 advance—saved him from ruin.

THE GOVERNMENT AS INNOVATOR

On the surface, the contract offered to Whitney by Wolcott and the government was absurd. Without tooling, capital, or a shred of experience manufacturing firearms, Whitney committed to make ten times the muskets in twenty-eight months that the Springfield Armory had manufactured in its first four years. Tench Coxe (1755–1824), the purveyor of public supplies, spoke for a chorus of skeptics when he wrote, "I have my doubts about this matter and suspect that Mr. Whitney cannot perform as to time." Indeed, Whitney's detractors attribute this plum deal to the saving grace of the good-old-boy Yale network, yet another indication that college may have done little for Whitney's mechanical prowess but everything for his entrepreneurial success.

Whitney had no illusions about what he was proposing to do. "A good musket is a complicated engine and difficult to make," he wrote, "difficult of execution because the conformation of most of its parts correspond with no regular geometrical figure." Indeed, in the modern world of the

American entrepreneur, where the assumption that everything (including the creation of new technology) will happen perfectly is routinely baked into audacious projections, Whitney proved ahead of his time.

This was the moment when Whitney crossed his own private Rubicon, becoming one of America's first *serial entrepreneurs*. The letter to Wolcott was proof that failure would no longer be an obstacle to progress, that the rules of engagement might have to be stretched, and that Eli Whitney had the grit required to succeed in the market.

With $5,000 and a contract in hand, Whitney paid his creditors and began the hard work of launching his second market innovation, this one based on an audacious business model designed to create an entirely new kind of mechanized factory. This meant purchasing a new water-power site and rebuilding its dam a few miles outside New Haven, fitting the water wheels and buildings to drive production, and designing machinery. As often happened with Whitney, nothing went easily. Unable to secure his mill site until mid-September, Whitney and his Connecticut neighbors were then hit with *twelve* snowstorms. These delayed completion of his facility until January 1799, just nine months from the promised completion of four thousand muskets. Then yellow fever struck Philadelphia, postponing delivery of critical raw materials. Whitney was suddenly playing to his skeptics, delivering just five hundred muskets in the first year.

Snowstorms and yellow fever were one kind of obstacle, but it was in November 1800 that real disaster struck: Oliver Wolcott stepped down from his post at Treasury. Whitney could absorb almost any loss but that of his personal network. It was again time to act boldly.

DAZZLING THE FOUNDING FATHERS

Whitney headed to Washington in January 1801 to win new friends—including Wolcott's replacement, Samuel Dexter (1761–1816), a *Harvard* grad—by hosting one of the most dramatic product demonstrations in American history. Specific details are lacking, but we can piece together the outline of what occurred.

Whitney's presentation probably took place at the War Department or the White House. President John Adams and President-elect Thomas Jefferson were both in attendance, as was Secretary of War Henry Dearborn (1751–1829), Whitney's congressman, and, presumably, Dexter. Whitney must have been nervous. His cotton gin business was failing, and he was now missing musket deliveries to the government and urgently short of capital. Perhaps he provided an update on the cotton gin litigation, hoping for sympathy. Once he began his demonstration, however, his goal was to reduce the emphasis on contractual obligations and place it squarely on advancements in mechanization.

Whitney set a complete musket and parts for a number of locks on the table before his distinguished audience. Then (so the story goes) he asked them to mix and match the lock parts in any combination to assemble complete, functioning locks. We are not certain how Whitney positioned his work—as an example of what could be done, what was about to be done at scale, or as a fait accompli. His congressman was clearly impressed, however, saying that the samples "met universal approbation." Likewise, Thomas Jefferson wrote that Whitney "has invented moulds and machines for making all the pieces of his locks so exactly equal, that take 100 locks to piece and mingle their parts and the hundred locks may be put together as well by taking the first pieces which come to hand." Jefferson even offered to write Governor James Monroe of Virginia to recommend hiring Whitney to make arms for the Virginia militia. This was a stunning recommendation for a contractor who had thus far failed to perform.

The ability to mix and match parts, creating a single, working musket from two or three that had broken in battle, could potentially change the course of war. The stakes around successfully devising a process for true interchangeable parts might, for the new nation, impact its very existence.

Eli Whitney arrived in Washington mired in litigation, out of cash, and negligent in his obligations. He departed Washington in a blaze of glory. Once home he wrote to Dexter, "My system I now consider as established and my theory successfully reduced to practice." He then asked for a further advance of $10,000 from the government and an extension in delivery dates—this time to five years. Whitney's prayers were answered.

Eli Whitney had prevailed in his showdown before the Founding Fathers. His factory would live another day, ultimately fulfilling its commitments to the federal government. His legacy would grow. "The long-term significance of his work," one historian offered, "was, indeed, not a well-made musket but a new approach to manufacturing." Pulitzer Prize–winning historian Allan Nevins (1890–1971) writes that "Whitney fathered the American system of interchangeable manufacture which shortly was producing quantities of cheap, serviceable clocks and watches, hardware, and sewing machines." Whitney's reputation was secure—until 1959.

ONE LAST BATTLE

That was the year that MIT historian Robert S. Woodbury presented a paper to the Society for the History of Technology that accused Whitney's biographers of failing to evaluate carefully the archival evidence. Woodbury was critical of Whitney's manufacturing practices, writing that even in 1825, the entrepreneur's factory was unable to deliver muskets at the rate promised the government in 1798. However, Woodbury found Whitney's real sin to be his demonstration of interchangeable parts before Jefferson and Adams—which the historian believed was a sham. "A test of a number of known Whitney arms in at least one collection proved that they were *not* interchangeable in all their parts," Woodbury wrote. "Some were not even *approximately* interchangeable." Whitney was a fraud.

Edward Battison, curator of mechanical engineering at the Smithsonian Institution's National Museum of History and Technology, examined lock parts manufactured for the government and found signs of traditional hand-filing "to the point that each Whitney lock was numbered and corresponded to a particular musket." This was the antithesis of interchangeable parts, the proverbial smoking gun. "The revisionist articles of Woodbury and Battison," historian Carolyn Cooper concluded, "effectively demolished the heroic Whitney myth among historians of technology, demoting Eli Whitney from Father of the American System of Manufactures to fast-talking arms contractor."

Time brought moderation, however. Historians agree that the definition of interchangeability is elusive. As late as the 1950s, for example, final adjustment of a typewriter full of "interchangeable parts" could last three hours. Even Woodbury struck a conciliatory note in 1977 when he admitted that "we still know far less about the part played by Whitney and the actual origin of manufacture by interchangeable parts than we would like to . . . [and] have a very limited knowledge of Whitney's actual methods."

This controversy was far away, however, when Whitney died in 1825. His passing was described as nothing short of "a public calamity." His cotton gin had revitalized the South and unleashed one of the nation's most profitable industries. His musket factory had defined the nation's industrial genius, while its steady supply of quality firearms after completion of Oliver Wolcott's federal contract ensured that Whitney would die not only famous, but wealthy.

BACK AT THE BAR

"I love your outsourced cotton-gin business model," one of the younger entrepreneurs exclaimed. "No capital, no money, no labor—just bring in five pounds of raw cotton and get back a pound of clean cotton, ready for sale."

Whitney chuckled. "It did sound good, didn't it? We had the world by the tail. The problem," he added, "is that you have to do what you say you're going to do. Our customers weren't the forgiving type. I don't suppose any customers are."

Then he turned to the larger group, many of whom were still trying to take in all they had heard. "It was my friends Phineas Miller, Catharine Greene, and Oliver Wolcott who deserve so much credit. They pulled me through some rough times. And maybe I should add one more person."

He smiled, looking over at another of the older entrepreneurs, dressed like him in knee-length breeches and tailcoat.

"When I visited the Springfield Armory in 1799 to learn their process for manufacturing muskets," Whitney continued, "I met with its first superintendent, David Ames. He was gracious and helpful. And he ran quite an impressive operation."

Then Whitney turned and said, "And his younger brother, Oliver, is here with us this evening." Oliver nodded. "Young Oliver was an apprentice at the Armory and had already earned a favorable reputation—though it wasn't muskets he cared about."

Oliver Ames rose from his chair and turned to face the barroom guests. "It's true, America needed plenty of guns in times of war," he said, "but in times of peace—well, we had roads to build, canals to dig, and railroad track to lay. In times like that, there was nothing more valuable than a shovel."

"Refill your glasses," Whitney said. "You're going to enjoy this story."

Chapter 2

OLIVER AMES:
RIDING THE PERFECT STORM

O liver Ames (1779–1863) was born during the American Revolution and died during the nation's Civil War, calamitous bookends that framed entrepreneurial life in the early republic. His business activities were centered in the quiet Massachusetts towns of Plymouth and Easton. Ames dabbled in several product lines early in his career, but his primary and lasting focus was on the design and manufacture of shovels.

Oliver's father, Captain John Ames, had used local bog iron and an eighty-pound trip-hammer located at the family's forge in West Bridgewater to produce a batch of iron-bladed shovels five or six years before Oliver's birth. Now the fourth generation in his family to practice ironwork, Oliver was married and in business for himself by 1803, manufacturing a few dozen shovels annually at a small factory in the nearby village of North Easton. Forty years later, Oliver Ames and his sons produced 410,000 shovels annually, and at the time of his death, some three-quarters of a million. These were volumes that he might have dismissed as impossible in 1803. Where Eli Whitney had benefited from a revolution in textile manufacture, however, Oliver Ames would find his own perfect storm in a country revolutionizing the speed and efficiency by which people and goods traveled.

THE ANNIHILATION OF SPACE AND TIME

Roads in America in 1800 were treacherous. President Thomas Jefferson's hundred-mile trip from Monticello to Washington, DC, forced him across eight rivers, only three of which offered boats or bridges. A trip from New York to Cincinnati took a hearty traveler nineteen days. A letter posted in Maine could take three weeks to reach Kentucky. Where a manufacturer might pay nine dollars to move a ton of goods three thousand miles by sea, that same nine dollars would purchase only thirty miles of transportation by land.

When Oliver Ames launched his business in the opening years of the nineteenth century, he was unknowingly perched on the crest of a series of consecutive and overlapping waves of innovation in transportation. The Turnpike Era (1800–1830) would be followed closely by the rapid growth of canals (1817–1840) and the rise of the river steamboat (1815–1860), all of which presaged the explosive development of the American railroad (1830 onward). By 1825, the nation would be awash in infrastructure projects, all of which relied on strong backs and an uninterrupted supply of that most basic commodity of progress, the shovel.

Turnpikes, or roads on which a toll is charged, were the backbone of hundreds of miles of intersecting rural roads that connected farm to town and facilitated commerce. By 1816, an American could finally travel on a single route from Maine to Georgia, and by 1820, cities along America's northern and middle Atlantic coast were more or less interconnected. By modern standards, the overland trip on toll roads was still slow (six to eleven miles per hour) and arduous, but it was now at least possible, and merchants were finally able to access dependable short-haul routes for their goods. By 1820, Oliver Ames was a beneficiary of this turnpike boom, producing nearly thirty-six thousand shovels annually.

In 1816, America had about one hundred miles of canals. The following year, the state of New York authorized the Erie Canal, breaking ground on July 4, 1818. Historian George Rogers Taylor called it "the demonstration of a spirit of enterprise by an organized government that has few parallels in world history." Opened in stages, the canal was fully complete by 1825: forty feet wide, four feet deep, and 363 miles long from Buffalo to Albany, with eighty-three locks. Beginning in 1835 it was enlarged to seventy feet wide and seven feet deep. "Digging a ditch . . . with hand labor through hundreds of miles of this primeval forest was the greatest challenge the builders of the Erie Canal would have to confront," wrote Peter Bernstein in his book *Wedding of the Waters*.

One fictionalized account of the work highlighted the role that high-quality Ames shovels came to play. Exasperated with an inferior product, one worker complained, "The damn blade bends in anything harder than sand, and breaks off completely if you bend it back to straight. A man can't get any work done with it at all." When asked for a solution, the worker suggested his employer "go back to North Eaton [*sic*], and buy some proper shovels from old Oliver Ames." Soon after, five wagonloads of Ames shovels arrived and sold out completely in two days, ending worker complaints.

The Erie Canal's success set off a wave of canal building, some of it virtually in Ames's backyard, like the forty-five-mile Blackstone Canal from Worcester to Providence. The economics were compelling in a country with no navigable river system reaching very far inland (save the St. Lawrence): Four horses could pull a one-ton wagon twelve miles a day or a one-hundred-ton barge twenty-four miles. By 1840, the United States had constructed 3,326 miles of canals at a cost of $125 million ($3.6 billion in today's dollars), and it would enlarge and improve those canals with another $75 million investment in the next two decades. This network was a tribute to American ingenuity, political foresight, commercial enthusiasm, and the Ames shovel.

The growth of towns along canals meant roads, homes, and farms—a multiplier effect for Oliver's business. Buffalo went from "five lawyers and no church" in 1810 to forty-two thousand people by 1850. No fewer than ten new towns sprang up between Albany and Buffalo. The Erie Canal also facilitated a steady migration of settlers to new cities like Cleveland and Chicago, and an entire generation of engineers who "went to school" on the canal, developing a new expertise in civil engineering for America and a new generation of projects requiring shovels. The business writer John Steele Gordon described the project as the "longest canal, in the least time, with the least experience, for the least money and to the greatest public benefit." For Oliver Ames, the Erie Canal was one of the great windfalls of his lifetime.

Of course, Ames was not the only shovel maker in the new republic to benefit from transportation improvements, but he was clearly a leading competitor. A federal report noted that in 1831, factories in the state of New York produced annually about sixty thousand shovels and in Connecticut about twelve thousand shovels. "A steel shovel and spade factory in Philadelphia consumed annually about fifty tons of American steel." In 1836, Pittsburgh had two establishments turning out ninety-six thousand shovels and spades annually. Meanwhile, *Niles' Weekly Register* reported in 1835 that Oliver Ames was now operating three extensive shovel works turning out 480 shovels a day, insufficient to meet demand.

As toll roads and canals improved travel, another powerful revolution in transportation was at hand. The first Western steamboat launched from Pittsburgh in 1811, and by 1830, the river steamboat had become the most important form of internal transportation in America. Steamboats helped turn boomtowns like Cincinnati into "Porkopolis" and enabled immigrants like William Procter and James Gamble to distribute their new soap. Kentucky farmers who sold their goods in New Orleans could, by 1826, return upriver to Louisville against the currents of the mighty Mississippi in just eight days. And, while steamboats themselves did not require shovels, the feeder systems that sprang from the steamboat routes, including new roads, turnpikes, canals, factories, farms, and towns, all meant a steady need for products flowing—farther and farther—from Oliver Ames's factories.

The closing act of the nineteenth-century revolution in American transportation, however, was also its most spectacular. In 1810, a three-quarter-mile, horse-drawn railroad was opened outside of Philadelphia to haul stone from quarry to dock. In 1828, it was Ames shovels that broke ground for the B&O Railroad in Baltimore, America's first railroad to offer scheduled freight and passenger service. By 1860, Americans had laid 30,636 miles of track, and the steam engine had become one of the wonders of the age. The fortunes of American rail and Ames shovels were tightly joined throughout; family historian Winthrop Ames wrote, "Nothing (except perhaps war) created such a demand for shovels as railroad building."

The country's transportation revolution seemed to reduce the size of a nation even as it was expanding. Coupled with the launch of the telegraph in 1838—a communications revolution to accompany the transportation revolution—Americans came to characterize their efforts at nation building as the "annihilation of time and space." In the midst of this "annihilation" sat Oliver Ames. "Ames shovels literally built America," historian Greg Galer writes, from farms, foundations, and wells to canals and railroads. "Remember the central role of shovels in building cities," he adds, "and in mining including the California Gold Rush and the coal mines of Pennsylvania." By the late nineteenth century, the Ames family had both shaped and ridden America's growth from coast to coast, turning a small factory in Easton into a multistate manufacturing operation that produced two-thirds of the world's shovels.

SPRINGFIELD ARMORY: PRECISION, VOLUME, AND QUALITY

While Eli Whitney fled the family farm in search of opportunity, Oliver Ames naturally assumed the occupation of his father. Likewise, Oliver's brother David (1760–1847), nineteen years his senior, was an expert ironmaster appointed by President Washington in 1794 as the first superintendent of the United States Arsenal at Springfield, the famous Springfield Armory. In 1797, Oliver joined his brother and apprenticed at the armory until the end of David's term in 1802. While we don't know Oliver's exact functions over those five years, this apprenticeship was possibly the single richest technology experience a young American entrepreneur could have in the early republic, comparable to an internship at Bell Labs in the mid-twentieth century or Google in the twenty-first century. Time at the Springfield Armory not only introduced Ames to a community of world-class craftsmen, but would determine his business model and commercial practices for the rest of his career.

Established by an act of the Third Continental Congress in April 1794, Springfield was the first national armory in the Western world outside France and the birthplace of small arms manufacture in the United States. Its single most important early activity was the establishment in 1795 of musket production—single-shot, smoothbore flintlock muskets, based on late eighteenth-century French models. With improvements over time, Springfield's renowned flintlock would be used in the Indian War of Ohio in 1799, the conflict with Tripoli in 1804, the War of 1812, the battles at Tippecanoe and New Orleans, the Seminole Wars, the Black Hawk War of 1832, and the Mexican War of 1845.

No early nineteenth-century product was more complex to manufacture or required greater precision and higher quality than the single-shot, smoothbore flintlock musket launched under David Ames's leadership. The locks themselves were perhaps the single most difficult item produced in the early republic; the very first one fashioned under Ames's watch took three days to be filed. Once these firing mechanisms were in use, they had to withstand powerful mechanical stresses. Gun stocking required the cutting of curved or irregular surfaces from hardwood, a process in which the finest mechanics were often "unable to produce two articles which were more than approximately alike." That left the rifled barrels, themselves an enormously challenging fabrication process of rolling, shaping, and welding iron or steel to produce a spiraled groove that would spin a musket ball and improve its accuracy. These barrels had to withstand intense, repeated shocks.

David Ames had taken on the most difficult industrial task in America. In 1796, a sample musket was sent for inspection to Samuel Hodgdon, the superintendent of military stores. His report was detailed and included criticism of everything from the weight of the barrel, the counterboring of the "Britch," the quality of the stock, the body of the "Cock and Lock," the joining of the "Pin and Pan," the raising of the "Trigger on a level with its plate," the length and temper of the bayonet, the welding of the socket, and the quality of steel of the ramrod. "The next you send me," Hodgdon demanded of Ames, "I expect to be perfect."

Production also required close coordination of a variety of raw materials, including walnut from New England and mid-Atlantic sources, coal from Virginia, and iron obtained both locally and from international sources. It was a supply chain that looked nothing like the eighteenth-century world of the typical American artisan blacksmith.

Ames's apprenticeship exposed him to dozens of highly skilled mechanics and armorers, a special group. As archaeologist Michael S. Raber notes, "Very few private armsmakers could even attempt to make arms along accepted military lines with predictable quality." In other words, Oliver Ames's first industrial experience placed him among some of the finest craftsmen of his time.

The production of about four hundred muskets a month turned out to be the high-water mark for a facility organized along eighteenth-century craft shop lines. With constant pressure but little additional growth in annual production through 1802, David Ames returned to private life to become the first papermaker in Springfield, leaving his successors to move the facility decisively into the nineteenth century.

Oliver returned home from Springfield having spent five years on the cutting edge of America's Industrial Revolution while working in community with its most talented practitioners. The Springfield Armory was a large, busy factory with complex inputs, precision manufacture, and national distribution. David Ames emphasized innovations that would improve processes, efficiency, and quality. This was metalworking for a new age and a forerunner of the role the American military would play in underwriting the nation's innovation. And it seems obvious in retrospect that this experience moved Ames decisively from the village blacksmith days of his father and grandfather into a new business model based on mechanization, one that emphasized precision, volume, and quality.

APPLYING THE LESSONS OF SPRINGFIELD

The implications of this new business model were far-reaching. By 1803, Ames was already focused on establishing water privileges to provide long-term power to his factories. He began to think broadly about how to assemble land, capital, and talent to meet expanding markets. His father had relied on local bog iron; Oliver searched globally for raw materials to feed his booming factories, becoming heavily reliant on imported iron. The development of new selling channels led to the increased use of middlemen and the reliance on distant management—led as often as possible by family members. Historian Greg Galer wrote, "Oliver and his sons demonstrate the transition from artisan to manager and industrialist, from general to specialized production, from small to large quantity production, and from local artisan to community leader and national figure."

There is scant detail about how Ames may have leveraged his Springfield apprenticeship into a lifelong, supportive community, but there are hints. The May 1796 payroll of armorers under David Ames listed his master armorer, Col. Robert Orr (1746–1811), and twenty-two men. Orr hailed from Bridgewater, Massachusetts, where he and his father, Hugh, were neighbors of the Ames family. It was Hugh Orr who made muskets as early as 1748, believed to be the first in America—a good reason for David Ames to hire his son in Springfield. It was the Orrs who first began to manufacture shovels in Bridgewater, perhaps the inspiration for Oliver's family. In any case, the Orr and Ames families were clearly part of a community of "millwrights, nail-makers and artificers in Iron" in and around Bridgewater, and it's possible that Oliver drew on this relationship, established across generations and strengthened in Springfield.

In time, Oliver Ames's focus on quality became the stuff of legend. "One aged shovel-maker used to tell of an occasion when he was tending a trip-hammer as a young employee," Winthrop Ames reports. "Suddenly he felt a mighty thwack across his shoulders and whirled about to see Oliver standing over him, with flashing eyes and upraised cane, expressing an opinion of careless workmanship."

Another aspect of Ames's genius, demonstrated time and again throughout his career, was an ability to balance—or perhaps, slightly *unbalance*—supply and demand. This skill, which created many an unhappy customer, might have been a hard-won lesson from the Embargo of 1807 when shipping and trade came to standstill. It might also have been a reflection of Ames's underlying resistance to being pressured by dealers and customers, or to extending production capacity in ways that threatened his credit. It also might have signaled a lack of trust in business relationships hampered by distance and slow communications. Whatever the reason, Ames consistently produced a little less product than his markets desired. "There are lots of letters with him lying to his customers about more shovels coming," Galer wrote, "as he carefully doled out what he had available to keep people on the hook and loyal to him, even though he wasn't completely filling orders. Other shovel makers went belly-up not doing this." Ames weathered the panics of 1819 and 1834; his record of a half-century of growth and market success speaks to the success of this conservative business approach, which served to balance his more aggressive innovations in technology and production.

In 1817, Ames received a patent for a back-strap shovel that further improved the ruggedness of his product. At some point, too, the famous "Ames bend" was introduced as a feature, creating shaped handles that made the job of shoveling considerably easier and undoubtedly differentiated the brand. By 1820, Galer notes, an artisan blacksmith might compete against O. Ames shovels on cost but not quality, or on quality but not cost. Eventually Ames shovels commanded a premium of a dollar per dozen wholesale. By 1837, the company offered at least twenty-two styles and sizes of shovels.

In California during the mid-century Gold Rush, Ames shovels were priced in gold dust instead of unreliable paper currency and could themselves be used as currency. In 1870, when the *Atlantic Monthly* spent "A Day with the Shovel-Makers" in North Easton, it referred to the Ames location as "works whose trade-mark has become a key to the markets of the world."

This brand equity was Oliver's legacy and, not surprisingly, that of the organization for which he had apprenticed, itself becoming a recognized national brand: The name "'Springfield Armory' on any weapon insured [sic] its value of dependability, ruggedability, versatility and overall effectiveness." The same could be said of Ames shovels.

When Oliver's focus on quality took the form of an occasional "thwack across the shoulders," we get a glimpse into his personality. Like many successful entrepreneurs, he was firmly convinced of his own opinions and highly suspect of everyone else's. His sons even felt the need to hide new machinery or devices; once Oliver stumbled upon a new apparatus for making handles and nearly smashed it in a fit of rage.

Another time the old entrepreneur was found on the factory floor bending an entire batch of shovels he felt were of inferior quality, until he was informed that they were trench shovels for soldiers and made light intentionally. As his sons gradually assumed control of the business, Oliver could be openly critical of their work. At one point his boys uncovered a batch of shovels made during the War of 1812 and decided to clean and mix them in with a batch of new shovels. When Oliver spotted and threw out all of the 1812 models, the boys admitted the hoax. After that, Oliver grew at least slightly more tolerant.

The historian of Easton, William Chaffin, looked back upon one of the town's favorite sons some twenty years after Oliver's death. "He was a man of strong and resolute will, of great force of character, indomitable energy, and persevering industry. He was the possessor of a splendid physique," Chaffin wrote, noting that "His manly and dignified bearing gave every one who saw him the impression that they looked upon a man of mark. He was such a man as a stranger, meeting him upon the street, would turn to look at a second time." His tastes were simple and democratic, Chaffin wrote, and to the extent Oliver had any defects, the historian concluded, they were merely those of "his limited culture and . . . the stern conflict and discipline of his early life." Of course, it's likely that Ames's formative experience as an apprentice at the Springfield Armory in "his early life" did not limit his growth but instead shaped his future success.

A GLIMPSE INTO OLIVER'S JOURNALS

Around 1842, as his career wound down and his sons took an increasingly active role in the company, Oliver secured a hardbound journal and began making two sets of notes in his precise, flowing script. One set concerned the activities of the shovel business, with a recap of his activities from 1803 that revealed the things Oliver found most satisfying in his career. The other was a weather journal, carefully noting each day's conditions, with special emphasis on the level of the various ponds that fed power to his factories. This second journal revealed the comings and goings of the Ames family, purchases and harvests on the farm, and an occasional election result or death in the neighborhood.

Oliver's first journal about his shovel business is remarkable in that it never mentions growth in revenue, customers, geographies, or employees, the information that a modern entrepreneur might capture. Instead, Oliver reveals himself to be the consummate mechanic. He is constantly improving his shovels, inventing machines and processes, or expanding facilities. For example, in Easton, around 1809, he established two new bloomeries that employed a new technique for "forcing the hammers to go over the Shaft, for which I got a patent." He also invented "a water Back & tie iron . . . and got a patent for it." In 1818, Oliver built an "ox wagon with iron hub wheels" and "began to make shovels by Back-strapping them," which, in both cases, he concluded proudly, "I suppose was the first ever built in that way." In 1827 he "put in a pair of iron Bellows which was the first we had of that kind," in 1830 "built a pare [*sic*] of shears for cutting iron," and in 1840 "built a tool for cutting out spades and got it going." His business was prospering by this time, becoming a dominant force in America, but his pride remained in the innovations he brought to mechanized production.

Oliver's diaries also suggest the fragility of nineteenth-century entrepreneurship. Eli Whitney had faced a devastating fire in his New Haven workshop. David Ames had suffered a similarly disastrous fire at the Springfield Armory in 1801 when precious tools, components, and five hundred finished muskets were lost. On April 7, 1844, Oliver wrote, "About half after one o'clock this morning the wood house and a small shop at Douglas were discovered to be on fire . . . we came very near losing all our shops but the wind happened to be the right way to keep it off the handling shop." Another fire in February 1849 at "the factory" was detected at one o'clock in the morning and constrained, but with damage. Then, two years later in March 1851, "Our finishing shop took fire and was all burnt up together with about a thousand dozen finish shovels. The hammer shop was also burnt . . . We estimated the loss at about $30,000 & there was $3,000 insurance on it."

Catastrophe could visit in other forms, as well. In 1845, a shipwreck off the coast of Hyannis, Massachusetts, cost the Ames company $1,200 worth of steel. And periods without rainfall regularly put production at risk, despite the sophisticated use of dams and reservoirs to enhance the precious flow of water.

NO ONE BOWED WITH MORE SUBMISSION

The Industrial Revolution advanced mightily at the Ames Shovel Works in the 1850s. In 1853, Oliver noted that he added a "60 horse power engine" to his factory operations. Two years later he noted that "the railroad from here to Stoughton is now so far done that the cars began to run on it today." Meanwhile, the size and needs of his workforce continued to expand; he built nine new single-family houses in the summer of 1856 and seven new residences designed for two families each in July 1859.

Oliver's last business entry was made on Easter 1863, just a few months before his death, when he described a new machine for grinding shovels that "promises to be a very valuable acquisition." It was a sign of his enduring faith in innovation, and recognition that his sons were capable of leading his business into the future. The next entry, on September 11, 1863, was made by his son, Oliver Ames Jr., who wrote, "Father died this morning about 2 O'Clock A.M. . . . He had been a great sufferer for some years from a water trouble and had for a year felt that to die would be gain. His mind was to the last clear and strong and he never showed any failing in his intellectual faculties."

Oliver Jr. continued his father's journal off and on for the next year, a simple but visible sign that the community Oliver Sr. had created in life would survive his death. His son brings the diary to a close on November 17, 1864, with a short entry, one that his father would have understood in terms of river depth, water wheels, trip hammers, and the ability to produce shovels: "Rainy."

BACK AT THE BAR

"I don't know how I would have built my business if my sons hadn't joined in," Oliver concluded. "I kept in touch through the years with many of the mechanics I met in Springfield—even employed some of them back in North Easton—but it was my family that made my success possible. Eventually," he mused, "I suppose you get big enough and run out of sons and must rely on people outside the family to grow. People you can trust."

A new voice joined the conversation, that of a man of color who seemed in dress slightly younger than Ames and Whitney. "It's good to have sons," he said to Ames, turning to the barroom to add, "Good evening, I'm Thomas Downing." Happy to yield the floor, Ames slid onto his stool and tried to locate his mug in the accumulation of glasses on the table.

"No disrespect intended to Mr. Ames or Mr. Whitney," Downing said, "but there was a lot of change happening in America that wasn't being produced in a factory. In fact," he added, "black men like me and my friend Mr. Grimes"—placing his hand on the man next to him—"were not welcomed in many places of employment. That made life difficult for us and for our families."

William Grimes rose and stood next to Downing. "But we found ways to get along. It didn't mean more cotton gins or shovels," he said with a smile, "but I think we made a difference anyway."

Chapter 3

AGAINST THE ODDS:
SOCIAL ENTREPRENEURSHIP
IN THE EARLY REPUBLIC

By 1815, more people had traveled to the New World from Africa by means of the slave trade than had emigrated from Europe. Blacks numbering 1.4 million were held in hereditary slavery under a Constitution that allowed individual states to regulate America's so-called "peculiar institution." In 1839, Kentucky politician Henry Clay (1777–1852) calculated that slaves represented $1.2 billion in capital, an amount so vast that preserving slavery was more important for some than preserving the Union. Free blacks in both the North and South inhabited an unfriendly world. When the Frenchman Michel Chevalier toured the country, he concluded that the American black, whether free or enslaved, was treated by most whites "as if he were infected with the plague."

Was it possible to operate as a black entrepreneur in such a culturally and constitutionally hostile country? Three stories of extraordinary men will help to describe the bounded world in which black Americans in the early republic labored to innovate and prosper—and how much a nation can lose when entrepreneurship is not fully inclusive.

WILLIAM GRIMES:
"THE HARDEST WORK I HAVE EVER DONE"

William Grimes (1784–1865), who in another time and place might have become a wealthy and famous entrepreneur, demonstrates instead the role racism played in excluding a segment of America from the supportive community necessary to be successful. A field and house slave, valet, stable boy, coachman, and eventual runaway, Grimes negotiated a world in which most free blacks were limited to occupations such as day laborers, seamen, or domestic servants. Black proprietors might sell clothing at retail, keep a boardinghouse, serve food, or operate a barbershop. In a life filled with frustration, Grimes tried a little of everything, eventually recording his experiences in America's first fugitive slave narrative. It was prepared and published in 1825, when Grimes was forty years old; the release of a book by a black author was itself a form of disruptive, social entrepreneurship.

William Grimes was born in King George, Virginia, to an unknown slave woman and Benjamin Grymes Jr. (1756–1804), a white man and lieutenant in the American Revolutionary Army. At age ten, William was sold to Colonel William Thornton of Culpepper County, Virginia, and by 1811, to his fifth master, who relocated him from Virginia to Savannah, Georgia. Grimes's ability to make something from nothing was astonishing. While laboring on the Savannah plantation, he raised a small crop of rice for himself, earning six dollars to purchase meat and other necessities. At another time, he carried a hundred pounds of wood on his head for three miles, selling it to supplement his diet. Eventually, however, he found his conditions intolerable: "I have experienced the sufferings of a slave in the Southern States. I have traveled from Frederickstown in Maryland, to Darien in Georgia and from there to Savannah, from whence I made my escape."

Sometime around 1815, Grimes's *tenth* master visited Bermuda, leaving William behind in Savannah with the understanding that he would contract out his labor until his master's return. When the brig *Casket* from Boston moored in Savannah Harbor, Grimes secured work loading it with cotton bales. As the Yankee sailors got to know Grimes, they hatched a scheme of carving a hole in one of the bales large enough for him and some provisions. On the night the *Casket* departed, Grimes slipped away with it, traveling to Staten Island, New York. From there, he headed north, fearful at every step of being recaptured.

Grimes arrived in New Haven, Connecticut, a free man but with just seventy-five cents in his pocket. He found work at a livery stable owned by a free black man and set about removing rock from a ledge for building. "This I found to be the hardest work I had ever done, and began to repent that I had ever come away from Savannah, to this hard cold country," he wrote. It was clear that the North and freedom were no panacea for a black person in antebellum America. Grimes eventually encountered a man known to his master and was forced to flee, this time to Southington, Connecticut, where he took a job on a farm. There he managed to crush his ankle and was forced to crawl on his hands and knees until finally acquiring crutches and resuming work at small tasks. "I found it much harder at this time to be a free man, than I had to be a slave; but finally got to be able to earn fifty cents per day."

Grimes took a series of jobs around Yale University, digging wells and cutting wood. He opened a barbershop in Providence, Rhode Island, and worked as a servant, barber, and grocer in New Bedford, Massachusetts. He was twice jailed on suspicion of break-ins but both times was acquitted. Apparently unwelcome in New Bedford, he passed back through Rhode Island and finally landed in Litchfield, Connecticut, where he established a second barbershop. He remained in Litchfield some four years before heading back to New Haven, where he opened a victualing shop for students and engaged in lending money, cutting hair, cleaning clothes, and trading in furniture. Grimes even advertised to help reestablish his former clientele, revealing a wry humor despite his many hardships:

> OLD GRIMES IS NOT DEAD,
> BUT YOU MAY SEE HIM MORE,
> CLEANING COATS AND SHAVING HEADS,
> JUST AS BEFORE.

In 1817, William Grimes wed Clarissa Caesar, a woman suitable for "such a fine Virginian like myself," he wrote. However, he soon found himself again being hunted by his old master from Savannah. In fact, with Southern students often in New Haven for college, Grimes grew certain that his former master would learn his whereabouts. William, Clarissa, and their growing family returned to Litchfield, but William was ultimately discovered and, in danger of being separated from his wife and children, sacrificed his home and savings to raise $500 to purchase his own freedom. Now destitute, he decided to write his life story and to offer it to an American public that often did not wish to be reminded of the brutal details of slavery or the harsh conditions faced everywhere by people of color. In 1825, *Life of William Grimes, the Runaway Slave, Written by Himself* was published in New York City.

Grimes was brutally honest about his experiences. "I would advise no slave to leave his master," he wrote. "If he runs away, he is most sure to be taken: if he is not, he will ever be in the apprehension of it." Living as a fugitive, Grimes added, had left him in a position to be "often cheated, insulted, abused and injured." In this sense, the life of William Grimes was one of continual frustration and hardship.

In another way, however, his life was one of triumph. Here was a man of talent and courage who repeatedly adapted to his surroundings and who sacrificed everything to maintain his freedom and protect his family. In a world where the act of a black man opening a business could itself constitute Schumpeter's "novel combination," Grimes's perseverance was herculean. I "have always been an industrious man," he wrote, "and have endeavored to get an honest living, and if I could not do it one way I have tried another." Never finding the supportive community so essential to entrepreneurial success, Grimes remains nonetheless an inspiration to generations of struggling individuals excluded from mainstream entrepreneurial opportunities.

THOMAS DOWNING: "HE KNEW NOT TIRE"

A generation younger than William Grimes and born to free black parents on Virginia's Eastern Shore, Thomas Downing (1791–1866) spent his childhood fishing, digging clams, and harvesting oysters, activities that would shape his life. At age twenty-one, he left Virginia to enlist in the army, serving in the War of 1812 before settling in Philadelphia. There, he married and spent seven years as a servant. We get a glimpse into Downing's proud and unyielding character in the advice he gave his five children, encouraging them to "stand up for [their] rights, as well as those of the weaker ones, and repel invasion, by force, if necessary."

When Thomas and wife Rebecca moved to New York City in 1819, they found themselves in the oyster capital of the world. The lower half of the Hudson River estuary contained 350 square miles of oyster beds; New York Harbor alone may have been home to half of the world's oysters. Pearl Street in Manhattan's financial district received its name because the road was once paved with native oyster shells. Familiar with oyster beds from his time in Virginia, Downing sensed opportunity, and realizing that food-service trades were open to blacks, he entered the catering and restaurant business in the heart of New York's financial and political world—a black proprietor catering to the city's white elite.

Downing was a hard worker whose son said he "knew not tire." Thomas awoke at two a.m. each day, rowed across the Hudson to the Jersey Flats, harvested as many oysters as he was able, and then returned to begin the selling day. By 1823, Downing listed himself as an "oysterman" in the city directory, and his fame spread, especially among New York's upscale white clientele. By 1835, he was established at 5 Broad Street with a busy dining room and a large vault to store oysters.

Success and New York's rapid growth brought competition. Downing responded by getting up earlier, rowing out at midnight to meet captains before they could dock, purchasing their best product, and then helping them later at auction by bidding up the remainder. He also treated the captains as special guests when they dined in his restaurant. Over time, his "oyster saloon and eating house" became famous for the excellence and variety of its food, offering everything from traditional raw, fried, and stewed oysters to oyster pie, scalloped oysters, and poached turkey stuffed with oysters.

Downing's "cellar" earned special status as "the only oyster house to attract the aristocracy as well as ladies in the company of their husbands or chaperones." Situated on the corner of Broad and Wall Streets near the Customs House, banks, and exchanges, and decorated with Persian carpets, gold-leaf carvings, and chandeliers, Downing's establishment also became a political and business meeting place, and from those powerful contacts Downing implausibly developed a white, wealthy, and supportive community. In 1842, for example, he catered the Boz Ball for the mayor of New York (at the fancy price of ten dollars per ticket), at which Charles Dickens and his wife met some 2,500 New Yorkers. Downing's fame and clientele created opportunities to ship product to locations such as Paris and London, where Queen Victoria was so pleased with his oysters that she sent him a gold chronometer watch.

Downing competed and prospered in a trade with universal appeal. As one observer noted, in New York City "everyone seems to eat oysters all day long." Industry sales in the city in 1842 were about $6 million.

Thomas used his money and fame to support both his business and the abolitionist movement, helping found in 1836 the all-black United Anti-Slavery Society of the City of New York. At a time when not a single high school in New York would accept a black student, he also served as a trustee of the New York Society for the Promotion of Education among Colored Children. Few knew that his restaurant, described as "the very model of comfort and prosperity, with its mirrored arcades, damask curtains, fine carpet, and chandeliers" was also an important stop along the

Underground Railroad. Escaped slaves could find nourishment and refuge in Downing's oyster vaults.

When Thomas Downing died on April 10, 1866, *The New York Times* described him as "the well-known colored caterer and oyster-man . . . [who] took a prominent part in all measures for the elevation of the colored race, and lived an active and useful life." The New York Chamber of Commerce closed for a day out of respect, and Downing's family extended viewing hours to accommodate his many admirers. His son George ran the Oyster House until at least 1871.

Ironically, his grandson Henry F. Downing, a newspaper editor and playwright, was refused service in a New York restaurant in 1895 because of his race.

By 1910, 600 million gallons of raw sewage a day were flowing into New York waterways. Seventeen years later, the city closed its last oyster bed due to toxicity. However, when the Clean Water Act in 1972 prohibited the dumping of waste and raw sewage, the fortunes of New York Harbor began to improve. In 2014, the Billion Oyster Project was founded to rebuild the region's oyster population in waters now clean enough to support shellfish. By 2019, this nonprofit, citizens-science initiative had created twelve reefs with some 30 million oysters—still a long way from the days of Thomas Downing, but a promising start.

JAMES FORTEN:
A FORTUNE MADE BY HIS OWN INDUSTRY

William Grimes was born a slave and fought bravely throughout his life for freedom and economic independence. Thomas Downing was born free and became prosperous through backbreaking work and social innovation, bringing new respectability to New York City's bawdy oyster cellars. A third entrepreneur of color in the early republic, James Forten (1766–1842), lived a rags to riches story so impressive that he became among the wealthiest businessmen in Philadelphia and a powerful voice for African-American reform.

Forten's future was cast the first time he accompanied his father to work at the sail-making business of Robert Bridges, a white Quaker. By age ten, Forten had acquired the basic skills of his lifelong trade while learning to read at a nearby Quaker school. Anxious to support the Revolution and perhaps get rich as a privateer, Forten enlisted as a powder boy on the 450-ton American *Royal Louis* captained by Stephen Decatur (1751–1808). During Forten's maiden voyage, the *Royal Louis* captured four British vessels. His second cruise was met by the British warship *Amphion*, however, and in October 1782, Forten found himself a prisoner aboard the *Jersey* in Manhattan's East River.

Conditions were wretched, and he barely survived his seven long months of captivity. Released in 1783, James walked barefoot from New York to Trenton, where he was given food, and from there, he hobbled home to Philadelphia.

In 1785, Robert Bridges welcomed Forten back to his sail loft, and within a year named the toughened, ambitious young man his foreman. In time, Forten learned how to outfit and repair sails for every kind of vessel that appeared in the port of Philadelphia. In return, Forten provided his older friend and boss with leadership and the wisdom of someone whose own life had once depended upon quality sails. When Bridges retired in 1798, he lent Forten the money to purchase his sail-making business, ensuring he maintained customers and his labor force. Bridges was clearly Forten's benefactor, but support from the greater Quaker community in Philadelphia made it possible for Forten to excel. By age thirty-two, he employed a workforce of thirty-eight men, half of them white, and in 1805 he was operating the largest, most complex enterprise being run by a black man in Philadelphia.

Sail making was technologically intensive and highly competitive. High-quality, cutting-edge product gave mariners an advantage in trade and battle. Around 1800, Forten patented "an improvement in the management of sails . . . brought him a good deal of money." This ability to innovate was also important after the War of 1812, when peaceful waters allowed traders to build bigger vessels to accommodate larger cargoes, requiring the design of a new generation of sails. Forten might have been even richer had he done business with slave traders, but that was work "he indignantly refused," abolitionist Lydia Child writes, "declaring that he considered such a request an insult to any honest or humane man." By 1820, Forten had likely become the largest sail maker in Philadelphia, his sail loft was a showplace, and he was a wealthy and admired man.

He was also actively investing in real estate and transportation stocks. In addition, he had become a writer and an important voice in the abolitionist movement of the early republic, "the head of a generation of black reformers," historian Richard Newman writes, "who viewed the written word as a critical part of the African-American struggle for justice." Forten was able to move in both black and white circles in ways few others could, a tribute to his own skill, the support and mentoring of Robert Bridges, and the cosmopolitan nature of Philadelphia, which, with fifteen thousand blacks in 1830, was America's largest northern urban black community. He took advantage of his biracial community, working to pass laws permitting black Americans to become citizens. "There was scarcely any initiative relating to the advancement of African Americans in Philadelphia from the 1790s onward," historian Julie Winch added, "that did not benefit in some way or another from James Forten's input." His home on Lombard Street became a stop on the Underground Railroad, and it is not unthinkable that slaves fleeing the South might have spent time sequentially under both Forten's and Thomas Downing's protection.

As an entrepreneur, James Forten brought a series of novel combinations to market. He was a literate black man who could prosper in white society. He was an inventive sail maker who adapted technology to the needs of his customers. He ran an alcohol-free, racially integrated workforce in a country where such establishments were rare. He refused to profit from the slave trade. He employed his pen as wisely as his capital. And he was as much social entrepreneur as shrewd businessman, becoming one of the nation's leading black reformers. By 1832, Forten was thought to be worth $100,000 (or $2.9 million in today's value) and owned a great sail-making enterprise. He was, as Pennsylvania merchant and former congressman Samuel Breck (1771–1862) wrote admiringly, "in possession of a fortune made by his own industry."

BACK AT THE BAR

"It may have been partly my own industry," Forten told his barroom audience, "but success would not have been possible without my friend Mr. Bridges and the Quaker community in Philadelphia. There were not many cities in America," he added, "that would have tolerated a black man owning a business that employed black and white laborers.

"Of course," he continued, "there were other people of color who were successful in America. I had a friend and business partner, Paul Cuffe [1759–1817], who was a whaler, trader, and wealthy shipbuilder. Another fellow by the name of Thomas Jennings [1791–1859] owned a dry-cleaning business not far from Mr. Downing's oyster establishment in New York City, and he became the first black American to receive a patent by inventing 'dry scouring' of clothes."

"And," William Grimes said, "we all heard about 'Free Frank' McWorter [1777–1854], who was born a slave, bought himself and his family out of slavery, and founded the multiracial town of New Philadelphia, Illinois. Maybe if I'd headed west instead of north," Grimes wondered aloud, "things might have been different."

"The world was changing fast," Thomas Downing continued, "and I lived long enough to see the war that ended slavery. That must have opened all kinds of opportunity," he added hopefully.

The room grew silent. A waiter slid between tables to replenish drinks. Nobody seemed to want to break the spell of the storyteller.

Then, a clean-shaven, sharp-looking man in a coat and tie stood. "Plenty of opportunity," he agreed. "But plenty of obstacles—always lots of obstacles." He adjusted his tie, smoothing his coat. "I can't pretend to know the horror of slavery," he continued, "or being held prisoner on a warship, or catching malaria, or watching my factory burn down. But if you want to know about hard times, about workers shooting at their bosses and bosses shooting back, and about businesses that got so big, so automated, and so powerful that they could subject their workers to *wage slavery*, then I've got a story for you."

Part Two

MASS PRODUCTION

Chapter 4

KING GILLETTE:
MASS PRODUCTION IN
AN AGE OF ANXIETY

In 1893, Wisconsin native King Camp Gillette (1855–1932) was a successful if obscure traveling salesman pitching rubber and cork bottle stoppers for the Baltimore Seal Company. A year later, nearly forty years old, he rose to sudden national fame with the publication of his book *The Human Drift*. Dedicating his writing to "all mankind," Gillette argued that capital and labor in America were at war. A nation crushed by the Panic of 1893 had watched fifteen thousand businesses close, hundreds of farms be abandoned, and unemployment in some states exceed 40 percent.

The root of this evil, Gillette told his reader, was unrestrained competition, a winner-take-all mentality that had led to the rise of massive, automated corporations. Oil, sugar, steel, and leather were just a few examples of industries that had consolidated and then mechanized their production, reducing the labor force to menial tasks or unemployment. He described the anguish of workers forced into a condition of "wage slavery," where weekly survival depended on the next paycheck, and employment hinged on the whims of a nonproductive class of owners. Gillette warned his reader that "the slaves of the South were in paradise compared with the position of those who will be dependent on the masters of the future."

This dire message resonated with many unemployed Americans, yet seemed completely at odds with the wonders of mechanization that entrepreneurs such as Eli Whitney and Oliver Ames had introduced to the nation in the first half of the nineteenth century. Why, if America's industrial capacity had only grown more productive and efficient after the Civil War, was there high anxiety and economic malaise? What had gone wrong?

MASS PRODUCTION AND THE ANXIETY OF BIG BUSINESS

While the term "mass production" would not become common in America until the twentieth century, the impact of high-speed mechanization had rippled through industry after industry beginning in the 1840s. The introduction of precision machining and interchangeable parts, first championed by the Springfield Armory, represented "the most prolific production technology the world has ever known," historian David Hounshell writes.

In the 1850s and 1860s, for example, Singer produced sewing machines one by one, the product of individual craftsmen. By the mid-1880s, the company had added specialized machinery capable of producing one million sewing machines annually. Likewise, the McCormick reaper, introduced commercially in 1840 by Cyrus Hall McCormick (1809–1884), was manufactured for a decade in the confines of a large blacksmith shop. By focusing on standardized parts, quality, and volume, and then adding a supervisor with experience in arms and sewing machine production, the company produced more than one hundred thousand machines in 1889. A generation later, as Henry Ford's moving assembly line dazzled the world by producing two million Model Ts annually, mass production had become, historian Allan Nevins concludes, "a lever to move the world."

It was this world in motion in the 1890s that King Gillette described in *The Human Drift*. Where America's farmers had generated $500 million more in annual output than industry in 1870, factories generated three times the wealth of farmers by 1900. The consequence of mass production was a wholesale shift of Americans from farm to factory, and the rise of business entities so large and controlling that they seemed a threat to the consumers they had been created to serve.

The Panic of 1893, a recession we now know to be part of the regular cadence of a capitalist economy, brought the fixed-cost, automated machinery of America to a screeching halt. Competitors in industries such as copper, wire nails, bicycles, tin plate, and newsprint could not discount or collude their way to recovery. There was simply not enough demand. The result was a wave of consolidations between 1895 and 1904 as organizations attempted to create the scale necessary to feed their machinery and survive. Some of America's iconic companies were formed in this period, including National Biscuit, DuPont, Eastman Kodak, International Harvester, and Otis Elevator. The formation of United States Steel Corporation with a market capitalization of $1.4 billion in 1901 would set off alarms with many Americans.

Could these enormous factories of mass production—and the wealthy who owned them—grow stronger than the federal government and *take over* America?

The solution proposed by Gillette in *The Human Drift* was to create a "united stock company" sufficiently large to control all national production and distribution. Gillette's plan was to rid the world of money and allow the only competition among men to be intellectual in nature and pursued for the common good. Gillette envisioned "Metropolis," a single city of glass towers built in a 135-by-45-mile rectangle stretching from Buffalo to Rochester, New York. It would be large enough to hold sixty million people, expandable to ninety million. The city would use Niagara Falls for electricity, Lake Erie for water, and feature porcelain construction for its strength and cleanliness.

While King Gillette wrote in earnest, even he must have been surprised when the radical-reformist magazine *Twentieth Century* formed a new company, named Gillette as president, and urged its readers to each buy a share of stock at five dollars. Fortunately for everyone involved, the idea was controversial among *Twentieth Century* readers, subscriptions to the new company were modest, and plans to build Metropolis languished over several years until *Twentieth Century* itself went bankrupt. Gillette still harbored utopian visions but was distracted by a second project that had come to occupy his spare time between visits with his bottling customers.

"AS LIGHTLY AS A BIRD SETTLING ON ITS NEST"

Joining the Baltimore Seal Company (later Crown Cork & Seal) in 1891, Gillette had become good friends with its president, William Painter, who had invented the bottle stoppers that his company sold. Gillette himself had dabbled with several inventions, "some of which had merit and made money for others," he wrote, "but seldom for myself."

Recognizing his friend's inventive itch, Painter issued a challenge. "King," he asked one day, "why don't you try to think of something like the Crown Cork which, when once used, it is thrown away, and the customer keeps coming back for more—and with every additional customer you get, you are building a permanent foundation of profit." This was a modern notion, one that set traditional American frugality against its new embrace of mass production: Make something expressly designed to be used a few times and then thrown away. Gillette became fixated with the idea of inventing what the modern world now calls "consumables."

In the summer of 1895, while shaving at his home in Boston, Gillette found his straight-edge razor dull beyond stropping. This meant another trip to the cutler for sharpening. Writing about the event a generation later, Gillette's origin story has a dreamlike quality. "As I stood there with the razor in my hand, my eyes resting on it as lightly as a bird settling down on its nest—the Gillette razor was born. I saw it all in a moment." However, Gillette knew little about razors and less about steel. I "could not forsee the trials and tribulations that I was to pass through before the razor was a success." Nevertheless, he wrote to his wife—just as an excited Eli Whitney had written to his father about the cotton gin nearly a century before—to announce that their fortune was assured. The path from invention to wealth seemed straight and true.

In 1895, Americans could choose from some three dozen straight-edge razor options ranging from sixty cents to $3.50. Straight-edge razors were made from forged steel and relied on thickness and mass to ensure that the cutting edge remained stable. Each was considered a long-term or lifetime purchase. Shaving with such "weapons" required a steady hand and both skill and time to keep the blade sharp. Those brave enough to shave at home still turned to a cutler to sharpen their blades. Others relied instead on the local barbershop, said to be "as thick as saloons" in 1900.

Gillette's idea was to make blades from thin sheet steel, reducing their mass and cost, and then create a locking mechanism in the razor handle to provide stability. From a consumer perspective, he wrote, "Blades could be constructed and made cheap enough to do away with honing and stropping and permit the user to replace dull blades by new ones." It was a novel idea in the nineteenth century, and it placed King Gillette in 1895 at the implausible crossroads of proposing a socialist takeover of capitalism to rid America of competition while launching an entrepreneurial venture designed to create competition and, if successful, a large and powerful business. His biographer, Russell Adams, says, "It was almost as if Karl Marx had paused between *The Communist Manifesto* and *Das Kapital* to develop a dissolving toothbrush or a collapsible comb." Gillette was both a big-thinking utopian and a big-thinking entrepreneur—either two sides of the same visionary coin, or a case in which "each side of his personality seems to have floated in separate, water-tight compartments."

There were innumerable obstacles between Gillette's epiphany in 1895 and the creation of a working disposable razor. He turned first to his professional community in the bottling industry, which listened intently but could not be much help in the earliest stages of his venture. Over the next six years, Gillette visited every machine shop and cutler in Boston, New York, and Newark, and even took his problem to the Massachusetts Institute of Technology, hoping to find someone who could harden and temper a thin piece of steel so that it would not warp. Most told him he was throwing money away. "If I had been technically trained I would have quit or probably would never have begun," he wrote. But, thanks to his community, he was about to stumble upon a breakthrough.

COMMUNITY FOUND, COMMUNITY LOST

The professional network around which Gillette had floated his idea included John J. Joyce and W. B. Holloway, customers and wealthy brewers. Gillette also approached Edward J. Stewart, another client and a soft drink bottler, who introduced the idea of a disposable razor to his neighbor, a Boston lamp manufacturer named Henry Sachs. This unexpected and serpentine series of connections—a good demonstration of how healthy entrepreneurial community often works—would prove pivotal. In early 1901, Sachs showed Gillette's patent idea to his friend William Emery Nickerson, an MIT-trained engineer. Nickerson was unimpressed and uninterested, but Sachs was unrelenting, and in the late summer of 1901 Nickerson agreed to spend a month thinking about how to create Gillette's disposable razor.

There were few people in America better qualified. An 1876 graduate of MIT with a degree in chemistry, Nickerson had taken his first job with a tanners' association and been given the assignment of improving yield of their tanning agents. Instead of tinkering with the chemistry of the process, Nickerson soon patented a successful, mechanized, bark-grinding mill. Thinking this would make him rich, he lost rights to the invention through the duplicity of his associates. Nickerson and his wife then moved to Georgia, where he was unsuccessful in gold mining and sawmilling. In 1886, they returned to Boston and, hearing of an elevator crash, Nickerson earned seven patents related to elevator safety and performance. His mechanical genius was undeniable, but so was his inability to successfully market or sell his designs. Discouraged and in debt, he joined a firm competing with Edison's light bulb that subsequently collapsed, and then he worked with a friend on automatic weighing machines for the food industry. Despite a series of inventions across a variety of industries, Nickerson had failed to cash in. He later wrote that he had encountered "natural obstacles, over which I have generally triumphed, and my brother man, by whom I have generally been vanquished."

In September 1901, Nickerson announced that he had solved the problem presented to him by Henry Sachs. "It is my confident opinion," Nickerson wrote, "that not only can a successful razor be made on the principles of the Gillette patent, but that if the blades are made by proper methods a result in advance of anything known can be reached." Without drawings or prototype, he was ready to construct machines that would create thin, inexpensive, sharp, and disposable blades. "I am as confident that I have grasped the situation and can guarantee, as far as such a thing can be guaranteed, a successful outcome."

Eli Whitney would solve a riddle with his cotton gin that others had tried to solve but failed. Nickerson, however, would solve a riddle that nobody except Gillette had even thought to ask, believing it impossible. And Nickerson's answer was not simply envisioning the design of a cheap razor blade, but the machinery required to mass-produce it.

Nickerson, Sachs, and Sachs's brother-in-law Jacob Heilborn set about calling friends and associates over the next four months to raise $5,000, enough to purchase the materials, tools, and labor to allow Nickerson to put his ideas into practice. Gillette, with his name on the patent application but still employed full time selling bottle stoppers, played almost no role in this early launch activity.

Nickerson was ready to begin manufacturing in May 1902. The first samples proved successful, and investors expected a steady increase in volume and revenue. However, Nickerson still had many problems to solve between these early prototypes and full-scale manufacture. By the spring of 1903, the company had run out of money and the investors had become disenchanted and ready to liquidate. That's when Gillette had lunch with his friend John Joyce, who offered to invest $100,000 in the company. In a sense, this was the last active contribution that King Gillette would make to the organization that bore his name and that would sell a product with his face on every package. Gillette's bottling community would make him famous and rich, but it would also force him out of any real operating role in the company.

In 1903, for example, Gillette was asked by Crown Cork & Seal to establish a factory in London. Already the unpaid president of his fledgling razor-blade start-up, Gillette asked his fellow directors to create a salaried position that would allow him to devote full-time efforts to the new enterprise. "But those in control refused to meet my wishes," Gillette wrote, "giving as a reason the need for every dollar for development of the business." Gillette resigned as president and assumed he would move permanently to England on behalf of Crown Cork & Seal, sailing with his family and all his household furniture. Six months later, however, he learned that Gillette was "selling all the goods it could make and that it was about to enter into a contract to turn over all its foreign interests on a royalty basis."

King raced to Boston, successfully stopped the royalty agreement, and—owning nine thousand of sixty-five thousand outstanding shares—insisted and was finally granted a salaried position, resigning from Crown Cork & Seal. As president of his namesake company, Gillette traveled to his office every day, but his role was fuzzy. "A contention developed between him and some of the directors," Nickerson wrote. It was a disagreement that apparently lasted until 1910, Nickerson adds, when "all differences were smoothed over peacefully and returned no more." But that was also the year that Gillette, now a millionaire, moved permanently from the company's home in Boston to California. For the next twenty-two years, until his death in 1932, he was president of the company in title only.

What happened is unclear. The year 1910 was when Gillette resumed his quest for utopia by announcing the creation of the "World Corporation," now incorporated in Arizona, and offering the presidency to former president Theodore Roosevelt for four years with a stipend of $1 million. The plan was to eliminate all human suffering by first acquiring all dividend-paying securities, estimated at $100 billion, to redeem all the shares, and then to turn them over to the "peoples of the world, as actual owners, in equal shares." Not surprisingly, Roosevelt declined. "A simple explanation of the plan," one journalist noted, "would be to compare it to a snake which defeated starvation by swallowing its tail." It was the kind of mockery expressed by observers who tried to come to grips with a famous, successful, millionaire industrialist who also seemed to be a socialist and crackpot.

Perhaps Gillette's departure from his company came because leadership found his utopian activities to be detrimental to the company's brand. Or, despite being a visionary, brilliant networker, and talented salesman, Gillette might have been a poor manager. One associate said that he could "wreck a company as easily as he could build one." In either case, Gillette's role after 1910 would be to visit the company a couple of times a year, speak at important events and anniversaries, and remain the face of the brand. He would draw a full salary until his death, but by 1910 it seems clear that the eponymous founder of the world's first disposable razor-blade company had been forced out by the community he had called upon to make his idea a reality.

GILLETTE'S MYTHICAL BUSINESS MODEL: RAZORS AND RAZOR BLADES

Meanwhile, Nickerson devoted most of his efforts to the company's production of razor blades. The employees working for him understood that they were involved in something special—and if there was any part of Gillette that felt like a modern start-up, it was in this department. In March 1904, for example, directors were told that blades, which they hoped to sell for a penny, cost five cents each just for labor. Nickerson and his team solved the problem by inventing a "bench grinder," which John Joyce later claimed saved the company.

The Gillette Company soon outgrew its first building, before taking a second in 1906 and a third and fourth by 1910. That year, King Gillette writes, "began the installation of new machinery which was to increase the capacity of the buildings to turn out our product fully one hundred percent." It was a grand leap from mechanization to complete mass production of both blades and handles. By 1918, he added, "We are able to produce with one thousand employees five times the output of product that we were able to produce in 1909 with 1800 employees." In absolute terms, the company's factory in Boston was producing 370,000 blades a day in 1918, or twenty-two miles of sharpened edges. And quality was flawless. "We talk of thousandths of an inch in the fitting of parts for automobiles, but when we come to a shaving edge, we cannot even consider millionths of an inch." By the 1930s, Gillette was selling a billion or more perfect blades annually and becoming the kind of company, ironically, that its founder had denounced in *The Human Drift*.

Even entrepreneurs who have never shaved with a Gillette product likely know the so-called razor/razor-blade sales model of selling at cost (or giving away) a handle and then locking a customer into a lifetime of purchasing expensive, consumable blades. It translates to "Give 'em the razor; sell 'em the blades," used today in everything from inkjet printers to video game consoles.

In April 1903, the directors of Gillette set a price of one dollar for twenty blades, and three dollars for twenty blades and a razor. John Joyce objected, however, saying that the razor was worth five dollars. He was certain the public would agree. The other directors were frightened to charge five dollars, equal at the time to about one-third of a weekly industrial wage. But, Joyce believed, Gillette had an ironclad patent and a mechanical mastermind in Nickerson, and that kind of genius (as Whitney and Miller had decided for their cotton gin) should never be discounted.

The median wage for US workers in the fourth quarter of 2017 was $857 a week. Using Joyce's 1903 recommendation, the cost of a Gillette razor would be about $285 today—two to three times the price of a full-functioned smartphone. Obviously, this is the exact opposite of the cheap-razor business model for which Gillette has come to be known. However, Gillette wrote, by *not* giving the razor away cheaply, Joyce showed great "foresight and courage," generating the capital Gillette required to power its growth.

The promise of the Gillette business model was not a low price but that "every razor sold by the Gillette Company represents a saving of half an hour of time spent in a barber shop, without saying anything about the money paid for service and tips." A perfect shave, Gillette told customers, was essential to cleanliness and the appearance of prosperity. And, Gillette told employees, the "stickiness" of the model was at work despite premium pricing. "Those who purchase the Gillette razor are willing victims of the Gillette habit, for they bind and tie themselves."

The company maintained its high-priced razor until its seventeen-year patent ran out in 1921. The patent was successfully defended throughout. Then, and only then, did the company launch a low-priced razor backed by a massive advertising campaign to fend off imitators.

A MASTERY OF MASS PRODUCTION

In Schumpeter's terms, Gillette offered a classic innovation. The company disrupted an economic flow by introducing American mass-production techniques using punched or cut sheet steel into an industry historically dominated by English and German forged products. Before Gillette, the razor industry was labor intensive, and after, capital intensive. Before Gillette, a quality razor was expected to last a lifetime, and after, blades were designed to be discarded. Gillette's promise of no honing and no stropping upended traditional competitors, stole share, and appealed to a new generation, which adopted Gillette products enthusiastically even as an older generation "tired of cutting themselves with old-fashioned razors" changed their lifelong habits, putting many barbershops out of business.

Despite their different talents and contributions, Nickerson and Gillette remained friends for life. Gillette wrote that Nickerson was "the only man in the world who could have perfected the razor." Nickerson, who had achieved little business success before meeting his friend, wrote that Gillette's "commercial triumphs were of no mean order since they involve, not so much the satisfying of an existing demand, as its transformation, and its adjustment to a new productive technique." Their innovative spirit continues to inspire the company, with Gillette now offering a customizable 3D-printed razor while still holding 54 percent of the global share for razors.

When we think of the Gillette Company's long record of success, we think first of the razor/razor-blade model. In reality, the company was anchored in the product vision and community of King Camp Gillette, the mechanical genius of William Emery Nickerson, and the business model and marketing savvy of John Joyce and his executive team. Gillette was a company driven by mechanization, aggressive pricing and marketing, determined patent defense—and the mastery of mass production.

BACK AT THE BAR

"So you're the razor and razor blades guy?" one of the younger entrepreneurs at the bar asked, clearly impressed. King Gillette grimaced inside but decided it was best to take credit, even if the story was more complicated than that.

The older entrepreneurs in the barroom were also impressed by Gillette, but for different reasons. The size of businesses in the twentieth century—*billions* of razor blades manufactured every year—was breathtaking. Oliver Ames, intrigued by the whole discussion of metal, was about to ask a question about the properties of sheet steel when the first female voice of the evening rose above the chatter.

"What about the women?"

The chatter softened a bit as a tall woman in a simple cotton day dress and a sturdy pair of mid-heel Oxfords rose from her chair. "Were there no female entrepreneurs among all of your shovels and razor blades?" She smiled, but in a no-nonsense way.

King Gillette returned the smile. "This, my friends, is Mary Evans Sharpe, but you might know her as Mary Elizabeth. Perhaps," Gillette added, "you have tasted her delicious candy or dined at one of her restaurants? She has a story about mechanization and mass production that is spectacular in its own way. Mrs. Sharpe?"

With a career spent taking care of hungry customers, Mary looked around at the faces in the barroom and said, "Before I begin—waiter, could we please get some menus?"

Chapter 5

MARY ELIZABETH EVANS SHARPE: THE INSTINCT TO *DO*

A spiring female entrepreneurs in America have always faced a
daunting set of economic and cultural obstacles. In the early
republic, historian Alice Kessler-Harris writes, "Marriage was
the natural and desirable role for white women." The unmarried and wid-
owed might teach, engage in an appropriate trade such as dressmaking,
or work as a domestic servant. Beginning in the 1820s, the growth of
America's textile factories attracted young, single women to millwork,
though few considered this kind of labor anything more than a temporary
step before marriage.

Women made inroads into the workforce throughout the nineteenth
century, but prejudice and discrimination persisted. One broadly held
assumption was that a married female laborer must surely be neglecting
her family. Another held that a single woman put her morals at risk when
she entered the workforce with men. "The wholesale employment of
women in the various handicrafts must gradually unsex them," the American Federation of Labor wrote in an 1897 policy, "while it numerically
strengthens the multitudinous army of loafers, paupers, [and] tramps."
In other words, common wisdom held, women in the workforce were
responsible for imperiling both themselves *and* the opposite sex.

By 1900, however, the term "New Woman" was in general circulation in the United States, capturing the radical idea that women should have a public voice and could aspire to be self-fulfilled in their work and personal lives. This transformation was reflected in the changing workforce. From 1890 to 1930, female clerical workers grew from 4 percent to 21 percent of all clerical workers, office life being more pleasant than factory or farm work. By 1910, women had established a toehold in the law while comprising 6 percent of all physicians and making significant advances in social work, science, and journalism.

In 1920, the US Department of Labor released a report that detailed the impact on the workforce from World War I, a conflict that had "wrenched the whole industrial machine with great violence." American women had been invited to work in industries—including heavy industry and the manufacture of armaments—that their fathers, husbands, brothers, and sons had vacated to serve in the war. The results were overwhelmingly positive. The president of a recording and computing machine company spoke for many of his peers when he told researchers that women outperformed men in a variety of activities involving punch presses, bench lathes, and milling machines. Quality was excellent, and turnover less than 4 percent annually.

By 1930, the percentage of wage-earning women between ages sixteen and forty-four in the American workforce was nearly 30 percent.

The call to traditional roles continued, of course. Author Constance Cary Harrison spoke for a nineteenth-century generation that found the 1900s to be a perplexing time when she encouraged women graduating from high school and college to consider the profession of home life. The cornerstone of civilization was the home, Harrison wrote, and when women did not fulfill their traditional roles, families suffered, and all of civilization was put at risk. This "home in peril" narrative surged in the opening decades of the twentieth century, a sign less of peril and more of educational and commercial progress being made by women.

One remarkable female entrepreneur whose career spanned this period was Mary Elizabeth Evans Sharpe (1884–1985). Sharpe was able to blend the old world of domesticity and the new world of industrial capitalism, launching a business in her kitchen that she mechanized, mass-produced, and marketed into a national brand.

SEEING THE BIG PICTURE

Born in Syracuse, New York, Mary Elizabeth Evans was the oldest daughter of Fanny Elizabeth Riegel and William E. G. Evans, a professor of vocal music at Syracuse University. When her father died in 1891, Mary Elizabeth, her mother, two sisters, and brother moved in with her maternal grandparents. This move brought under one roof the two individuals who would most shape Evans's future entrepreneurial success.

Her grandfather, Henry Riegel (1825–1897), was a lawyer and judge. "He was well-known and much beloved, and a very wise man," Evans said in 1979 when, as a still vigorous ninety-five-year-old, she sat for a set of interviews at the Schlesinger Library at Radcliffe College. Grandfather "educated me in a conceptual way," she said. "I think I'm apt to be able to see the whole thing rather than the details—to think big and not be afraid of the issue. Don't scuttle away."

Mary Elizabeth's ability to see the big picture was complemented by a strong dose of her mother's courage. My mother's "great quality was her fearlessness," Evans said. "She never looked back. I never heard her regretting or being sorry for herself. She always looked forward."

It was her grandfather Riegel who first set in motion Mary Elizabeth's future career. "He did not approve of our buying cheap penny candy," Evans said. "He thought it was not good for us . . . so he told us that we could have all the candy we wanted, if we'd make it ourselves." For Judge Riegel, this dictate was common sense. In the unregulated market of nineteenth-century America, before passage of the Pure Food and Drug Act in 1906, store-bought candy was often unhealthy and sometimes deadly.

FUSEL OIL AND GLUCOSE:
"FOOD FOR CHILDREN"

At the turn of the century, America's candy manufacturers boasted of an annual business in candies and sweets that exceeded that of beer, wine, and liquor combined. A British newspaper declared that Americans "make their sweets as we make our bread, practically for a day's consumption," and that a gentleman escorting a young lady to the theater had best bring her not a bouquet but a box of sweets. Strong demand attracted quacks and crooks. Chocolate drops full of brandy were indiscriminately sold to children. Some candy was found to contain fusel oil, an ingredient used in lacquer solvents. Other manufacturers added glucose to honey, brightened candies with the use of aniline colors (used in the manufacture of the precursors to polyurethane), and added terra-cotta, a clay commonly used to make bricks.

In 1899, the American Confectioners' Association assured the public that "poisonous candy has entirely disappeared from the market, and laws against such products are strictly obeyed in almost every State in the Union." Nevertheless, time and again, children were sickened and killed by adulterated candy.

Judge Riegel bought a candy hook and put it up in the kitchen so his grandchildren could make molasses candy and vinegar taffy. "And then my mother had a friend," Sharpe recalled, "who knew how to make chocolate creams." As Mary Elizabeth and her younger siblings became more adept at candy making, they began giving it away as presents at Christmas.

When Judge Riegel died in 1897, the family found itself saddled with heavily encumbered farmland that generated only modest rental income from a settlement of seventy-five workers' cottages constructed by the judge. Mary Elizabeth and her family moved into two of these small homes and soon found themselves in a struggle to make ends meet. They accepted used clothes from friends, and vegetables in lieu of rent from neighbors occupying the cottages around them. It was Mary Elizabeth's mother, however, who hit upon the idea of opening a small drugstore.

From this modest beginning, the family called upon a cousin in the wholesale grocery business to extend credit, allowing them to launch a larger grocery store. "Lizzie [the former maid of Mary Elizabeth's grandmother] and I lived there at the store," Mary Elizabeth said. "And then we began making a little molasses candy and whatnot." The store began to grow. "We put a sign up, 'M. E. Evans.' And one of the reporters on the *Syracuse Herald* . . . came out and made a big splashing article about us. This helped people to remember us."

By 1900, at age fifteen, Mary Elizabeth found herself a full-fledged merchant in charge of a grocery store with a meat shop, drug department, and ice cream parlor, generating income for a family of five. In an inauspicious way, she had begun what was to become her true entrepreneurial calling. "We didn't sell much candy at that time [but] occasionally, when we made candy, we'd take some around," she recalled. "We had three or four neighbors that would always buy a little; it was more a fun thing than it was really for the money. But I think that this gave us the idea that we *could* sell candy."

It was this local community of friends that embraced the Evans family and launched Mary Elizabeth's entrepreneurial career. One day, her Sunday school teacher asked to purchase some candy, boxed in such a way that she might take orders at a party she was attending. "This gave me an idea that maybe I could start a club that would give regular orders," Evans recalled. "So I wrote a little advertisement and said, 'Would you like to become an interested outsider? If you'll pay me $4.00 a month, every Saturday I will bring a pound of candy to your house.'" Several customers subscribed. Mary Elizabeth purchased white folding boxes and wrote, "Mary Elizabeth's Homemade Candies" on the outside. "And that's the way the name began. And it wasn't much of a thing, you know. Very, very precarious and small."

These efforts were barely enough to support the family. "We struggled along," Evans recalled. "There didn't seem to be any way that we could climb out of it, you know." Finally forced to rely on the charity of a friend, the family relocated to Syracuse proper. This move became another turning point, however. In a more spacious apartment, the family had, for the first time, enough room to expand their small enterprise. They used the basement for candy making and the second floor as a display room. And they took advantage of the extra space to take the first small step in mass production, purchasing a huge kettle that could cook fifty pounds of taffy at a time.

Less a stroke of genius or entrepreneurial vision than an act of desperation in a world without a social safety net, Evans explained, "Why did I go into the candy business? Why, simply because we were so poor we had to do something, and candy-making was the only thing I knew how to do *well*."

In the fall of 1901, Mary Elizabeth and her mother placed a tiny candy cupboard, "barely six feet long under the stairway of the University Block building in Syracuse for a hefty ten dollars a month." This eleven-story office building had steady foot traffic, including students, teachers, and administrators of the Syracuse University College of Law. Mary Elizabeth chose to make it a "help yourself booth" where patrons were asked to pay and make change on an honor basis. "Everybody warned us against putting the stand on any such basis, predicted that we would be robbed right and left, and said it was foolish and opposed to all business sense." Undeterred, the young entrepreneur left a sign on the self-serve booth that said,

> OPEN THESE DOORS
> TAKE WHAT YOU WILL
> LEAVE COST OF GOODS TAKEN
> MAKE YOUR CHANGE FROM MY TILL
> RESPECTING CUSTOMERS' HONOR,
> MARY ELIZABETH

This first retail candy effort would become a key feature in the company's future branding, both for the exposure it provided and for the sense of customer trust it embodied. "This was written up not only in Syracuse, but in Buffalo," Sharpe recalled. "Even a national candy magazine wrote up an article about 'this little girl.'" The press loved the story and ran with it. "The Evans sisters had a profound belief in the honesty of human beings," one reporter wrote, "or they would never have started a Help Yourself Booth . . . And it's to the credit of Syracusan morals that the three sisters were never cheated." A Buffalo paper reported that Mary Elizabeth "is very girlish in manners and appearance," and, added a customer, "the person who would cheat her must be a cur."

MECHANIZING PRODUCTION

By March 1902, the Evans family had sold twelve thousand boxes of candy. In 1903, *Grocery World* referred to Mary Elizabeth's business as "probably the most famous retail candy business in the United States." With this success, Mary Elizabeth generated enough capital to move to a larger and more visible candy shop in Syracuse, this one leased at the princely sum of twenty-five dollars a month.

Evans's entrepreneurial community was built around family and friends. Her brother, for example, discovered a gift for mechanization, developing a candy-wrapping machine and running the family's shipping operation. Her mother and sisters worked side by side making candy. And with growth, this community expanded. "We began to hire some people to help stir the batches while they were cooking and so on . . . It was the first time we did that. Until then it had been just family."

As the business grew, the task of manual candy making became onerous. One Christmas, a mysterious card appeared addressed to Mary Elizabeth with a gift of $250 from friends in the Syracuse community. The funds allowed the family to pay down its debts and invest in its first piece of mechanized equipment, a Ball cream beater. "Oh, a tremendous difference," Evans recalled. "We could make 250 pounds at a clip. And that was enough for a week or maybe a two-week supply." This gift was a testament to the power of both mechanization and community—one that had obviously been won over by the industriousness of Evans and her family. "They were tiny steps for tiny feet," Evans said, "and they, of course, seemed to me to be much bigger than they were."

As Evans's business grew beyond its neighborhood, it began to experience troubling seasonality. Trade was strong in the spring and winter but declined markedly in the summer, when upscale customers fled to the shore and mountains. Evans elected to follow her customers, launching a new store in Newport, Rhode Island, and placing candy in the summer resorts of New England and New York. Developing these new trade channels was difficult.

> I went way up into the Rangeley Lakes in Maine, and I went to the Adirondacks . . . Yes, every step was a vague and trying thing to go to strange people and ask them to buy my candy . . . Naturally, I was not a pushing kind of child. I was ready to do what I had to do, but I don't think I was really full of pizazz . . . I'd say, "God, please help me, please help me." . . . It was a very, very difficult thing for me to do psychologically. I felt I was just a tiny little ant in a great big world. Why should anybody be interested in buying anything from me? I was timid about saying what I had to sell, you know. But my mother created the atmosphere behind me that kept me going.

About that time, Evans designed a marketing piece, *The Story of Mary Elizabeth*. It described her "Candy Kitchen" in Syracuse in terms that a traditional, upscale female customer would appreciate. The business was, after all, "simply the true story of a sweet young girl without business experience, without capital, but with an *Idea*, courage, and a sincere belief in human nature and herself." Mary Elizabeth, the brochure noted, was "the youngest successful merchant in the United States . . . [a] 'slip of a girl,' bright-eyed, and rosy cheeked," who launched the enterprise at fifteen years of age and is now "willing and happy to devote all the long joyous days of youth to the one vital object of her existence—making her candy business a success." She was also, her literature failed to disclose, willing to add mechanization to the production and shipping process, and unafraid to look beyond the confines of her small Syracuse kitchen.

SUCCESS IN NEWPORT

While mountain resorts offered only modest success, it was in Newport, Rhode Island, where Evans finally struck gold. Seeking an upscale summer retail outlet, the family stumbled upon a run-down and abandoned flower shop in the center of town. It was big enough to set up tables and serve tea and cake, along with their candy. "We took some of my grandmother's beautiful china down there to serve tea in," Mary Elizabeth said. "Well, of course, the Newporters were very surprised to see that beautiful china used, and I think that they were amused that these little girls were making tea and serving things . . . People in those days who had grand dinner parties always had plates of candy all over the table, and these people sent their butlers in to buy our candy. So we had very, very good business between the tea and the candy."

It was this success in Newport that encouraged Evans's next stage of commercial growth. "By then it was getting to be a complicated bookkeeping problem," Mary Elizabeth recalled, "so I got an expert accountant to teach me double-entry bookkeeping . . . I always wanted to be in control of the operation." Meanwhile, Evans moved the "Candy Kitchen" to a larger and more open factory space in Syracuse. It was another instance of homespun marketing meeting the realities of twentieth-century production. The company's branding material suggested to customers that, upon entering the kitchen, "you have left the old commercial world *far* behind, and are in a place of ideals where the heart and the hand and the head work together." The kitchen presented in the company's new marketing material featured white-frocked girls, delicious odors, harmonious color schemes, and women that "bring their environment up to their own ideals. Not a single copper kettle is discolored. There is an air of calm and cheerfulness."

In fact, the "Candy Kitchen" in Syracuse had become a high-production facility employing fifty workers expected to supply dozens of locations in New York, Philadelphia, and throughout the East. The Ball cream beater had many mechanized companions by then. Evans wrestled with the distribution of a highly perishable product before the availability of reliable refrigeration. She also faced human resource issues, balky suppliers, and commodity pricing risk—in short, all of the issues of the modern American enterprise. And yet, as one admiring fan wrote about the Evans family, "This earnest, honest, healthy, intelligent, active, alert and loving little group produces candy of a most superior kind and quality. The candy they make is like themselves."

An article in the *Pittsburgh Press* played into this homespun image, describing Mary Elizabeth as "wonderfully neat, wonderfully house-wife-y in appearance and wonderfully in earnest about all she does." By then, this yet-to-be-married "housewife" was growing increasingly wealthy and was sweating out the daily issues of a growing entrepreneurial enterprise.

Success in Newport also set the stage for the most important move of all. Mary Elizabeth and her mother traveled to New York City and located for rent an old brownstone at 28th Street and Fifth Avenue. At about that time, the English fashion of tearooms had invaded America. Evans saw the demand and answered it in 1908 by placing her trademark signature over the door and launching her first tearoom. Four years later, Evans moved into a bigger facility with a basement large enough to move candy production from Syracuse to New York. "It was a terrific undertaking," she remembered.

The new shop employed one hundred women—sixty in a state-of-the-art candy and bakery kitchen—while the total company had three hundred employees on its payroll. Other locations included a Tea House and Italian Garden in Hartsdale, New York, and two prosperous shops in Boston. It was now a very different company from the one launched around a kitchen table in Syracuse. "I always liked to enlarge," Evans explained modestly.

WE MANAGED TO GET ALONG

When World War I broke out, Mary Elizabeth again demonstrated her entrepreneurial resourcefulness. "We began to be limited with sugar, and in a very direct sort of way I decided I would go down to Washington and talk to Mr. Hoover [Herbert Hoover (1874–1964), head of the US Food Administration during World War I] and ask him what this really meant for people like us," she recalled.

> *I don't know why it is with me, but this is what I always have the instinct to do. Go to the top . . . Well, anyway, I managed to get an appointment with him. We were supposed to save wheat and beef and sugar and they were to be rationed. I told him that I had this $50,000 a year lease and I had just begun to get established, but I didn't come down to plead for any extra. I said, "I want suggestions. What can I do? Can I make candy out of honey? Is honey going to be on the list? Are dried fruits and nuts and things like that going to be available?" And I said, "I sell cakes, and I sell tea. If I can't have flour, can I use rice flour or other things of that kind?"*

Hoover was more than impressed, saying, "You're the only person who has come down here with any constructive ideas. I will see to it that you get your full allotment." But Evans knew that allotments and actual deliveries were two different things, so she experimented with recipes that used the raw materials at hand, and when successful, gave them to customers and friends. "So I got a big editorial in the *New York Times* on having done this. Without seeking it . . . That, of course, gave extra publicity and extra income as well."

In the summer of 1918, Hoover sent Evans to Paris to oversee the US

Central Diet Kitchen. Full of energy and ideas, she published two books during the war, one that explained her candy-making techniques, and one with a collection of wartime recipes that was so popular it was reprinted during World War II to help homemakers faced with rationing. Her gift for "making do," which had served her family so well, was now obvious to the general public.

In 1920, Mary Elizabeth married Henry D. Sharpe (1872–1954), the president of Brown and Sharpe (one of the most successful machine-tool companies in the world), moving from New York to Providence, Rhode Island. By that time, her enterprise—in which family remained central to her community, her sisters still active participants—included candy stores and tearooms located in a half-dozen cities, and annual company revenue in the hundreds of thousands of dollars.

At its peak, the Mary Elizabeth Tearoom on Fifth Avenue served a thousand luncheons a day, many patrons leaving with candy and cake orders. Sharpe's operations and success were now substantial enough that some competitors believed she was the figurehead for a giant corporate trust. Despite growth, however, she never lost sight of her brand. When interviewed by *Fortune* magazine, Sharpe said that she expected the hundreds of women in her employ to "live up to the ideal of doing everything as well as men would do it—and always with that extra touch of feminine charm which women give to their work when they take the right interest in it."

When the Great Depression struck, Sharpe was again called into action by her family, despite her distance from New York City, marriage, and young son in Providence. "So I started in going [to New York] on Mondays and coming home Fridays. And for three years I practically ran the business," she said. The Depression required "novel combinations" and a willingness to take chances—not entirely unlike Mary Elizabeth's earliest years in Syracuse.

We had never served a dinner, but we added that now. I man-
aged to keep most of the crew by dividing it up and having some

*of them serve dinner and some serve as daytime people. Then
we also opened a little section, because we weren't busy all over
this large place. We called it "The Soup Tureen," and we served
peasant soups . . . It was a very good, satisfying lunch, and we
had it at a fixed price so that people knew what they were going
to spend.*

With the crowds thinned by hard times, Sharpe saw opportunity
among the lonely dining tables. "I used some of the empty space and put
in some card tables and a couple of ping-pong tables, and advertised for
the first time in my life in the *New Yorker* magazine . . . It was the first
time I had ever done any paid advertising other than the little booklets
and things."

Despite the Depression, Mary Elizabeth kept the business on firm
footing, and by the mid-1930s, she and her family had made enough to
retire comfortably. With a husband, son, and philanthropic ventures in
Providence, Mary Elizabeth donated shares of the business to her sister
Martha's family, who moved the New York City restaurant to a smaller
venue and raised two generations on its profits.

Mary Elizabeth Evans Sharpe left an impressive legacy, remaining
active in a wide variety of political and social causes until her death in
1985 at age one hundred. As an entrepreneur, sometimes under pressure
to feed her family, she founded and grew a complex, competitive consumer business at a time when American women had few opportunities
to do so. She mechanized and automated while marketing her candy
business in a way that played to traditional nineteenth-century values,
all while scaling distribution to cities around the country. She survived
war and economic depression: "We got this habit of facing up to a situation and doing something, maybe doing something very peculiar, but we
did something." It was a tribute to the community of family and friends
who launched her, and to an entrepreneur who wove together the best
features of a traditional world of domesticity and a mechanized world
of scale and competition.

BACK AT THE BAR

Food was arriving just as Mary Elizabeth finished her story, perfectly timed—as she had known it would be. "Enjoy your meals," she told her audience. "The night is young, and there are many good stories left to be heard."

Spying Thomas Downing, she asked, "Were there no oysters on the menu, Mr. Downing?"

The entrepreneur looked up. "Such a menu! Buffalo wings! Sliders! What are sliders? Such variety! So much has changed from what I remember, so much improvement. And," looking admiringly at Mrs. Sharpe, "even women being successful in businesses where only men could compete in my day. I wonder," and he looked around the barroom, "if people of color saw the same kind of progress?"

Surely one or two of the assembled entrepreneurs had some good news for Downing? What progress had black entrepreneurs made in the later nineteenth and early twentieth centuries, as mass production and America's population grew?

John Merrick rose, not entirely content to leave his just-arrived hot meal but happy to respond. "Please, let me introduce myself."

Faces looked up from full plates.

"My name is John Merrick, and my story starts in Mr. Downing's world but ends in Mrs. Sharpe's. And that," he added, "covers a lot of ground. Can you all eat and listen at the same time?"

He saw heads nod, and so he began.

Chapter 6

JOHN MERRICK:
BUILDING A GREAT INSTITUTION

On June 7, 1892, Homer Plessy, considered by Louisiana state law to be a black man despite having seven white and one black great-grandparents, entered the white compartment of a passenger car of the East Louisiana Railroad in New Orleans. Challenged by the conductor under an 1890 state law that required segregated accommodations for each race, Plessy was arrested and brought before Judge John H. Ferguson of the Criminal Court for New Orleans. Ferguson upheld the state law despite the 14th Amendment, which guaranteed equal protection. Plessy fought on in the courts. Six years later, the United States Supreme Court issued its decision in *Plessy v. Ferguson*, ruling that Louisiana's state law was constitutional, making "separate but equal" the law of the land.

This was the world of the black entrepreneur in America in 1900. Many of the political and social advances enjoyed under post–Civil War Reconstruction had evaporated. African-Americans, who made up 11.6 percent of the population, were often denied living wages and adequate housing. The black American was "a marked man," historian Robert Wiebe writes, who "became everyone's inferior by standards of either power or prestige."

Reformer and statesman Frederick Douglass (1818–1895) made an eloquent and courageous case for the plight of post-Reconstruction African-Americans when he wrote, "While we recognize the color line as a hurtful force, a mountain barrier to our progress . . . we do not despair. We are a hopeful people." Often that hope translated into action, and sometimes, despite the odds, into entrepreneurial success.

Among the most impressive of black entrepreneurs in this period was John Merrick (1859–1919). His rise in a world of brutal segregation included the founding of one of the largest black enterprises in America. Merrick's innovation involved bringing a service to a segment of America that previously had been excluded. In the process, he disrupted a traditional industry, created new and substantial economic flows, strengthened community, and raised the standard of living for thousands of Americans.

CREATING A BIRACIAL COMMUNITY

Born a slave in Clinton, North Carolina, and emancipated by the Civil War and passage of the 13th Amendment in 1865, John Merrick found himself at twelve years old working in a brickyard in Chapel Hill, learning the construction trade. Six years later, he moved with his family to Raleigh and helped to build the campus of Shaw Collegiate Institute (later Shaw University), rising from assistant to brick mason.

When construction slowed, Merrick grasped an opportunity that was to change his life, accepting employment as a bootblack, shining customers' shoes in the barbershop of W. G. Otey, in Raleigh. From there, he learned the barber's trade, married, and had the first of five children. When, in 1880, one of Otey's barbers, John Wright, decided to open a shop in Durham, he invited Merrick along. Six months later, Merrick purchased a half-interest in the business.

From slavery in 1859 to coproprietor of a business at age twenty-one in 1880, John Merrick's rise was meteoric. His and Wright's barbershop grew from three to five chairs. "We got into the hearts of the people of Durham," Wright said, "and they had great confidence in us. After so long a time we decided to buy a lot and we built our homes side by side." In

1892, Wright sold his share of the business to Merrick, who now, as sole proprietor, continued expanding, growing (in this "separate-but-equal" world) to "three shops for white patronage and two for colored patronage." He also began to buy land and, with his background in construction, build new homes for rent as the population of Durham increased.

The fact that Merrick could serve white customers was a testament to the fact that there were few less-threatening opportunities for community in turn-of-the-century America than a barbershop. Merrick's biographer, Robert McCants Andrews (1891–1932), refers to it as the "original chamber of commerce, men's clubs and civic forum . . . It requires no stretch of the imagination to see how a wide-awake, energetic, and industrious barber could appropriate and absorb information and business methods thru [sic] such contact." Merrick's work cutting hair allowed him to build a biracial community, putting him in intimate contact with both poor black people and some of the wealthiest white businessmen of Durham, including Washington Duke (1820–1905), organizer of the American Tobacco Company. Writing in the racially fraught 1920s, Andrews remarks, "Now that the two races have become so estranged, it is hard to realize how close John Merrick stood to these men. There was no time that he needed help that he did not get it."

A HEALTHY "THIRD PLACE": THE BARBERSHOP

In 1989, sociologist Ray Oldenburg wrote about the need in healthy communities for what he called "third places," those locations where people meet after home (first) and work (second) to come together for casual companionship. These informal meetings often create other meaningful associations. "There must be *neutral ground* upon which people may gather," Oldenburg writes, and "where individuals may come and go as they please, in which none are required to play host, and in which all feel at home and comfortable." John Merrick's barbershops, in which he served both black and white customers of every rank and status, were as close to a healthy "third place" in segregated Durham as society would allow. And it was this community, where black and white locals could momentarily connect as friends in a relaxed, intimate way, that may have been as important to John Merrick's growth as an entrepreneur as any other external factor.

Having access to benefactors like Washington Duke was only a start, however. It would require Merrick's energy, gifts for organization and promotion, and ability to instill confidence in those around him that would help to create the kind of lasting enterprise for which he became famous.

His next important opportunity came in 1883, when a minister from Georgia arrived in Durham intent on selling the rights to an organization called the Knights of King David, a fraternal order that provided friendship and support, promoted black self-reliance, and, among other things, wrote private insurance for its members. Merrick was part of a group that decided to purchase the rights for the state of North Carolina. Within a year, Merrick and his enterprising partners had increased insurance collections from $14 to $430 per month in North Carolina and had expanded into Virginia. Merrick was appointed the Supreme Grand Treasurer.

Sensing the opportunity to move from a limited fraternal organization to a full-fledged commercial venture, Merrick and six other black community leaders founded North Carolina Mutual and Provident Association in 1898. Their intention was to provide a service to the poorest of Durham's black population, many of whom might be thrown instantly into poverty by the loss of their breadwinner. White insurance companies were often unwilling, or willing only at onerous rates, to insure black families because of higher mortality rates. Andrews notes, of course, that "this high death rate is the most damning result of the segregation of the race into inferior living quarters." In fact, the idea of universal insurance coverage for African-Americans seemed so preposterous—and therefore the sign of genuine innovation—that some black consumers themselves believed it could not be done.

John Merrick served as the association's first president. He was joined in the organization's development by Dr. Aaron McDuffie Moore (1863–1923) and Charles Clinton Spaulding (1874–1952), men who had their own remarkable careers and would become important partners in Merrick's entrepreneurial ventures. When Spaulding was sent into the field to write policies for sick and death benefits to black consumers who had never been offered such services, he had to educate before he could sell. Business was so slow at first that Spaulding sometimes had to sell a policy and collect the first payment in order to purchase the train fare home. He was paid commission only. Likewise, Moore and Merrick took no salaries. The first death claim, for forty dollars, caused a crisis, with the company's board assembling in Merrick's barbershop and voting to fund the claim from their own pockets. By 1900, however, the firm had enough capital to rent two rooms on Durham's Main Street and advertise in black newspapers. Interest grew, and Spaulding began receiving invitations to speak.

A second agent, T. J. Russell, an employee of the Duke Tobacco Factory, began to write policies in his free time but finally elected to join full time. Here, we see a glimpse of Merrick's charisma. Two weeks after Russell quit the factory, he ran into his old boss on the street, who offered him twelve dollars a week—twice his former salary—to return to the plant. Russell told his boss he needed to chat with Merrick.

> *Mr. Merrick always had a smile and always could see the bright side of things; that is the reason he succeeded so well. When I told him of the offer I had had he said that was pretty good and that I was worth it. Then he put his hand on my shoulder and said: "Why don't you brighten up and take fresh courage and make fifteen dollars a week out of your job with us?"*

> *Russell added, "I worked much harder and increast [sic] my earnings and never looked for a better job after that; but always tried to make my job a better job."*

Andrews tells us that Merrick was unselfish, simple, honest, unaffected, and generally quiet. He often presided as president of the North Carolina Mutual and Provident Association in the rear of his barbershop, in his barber coat. Merrick was devoted to his church. His extravagances were few but included the first automobile owned by a person of color in Durham, and a pool table placed in his garage to entertain friends and nurture community.

John Merrick's career demonstrated that often the win is in the pursuit. For the first six years North Carolina Mutual made no money. It was not until 1905 that the business was able to pay the president his salary. Notably, too, none of the founders had insurance experience. They were learning and carrying the business as it grew. For the first eighteen years, the officers met every day at noon to oversee the business. Each was willing to hit the road and sell policies if required. They practiced and preached absolute honesty: The simple existence of a policy in North Carolina Mutual became sufficient guarantee of burial costs.

EVERY HEART WAS INSPIRED

Merrick and his partners also began to understand and appeal to America's emerging consumer culture. They studied advertising and distributed novelties, from pencils, matches, fans, and thermometers to spittoons, blotters, paper weights, and art calendars.

In time, the company expanded both its product line and its geographic reach while weathering substantial obstacles. In 1906, for example, a year after North Carolina Mutual entered South Carolina, that state's legislature passed a law requiring all foreign insurance companies to deposit $10,000 with the insurance commissioner. Undeterred, Merrick and Moore mortgaged some of their personal property and, ten days after the law was passed, North Carolina Mutual deposited $10,000. "Every black heart in South Carolina was inspired," Andrews wrote, "and it immediately won the confidence of the people and added a great volume of business to the new Company." Merrick's firm was one of just two companies out of thirty still able to operate in the state.

In 1908, the company erected a $10,000 brick building and established its own offices and space for black businesses, adding a shoe store and hat store, men's furnishings, a bank, drugstore, and barbershop. It was emblematic of Merrick that he worked tirelessly to build community in Durham that would give African-Americans access to the services and opportunities of their white neighbors. In 1901, Merrick served as the first president of the board of trustees for the Lincoln Hospital, the first freestanding black hospital in Durham (thanks to considerable support from Washington Duke). It not only gave black doctors and nurses a place to practice medicine and pursue their careers, but it was instrumental in helping the black population weather the 1918 influenza epidemic. In that year, Merrick's Mutual Association paid nearly $100,000 in flu claims, the heaviest single charge to the association, but of untold benefit to the black community.

In 1907, Merrick was influential in the establishment of the Mechanics and Farmers Bank, the first black bank of Durham to meet the needs of African-American businessmen unable to borrow at white-owned banks. In 1908, finding no drugstores were conveniently located, Merrick and five other men founded the Bull City Drug Company.

As African-Americans acquired property in Durham, many wanted to purchase property insurance. Merrick, with his experience in the construction trade and real estate, persuaded his business partners to join him in forming a company that offered such a product, founding the Merrick-Moore-Spaulding Real Estate Company in 1910.

Meanwhile, North Carolina Mutual grew. Premium income increased from $70,000 in 1905 to $416,000 in 1915. In 1918, the company subscribed to $100,000 of Liberty Loan bonds, causing Treasury Secretary William McAdoo (1863–1941) to remark that "the Treasury Department had never received a more substantial expression of the patriotism of the Negro race in the South than evidence in this subscription." Merrick's biographer Robert Andrews added, "Secretary McAdoo is a southern man and his tribute to the colored people may be taken as a model for any timid white man who would deny to them any of the credit for the large things they so often do." By 1919, the association was in ten states, the largest black-owned business of its kind in the United States, a distinction it held for much of the twentieth century.

Merrick led an extraordinary career, from slave to president of an insurance company, a hospital, a bank, and a real-estate firm, and as benefactor of an entire community. He died in 1920 at age sixty, his success proof to an often skeptical white public that black entrepreneurs could operate large business enterprises. Merrick's gift was combining commercial and social entrepreneurship, working "to build a great institution which would teach by its example what the Negro could achieve in the world of finance." He took on the burden of both business and his times.

A plaque placed in Durham in 2004 by the North Carolina Office of Archives and History reinforced this rich legacy, recalling that Parrish Street, lined with black-owned businesses inspired by John Merrick and his associates, supported a culture so entrepreneurial in the early twentieth century that it became known as the "Black Wall Street."

BACK AT THE BAR

"And so," Merrick concluded, "it wasn't just businesses like Mr. Gillette's razor blade factory that had to 'mass-produce' its product. Selling thousands of insurance policies across numerous states required new systems for marketing and selling, finance, risk management, and organization."

"Try serving a thousand lunches a day without a well-oiled system," Mary Elizabeth Sharpe added, "or making a thousand orders of butter cremes to be shipped up and down the coast."

Gillette agreed. "We were all just trying to keep up with the American public, which was growing in leaps and bounds—more than 100 million of us by 1920," thinking to himself, "and half eventually needing to shave their faces every day!"

A new voice joined the conversation, that of a gray-haired man with kindly eyes, dressed in a suit and tie. "Here's a riddle for my new friends around the barroom: Can any of you think of a *service* that is delivered by a *product* that allows other products to be mass-produced?" The room went quiet. A hand slid up, and then down.

"How about air-conditioning?" The man watched for a reaction, but there was little. Half his audience had probably never experienced it. The other half had probably lived with it for so long that they never thought much about it—the way a fish stops thinking about water.

King Gillette walked over to the man and placed a hand on his shoulder. "In 1918," Gillette announced, "Mr. Willis Carrier and his engineers helped save my business when they installed an air-conditioning system that stopped rust spots from forming on my fine steel razor blades. If you want to mass-produce a standard product," Gillette added, "you'd better be able to produce a standard environment."

"Mr. Gillette is very kind," Carrier said, "and it's nice to be with you all this evening. My story," he began, "is about selling something that nobody at first wanted because they couldn't understand what it was. But once they figured it out," he chuckled, "they didn't want to live without it." He had the attention of the barroom now.

Chapter 7

WILLIS CARRIER: MASS PRODUCTION MEETS CONSUMERISM

In 1881, Robert Sackett and Charles Wilhelms founded a printing company in New York City that produced advertising cards, stock certificates, and other fine-quality work. Sackett & Wilhelms Lithographing & Printing Co. employed thirty-five skilled workers and ran some of the country's first steam-powered presses. In October of that same year, another start-up, *Judge* magazine, premiered its first issue, specializing in humor and political satire.

Twenty years later, Sackett & Wilhelms moved its printing operations into two interconnected buildings in Brooklyn. The second floor of the smaller building held sixty multicolor presses that, by 1902, were churning out thousands of issues of *Judge* every week for the magazine's enthusiastic subscribers.

In the spring of that year, Sackett & Wilhelms's consulting engineer, Walter Timmis, visited the Manhattan office of Joel Irvine Lyle (1874–1942), the head of sales activities in New York City for the Buffalo Forge Company. Headquartered in Buffalo, New York, the twenty-four-year-old firm had developed a reputation for expertise in facility heating and ventilating. Timmis told Lyle that his printing client had a serious problem: The humidity at the Brooklyn plant played havoc with the paper used in its high-speed, multicolor printing.

The trouble was especially acute in August and September, when air was saturated with as much as nine grains of moisture per cubic foot, Timmis said. Optimal printing required five. He described to Lyle how a variation of 1/175th of an inch in paper size could throw off the alignment, or *register*, of multicolor work; how paper sometimes had to be run through the press without ink simply to season it; and how presses were sometimes held up for several days in hopes that atmospheric conditions would improve. The effects of inconsistent humidity led to poor quality, waste, and lost production time. *Judge* magazine's exacting schedule was at risk. Timmis needed help. Was Buffalo Forge interested?

Kentucky native Joel Irvine Lyle was gracious and outgoing—a natural salesman. Lyle had earned a degree in mechanical engineering from Kentucky State University (now the University of Kentucky), where he left a legacy as a talented student and athlete. Having joined Buffalo Forge in 1899, Lyle was already beginning to exhibit a genius in selling and in sizing up business opportunities. He understood that nobody yet had mastered control of humidity. He also recognized that the first practical solution would create new business opportunities. Lyle thought he knew the one person to tackle the problem.

At a meeting of Buffalo Forge engineers that previous December, a recently minted Cornell engineering graduate had presented a rigorous study establishing the improved efficiency of boilers when fans supplied air at optimum rates. Like many smaller American companies, Buffalo Forge had yet to invest in a research and development function. Its owners were generally skeptical of abstract research work. The December presentation proved unique, however, in pairing analysis and application, resulting in a scientific approach that provided new ways for Buffalo Forge salesmen to pitch opportunities, save money, and win customers.

The author of this study was twenty-five-year-old Willis Haviland Carrier (1876–1950). When Lyle accepted the challenge of humidity control at

Sackett & Wilhelms and sent it to Carrier, it was the first step in what was to become—like Eli Whitney and Phineas Miller a century before—one of the most fruitful business partnerships in American industry.

THE AGE OF ENGINEERS

Born in November 1876 on a farm outside Buffalo, Willis Carrier exhibited early signs of the intellectual curiosity and analytical abilities that would come to define his career. He worked school geometry problems in the snow and sometimes would complete math problems that baffled his teachers. A young Willis impressed his family by assembling a new thrasher that arrived in parts at the farm.

In June 1897, Carrier was awarded a four-year scholarship to Cornell University. He soon earned a reputation for outstanding academics and exceptional powers of concentration, losing track of time and place when engrossed in a problem. His class of 1901 printed a complimentary, humorous prophecy in its yearbook, saying that Carrier would become the first president of the great National College of Engineering but would succumb to starvation by forgetting to eat while absorbed in the solution of an intricate mathematical problem. Some of Carrier's colleagues later would say that he could carry a problem in his mind for fifteen years, wrestling with it off and on until it was solved.

In the summer between semesters, Carrier sold stereoscopes and viewing cards door-to-door. In 1899, the first signs of entrepreneurial talent appeared when he and a partner launched a student laundry business. At graduation in 1901, he accepted a position with the Buffalo Forge Company, where he found himself at a drafting board, churning out drawings for projects such as a heating plant at the Erie City Boiler Company and a dryer for a San Francisco coffee producer.

It was these first jobs that convinced him that there was insufficient data to design efficient, high-quality systems. He began working in his spare time on the revised tables he would present successfully that December to the company's sales team, the analysis that had so impressed Lyle.

Buffalo Forge provided a dynamic business environment for Carrier and his colleagues. Founded in 1878, the company's first product was a revolutionary portable blacksmith forge that competed successfully against traditional bellows. By the turn of the century, Buffalo Forge was selling a variety of heating and ventilating products throughout much of the world, including North America, Russia, Australia, India, and China. One of the company's important lines, heavy-duty power punches and shears, offered customers the audacious guarantee that the frames of its machines would be "Unbreakable Forever." An emphasis on the steady release of new products, expansion into new geographies, and bold statements to customers would become hallmarks of Carrier's future enterprises.

Buffalo Forge was owned by William Wendt (1858–1928), whose leadership featured a strong financial focus and an occasional iron fist. Both respected and feared, Wendt generally disliked college-trained engineers but grudgingly saw their value if they were "practical," which he deemed Carrier to be. It was his brother Henry Wendt (1863–1929), however, who saw the real value in employing college-trained engineers. Henry was a multidimensional talent, serving for some years as Buffalo Forge's lead salesman and designer while overseeing manufacturing, which he learned from the bench up. His reputation as a gifted foundryman made him a valued consultant at some of the largest jobs in the United States and Europe.

Henry Wendt seemed to grasp that Buffalo Forge had arrived at "the beginning of the 'Age of Engineers.'" He encouraged his newly hired Cornell grad to pursue the more theoretical aspects of the heating and ventilating business. It was also Henry who supported the establishment of an R&D function at the company, putting Carrier in charge of a new department of experimental engineering in 1902. Henry would consistently champion the work being produced by Carrier and create an environment that allowed Buffalo Forge to one day call itself the "Birthplace of Air Conditioning." He was a role model and mentor for Carrier and the anchor to the young engineer's growing professional community.

THE IMPROBABLE BIRTH OF A NEW INDUSTRY

When Lyle forwarded the Sackett & Wilhelms challenge to Buffalo Forge in the late spring of 1902, Carrier was energized but in uncharted territory. After several false starts, he experimented with forcing moist air against a cold metal surface, drying the air through condensation. He then devised a set of calculations that allowed him to regulate this process, what he would later call "dew point control."

The method seemed promising enough that a full design was approved and installation completed. The world's first modern industrial air conditioner, mounted in the press room on the second floor of Sackett & Wilhelms's Brooklyn facility, included eight thousand feet of one-inch cast-iron pipe and two fans driven by a steam engine. Cool water was first sourced from a nearby well, supplemented in 1903 by a thirty-ton ammonia compressor. This system of chilled coils designed by Carrier had the equivalent cooling effect of melting 108,000 pounds of ice a day.

A decade later, Timmis, then president of the New York chapter of the American Society of Heating and Ventilating Engineers, presented a paper highlighting the success of Willis Carrier's first installation. Tests made on September 13, 1904, Timmis said, established that "the temperature of all rooms was maintained 71° to 73°F, with humidity at 54 percent to 57 percent, only 3 percent variation in the four large press rooms all day long from 10 A.M. to 3 P.M." The installation had cost $6,500 and "paid for itself in the first year," he added.

Carrier himself put this first installation in perspective, writing, "These early experiments, prompted by a problem based upon a comparatively small printing establishment, started the trend of investigation through which many of the fundamental laws of evaporation, of humidity control, and of heat transfer were established." In other words, the installation at Sackett & Wilhelms was a first, rudimentary solution—but one that provided a lifetime of innovation and entrepreneurial motivation for Willis Carrier.

Carrier and Lyle had complementary skills and became fast friends, together pushing the technology and business applications of their innovation. When Buffalo Forge won the opportunity to install an air-conditioning system for the Huguet Silk Mills in Wayland, New York, Carrier and his team were ready to take the next step. They had now improved their system to the point where it could adjust automatically to changes in heat and humidity. In May 1907, they proposed to Huguet Silk Mills a guarantee *not* on equipment capacity but on *results*—a pledge of *year-round environmental conditions*. For example, "in summertime," Carrier's team promised, "we guarantee that you will be able to obtain 75 percent humidity in the mill without increasing the temperature above the outside temperature." This modest, $3,100 contract demonstrated that Carrier now had enough confidence in the equipment, design, and performance of his systems to offer this new technology with an iron-clad guarantee. He had shifted the focus from hardware to performance.

"For many years, we refused to divulge the air-handling capacity of the system and revealed only its requirements for floor space, power, water, and steam," one Carrier colleague recalled. "We agreed that if guarantees were not met, we would remove the equipment and refund all moneys previously paid—and there were few instances in which this was done." No other consulting engineer could match this promise, and for years, Carrier and his teams enjoyed a virtual monopoly on air-condition-ing know-how. Architectural critic Reyner Banham calls the installation at Huguet Silk Mills "one spectacular exercise of comprehensive environ-mental quantification"—backed by money.

Carrier, Lyle, and their teams had shaped a substantial and differ-ent enough business that the Wendts proposed the creation of a wholly owned subsidiary, the Carrier Air Conditioning Company of America (CAC), officially incorporated on April 18, 1909.

BECOMING THE
"FATHER OF AIR-CONDITIONING"

There were several promoters of modern air-conditioning in the early twentieth century, but only one is known today as the "father" of the industry. While the title is indicative of his lifetime body of work, Willis Carrier assumed paternal rights in one dramatic act of competitive generosity in early 1911, when the American Society of Mechanical Engineers (ASME) invited the thirty-five-year-old engineer to present a paper at its annual meeting in New York City. The invitation was important because it recognized air-conditioning as a distinct branch of engineering, and it also recognized Willis Carrier and Buffalo Forge's leadership in the field.

Carrier knew he would be presenting to academics and scientists as well as to practicing engineers. He chose psychrometrics—the study of gas-vapor mixtures—as his topic because he considered the current science fuzzy and the practical applications inadequate. He worried that if the industry continued to rely on erroneous data to determine measures such as relative humidity, its legacy would be thousands of poorly designed systems. Carrier wanted to revise the underlying science to improve the practical art. It was an ambitious objective, requiring that he prove inconsistencies in existing data, propose new theories based on sound science, and then demonstrate the practicality of those theories.

By July 1911, the paper was complete, prompting ASME to request a second paper on the state of air-conditioning apparatus. Again, Buffalo Forge responded, delivering in early November a seventy-five-page treatise by Carrier and a colleague on the products used in the industry. This work made practical the psychrometric formulae outlined in the first paper.

The fact that the Wendts approved both the topics and the time demands on their star engineer was a magnanimous gesture. Together, the two works would strengthen every competitor of Buffalo Forge and undoubtedly launch new competitors. It would result in the creation of an enormous community of professionals capable of advancing an entire industry. And from Carrier's perspective, it was the surest way to see his "baby" grow—something only a father would do.

ENTREPRENEURIAL LUCK:
THE BIRTH OF CARRIER
ENGINEERING CORPORATION

Meanwhile, the Carrier Air Conditioning Company of America was growing rapidly, booking sixty-three new installations in 1912, ninety-three in 1913, and 130 in 1914. Carrier and his team continued to deliver patents, technical papers, and an abundance of educational marketing materials to potential customers in dozens of industries. Consulting engineers and architects became increasingly interested in specifying air-conditioning equipment. The company's ecosystem was growing rapidly, while new competitors emerged. The industry was on its feet and gaining converts. But then, in August 1914, war erupted in Europe, a shock to industries around the world.

International trade ground to a halt in the opening months of World War I while America sought to remain neutral in European events. Sentiment changed in May 1915, however, when German torpedoes sunk the British ship *Lusitania* in the North Atlantic, killing 128 Americans. Carrier remembered:

> *The elder Wendt, who was really the proprietor of the company, thought that the Germans were going to win and that there would be very hard times ahead for America. In fact, hard times had already begun due to uncertainty and disruption of business caused by the outbreak of the War. In order to prepare for the gloomy future that he envisioned, Wendt started an all-around retrenchment in his organization. This retrenchment included, by the spring of 1915, a decision to liquidate the Carrier Air Conditioning Company of America and focus instead on Buffalo Forge's more traditional heating and ventilation lines.*

Carrier was distraught. Even though his and Lyle's jobs would be preserved, virtually everyone who had built the air-conditioning subsidiary—their closest friends and hard-won community—was scheduled to be terminated. Carrier tried unsuccessfully to change Wendt's mind and then considered quitting. "I saw that this wrote 'finis' to all of our air-conditioning opportunities and henceforth that others would be leaders in this art which we had so laboriously built up," he concluded.

In terms of fatherhood, the child was about to become an orphan. Not only would thirteen years of intellectual capital and a competitive lead be squandered, but the engineers who had built that lead would now disperse and enrich every competitor in the business. Given this, Carrier was unwilling to let the company slip away. Lyle concurred. One had the technical genius while the other possessed the selling, marketing, and team-building brilliance. Both felt wounded and unsure, but Carrier was convinced that "if Irvine Lyle is willing to take the chance, and if we can get his staff of engineers to come along with us," they could make a go of it.

On June 15, 1915, Carrier and Lyle reached an agreement to form the Carrier Engineering Corporation (CEC), with each equal in status, stock, and salary. They then invited five additional cofounders, gathering the community of talent they would need to succeed. The new company struck an agreement with Buffalo Forge that assured CEC access to product.

Carrier Engineering Corporation opened for business on July 1, 1915. It was a classic start-up. Willis Carrier rented two rooms in the Mutual Life Building in Buffalo for himself, a secretary, and one draftsman. His secretary recalled, "We ended up with second-hand furniture—two desks, a drafting board and stool and a few files. We had two wicker chairs for visitors, and Mr. Carrier's friends would ask him if he had swiped them from a tavern." The father of air-conditioning had made the leap from "intrapreneurship" within a larger, diversified company to betting his career on a set of fundamental technological innovations whose ultimate market success was still unproven. He also bet on Lyle, on the community of cofounders he and Lyle had gathered around them, and on the larger ecosystem they had helped to launch in 1911.

Carrier Engineering raised enough cash to run the business for six months without a sale. "This was certainly cutting it pretty fine," Willis recalled. And, for eighteen days, the new company languished, just as

William Wendt had anticipated. But what World War I had taken away, it suddenly returned.

The first contract booked by CEC was with the American Ammunition Company in Paulsboro, New Jersey. The fourth job was for the International Arms and Fuse Company in Bloomfield, New Jersey. Ten of CEC's first twenty-nine jobs were for fuse-loading plants and totaled nearly $150,000. Pricing was robust because only Carrier had the skill and speed to complete the installations for such critical wartime work.

These contracts ensured the start-up's success. In December 1918, Lyle reported that CEC had equipped sixteen fuse-loading plants in the United States and Canada with air-conditioning apparatus. These installations reduced dust and the risk of explosion by providing cool, dry, consistent air—allowing delicate manufacturing operations to continue twenty-four hours a day. Those not acquainted with development of the art of air-conditioning over the previous few years, Lyle said, would have considered this feat impossible.

Carrier and his talented team of engineers found themselves with a wide-open playing field, the result of innovation and intentional community building. But it was also the result of sheer entrepreneurial luck.

"Looking back at those uncertain days," Carrier said, "I have often thought that—had we not decided then and there to go ahead at once—we never would have formed the Carrier Corporation. Lyle was all for waiting until September or even the following spring to see how business conditions looked. If I had waited another month, the whole project would have been doomed." In fact, a Carrier associate believed, if William Wendt had known that business would pick up as it did, "he would have made all of us such attractive propositions we would have found it impossible to say 'No.'"

Instead, Carrier and Lyle launched a start-up at one of the single worst entrepreneurial moments of the twentieth century. Their intent was to sell a still expensive, often misunderstood product in markets that seemed to be imploding under wartime stress. In retrospect, Willis Carrier knew that the gods of chance had smiled upon him, and he recalled,

"What neither of us saw was the business in munitions, which came along and saved our bacon."

By the 1920s, Carrier and Lyle had successfully installed their "manufactured air" in more than two hundred industries. The sale often involved a skeptical buyer asked to absorb new capital and operating expenses. Pioneering customers purchased a product that was invisible and could seem frivolous to traditional managers. Nevertheless, early successes in textile, tobacco, confectionery, and munitions factories led to increasing acceptance across industries and provided proof that the CEC partners had identified a profitable, long-term business opportunity.

Born on the factory floor, modern air-conditioning remained there almost exclusively for its first twenty years, helping companies to mass-produce their products in stable, predictable environments. Meanwhile, "comfort air," designed purely for human comfort, made only limited progress in consumer acceptance. Some of this could be blamed on technology; air-conditioning units were still large, often complex enough to require a trained engineer, and required high pressures and volatile refrigerants such as ammonia. Carrier had one success at a bank in La Crosse, Wisconsin, and another at a library in St. Louis. But even as the technology grew more compact and less complicated, the owners of banks, libraries, retail stores, and restaurants struggled to justify the need for cool, dry air in a world where hardy Americans had always found ways to cope with the weather.

If Willis Carrier was going to succeed beyond the factory floor and move from supporting mass production to directly touching the lives of consumers, he would need opportunities to demonstrate that his innovations were as much social as technological. Fortunately, opportunity was springing up on Main Streets all across America.

WITHOUT ONE SINGLE REDEEMING FEATURE

A 1911 report on the "Condition of Moving Picture Show Places in New York" found that most of the fifty theaters surveyed offered patrons an unrelentingly foul experience. One venue on Third Avenue was reported to be so vile that an attendant with a giant pump-atomizer sprayed "perfumery to allay the odor." At the Pitkin Avenue Theater in Brooklyn, auditors reported that "the air was fetid and stifling." Fights broke out among unhappy patrons. This "place is without one single redeeming feature," the report noted.

While technology historians tend to draw a distinction between process air (used to improve factory productivity) and comfort air (designed to cool people), Carrier and his engineering teams encouraged movie-theater owners to approach their decisions with both perspectives in mind. Like confectionery or pharmaceutical companies, theaters worked with raw materials that wilted in heat and humidity. In the case of moviegoers, however, the raw material could vote with its feet. Because of that, the industry experienced a summer slump that was so severe that some theaters closed. Hollywood released popular films in cooler months, the idea of a "summer blockbuster" being an oxymoron.

The solution encouraged by CEC was to improve the "process flow" of a theater's patrons. Improvements in the "yield" of movie audiences could be measured in tickets purchased and seats filled.

Most movie theaters in the opening decades of the twentieth century were constructed with some form of mechanical ventilation, often in the guise of fans that did nothing except replace the foul air of the theaters by drawing in the dirty and hotter air from the outside. One theater owner pasted fake icicles on his windows and spread marble-dust snow in his foyer. Prior to a showing of *Call of the Wild*, another operator created a travel booklet that emphasized "the scenic and cooling aspects of the film."

At the other extreme, air-conditioning received a bad name when inexperienced players offered quick fixes. Chicago's first fully air-conditioned theater, installed by a Carrier competitor, had been successful in reducing indoor temperature to 78°F when the outside temperature was 96°F. However, without effective humidity control, patrons went from being hot and sticky to cold and clammy, accompanied by condensation running down the walls and curtains.

A NEW ERA IN AIR-CONDITIONING

At the heart of CEC's movie-theater solution was one of the most important technological innovations of Willis Carrier's long career, the centrifugal chiller. Unveiled in May 1922, it was quiet, smaller, easy to operate, and used a "non-poisonous, non-corrosive, incombustible, *safe* refrigerant." The centrifugal chiller allowed CEC to make a bold leap into the consumer economy, with the premiere of comfort air coming in 1923 at the Metropolitan Theatre in Los Angeles. Described as "the first example of a well-engineered theater system," the Metropolitan installation included service to the basement of the theater, which delighted musicians, ushers, and staff. Carrier's encore was to install systems in 1924 in the Palace Theatre in Dallas and the Texan in Houston. The owner of the Texan suggested the disruptive nature of comfort air when he telegraphed CEC to say, "The house feels and smells like a spring day."

Modern air-conditioning's most spectacular opening was its Broadway premiere on Memorial Day 1925 at the Rivoli Theatre, one of the newest and most luxurious of big film palaces, seating 2,400 patrons. "Long before the doors opened," Carrier recalled, "the line-up at the box office looked like a World Series crowd waiting for bleacher seats. The people were curious—and skeptical, too—as most of the women and some of the men carried palm leaf fans, a standard accessory for summer days." In the audience that day was Adolph Zukor, the founder of Paramount Pictures, visiting from Hollywood and destined to become another "father"—of "the feature film in America." Carrier recalled, "The doors opened before we got the air conditioning and refrigerating systems turned on." His team struggled to make last-minute adjustments. "People poured in—stood seven deep in the back of the house . . . From the wings we watched hundreds of fans flutter back and forth, and we felt Mr. Zukor was watching them, too."

Like every good Hollywood classic, this one would have a happy ending. "Soon the effect of the air conditioning system became evident," Carrier said. "Fans dropped into the laps of their owners, even those of chronic fanners. We breathed a sigh of relief, and later actually became jubilant when Mr. Zukor gave his endorsement, 'Yep, the people are going to like it.'"

The impact was immediate and extraordinary. "Last week," the press reported, "while Broadway sweltered in the terrific heat wave, one theatre, the Rivoli, was well filled day in and day out." Admissions, which generally ran at ten thousand in a week, had exceeded twenty-seven thousand. In July came the first inkling of the summer blockbuster: "It has now been demonstrated that the hotter the weather here, the more people attend the Rivoli."

Carrier installed comfort cooling at a steady clip in theaters around America for the remainder of the 1920s. Rarely had two such different industries—Hollywood and modern air-conditioning—fallen into such a happy marriage. By 1929, 95 million movie tickets were being sold each week to a total population of nearly 122 million people—suggesting, on average, that every American attended a movie every nine days or so. Carrier's marketing team summarized the impact on Hollywood, writing, "We couldn't improve the pictures, so we improved the theatre."

FROM MASS PRODUCTION TO CONSUMERISM

Modern air-conditioning transformed twentieth-century America no less than Eli Whitney's cotton gin transformed the nineteenth century. Consumers began to enjoy comfort air not only at the theater, but in restaurants, trains, and stores. By 1957, an Arkansas court concluded that "air conditioning is becoming standard equipment in homes, offices, and public buildings; it contributes to the comfort and efficiency of all those people who have occasion to utilize its benefits and is as necessary as telephones, heating, etc., in courthouses." The 1970 Federal Census, sometimes called "The Air-Conditioned Census," showed modern air-conditioning as having circulated people along with air, pushing the American population southward. Today, some 90 percent of American homes have central or room air-conditioning.

In 1999, *U.S. News & World Report* named Willis Carrier one of twenty-five Americans who shaped the modern era and "the coolest American of the century." The magazine added, "Carrier, the 'Father of Air Conditioning,' is the man who made the Sun Belt—as well as the factory, the movie theater, and the modern home—tolerable in summer." From the mass production of automated factories to the homes of American consumers, Carrier, Lyle, and the industry they built span two of the great themes of American entrepreneurship.

BACK AT THE BAR

"I always tried to envision the future," Carrier concluded, "but even I couldn't anticipate that a problem with smudged ink in a Brooklyn printing shop would one day grow to become a multibillion-dollar global industry."

One of the young entrepreneurs in the barroom spoke up. "It was unbelievable that you gave all of your intellectual capital away, Dr. Carrier. It's like when Elon Musk donated all of those battery patents."

Carrier paused for a minute to consider, not entirely sure who Musk was. "We had a strong company with great engineers, and Lyle was a sales genius. But we had to explain what air-conditioning was to *every single customer*. How it worked. *Why* it worked, and why it would make them money. We needed help, and that meant a larger, stronger community. Only by educating our competitors would we ever build an important industry."

That was when a new voice boomed from the back of the barroom. "Air-conditioning. Razor blades. Shovels. Sails. Cotton gins. Panics. World wars. *Insurance*. Doesn't anyone in this joint know how to have a little fun?" That was when the tall, slender speaker picked up the cornet resting on his lap and blew a couple of beautiful notes that Carrier thought might shatter the glasses and mugs on the tables.

"Time to call my children home," the musician announced.

The Father of Air Conditioning was happy to yield the floor and finish his meal. In any case, it didn't look like he had a choice.

Chapter 8

CHARLES "BUDDY" BOLDEN: THE SOUND OF INNOVATION

The career of Charles Joseph "Buddy" Bolden (1877–1931) was short, spectacular, and heartbreaking. Fueled by a prodigious natural talent, Bolden pursued one of the few entrepreneurial opportunities available to a black American living at the margins of early twentieth-century New Orleans society. Like Thomas Downing, Bolden produced a novel combination that fell outside the dominant entrepreneurial themes of his time. In the process, he helped to create jazz, a new musical form that was distinctly American and would soon float in the air around the nation every bit as much as Willis Carrier's remarkable atmospheric innovation.

Before turning thirty years old, however, Bolden became ill and unable to play his music. Over time, his name faded from memory. Thanks to the careful work of music historians such as Donald M. Marquis, Bolden is celebrated today as one of the most influential of New Orleans's founding jazzmen.

The son of a drayman and grandson of a slave, young Buddy Bolden found a way to innovate that was based on talent, not race or social standing. Even so, his extraordinary musical gifts might have been insufficient had he not been born into one of the great innovation communities in the history of America.

NEW ORLEANS:
A CLASSIC INNOVATION COMMUNITY

For a black musician in 1900, the musical community of New Orleans was as powerful and nurturing a force as the machine tool community in New England was for a mechanic in 1800, or the software development community in Silicon Valley was for a developer in 2000.

Buddy Bolden grew up in a world where musicianship was a collegial and competitive sport driven by black, white, and Creole men who competed intensely for crowds, status, money, and the affections of the fairer sex. New Orleans welcomed the poor and disenfranchised from every race, not just to participate but to lead the creative and commercial development of something brand new. As an innovation community, the city was able to attract and nurture talent that would surely have been lost in almost any other setting. New Orleans music exemplified innovation from the *bottom up*. For Jelly Roll Morton (Ferdinand Joseph LaMothe, 1890–1941), who grew rich playing piano in the brothels of New Orleans, the new sound being created "was not just music . . . It was security and acceptance; it was the path to wealth and glory; it was power."

Nevertheless, the New Orleans musical community was far from perfect. Women were largely excluded from the creative process. Black, Creole, and white musicians were forced to meet and share ideas in the "interstitials" of the community—after hours and behind the scenes, sometimes in violation of the segregation laws that governed public performance. Few musicians could make their living solely from their craft. Community thrived anyway. Talent was the great leveler. Frank Walker, the recording director for Columbia Records in the 1920s, said, "New Orleans is what I like to call 'The University of Jazz.' Oh, lots of musicians and bands came from places like Kansas City and Chicago, but there was something—a certain combination of hot weather, dumps and dives and people that only New Orleans could provide."

As the city became a magnet for musicians from all walks of life, it also became a melting pot of musical styles. In 1900, New Orleans was known as "The Opera Capital of North America"; orchestras and string bands flourished. Meanwhile, ragtime was seeping into the city as America's newest music sensation. Something called "the blues" had arrived in the songs of black refugees from the surrounding farms and sugarcane fields who were seeking employment in the city. The Baptist church that Bolden attended was finding new ways to "swing" hymns and spirituals. One contemporary recalled that music was everywhere, from "private affairs, balls, soirees, banquets, marriages, deaths, christenings, Catholic communions, confirmations, picnics at the [Lake Pontchartrain] lake front, country hay rides, and advertisements of business concerns. During the carnival season (Mardi Gras), any little insignificant affair was sure to have some kind of music."

Day after day, entrepreneurs combined the raw material of note and tempo to create new music, tested their creations on live audiences, and readjusted to meet the pressing demands of commerce. The competition for ears and dollars was fierce, though older musicians could often be found teaching the young and mentoring protégés. Kings were anointed and dethroned. Talent was fluid, moving from band to band, carrying new ideas throughout the community. Back rooms, attics, and front stoops became places of constant musical invention, which soared on the breeze, available to any aspiring talent. Musical entrepreneurs ate, drank, and slept their craft.

Competition for audiences was relentless and often colorful. Brass bands paraded through the streets by day, sometimes in step with a funeral and sometimes simply to advertise a dance where they would play that evening. It was not uncommon for two bands advertising different events to meet at an intersection and engage in a "cutting" or "bucking" contest. Winners received bragging rights and a larger paying crowd that evening. As one participant noted about the rough-and-tumble matches, "If you couldn't blow a man down with your horn, at least you could use it to hit him alongside the head."

THE BLOWINGEST MAN EVER LIVED

Sometime around 1894, Buddy Bolden settled on the cornet as his instrument of choice. He may have first picked it up at a nearby barbershop, an important "third place" in New Orleans just as it was in Durham for John Merrick. One shop close to Bolden's home was operated by Charley Galloway, who played the guitar and had a steady stream of Irish, German, and black musicians in and out of his shop. It was a place where Bolden could find free instruction, job offers, acceptance, and impromptu jam sessions.

At age seventeen, Buddy began to play in earnest, his mother recalling that her son would rather play than eat. By 1897, Bolden and his band were booking jobs steadily for a young, hip, black, and growing crowd. He was described by a peer as "one fine-lookin' brown-skin man, tall and slender and a terror with the ladies." One story claims he could be seen walking down the street with one woman holding his hat, another his coat, and sometimes a third his handkerchief. Nobody but Bolden, the story went, ever carried his cornet.

Buddy's personality and playing were big, flashy, distinctive, and mythically loud. One contemporary remembers Bolden blowing the tuning slide from his cornet twenty feet across the room. When Buddy and his band played "Home, Sweet Home" on the New Orleans docks for a black regiment bound for Cuba during the Spanish-American War, legend says some of the men were so moved that they jumped overboard and swam back to shore. Jelly Roll Morton claimed that Buddy Bolden was the most powerful trumpeter in history.

I remember we'd be hanging around some corner . . . then we'd hear old Buddy's trumpet coming on and we'd all start. Any time it was a quiet night at Lincoln Park because maybe the affair hadn't been so well publicized . . . he'd turn his big trumpet around toward the city and blow his blues, calling his children home, as he used to say. The whole town would know Buddy Bolden was at the Park, ten or twelve miles from the center of town.

Morton's summation would eventually get chiseled into Bolden's tombstone: "He was the blowingest man ever lived since Gabriel."

Buddy appeared in the New Orleans city directories as a plasterer, music teacher, and from 1902 to 1907, musician. By age twenty-two, he was leading a well-known band and, by 1904, was popular and celebrated enough to be promoted from "Kid Bolden" to "King Bolden." If the job of an entrepreneur is to bring new combinations to market, Bolden was a sensation. "When you come right down to it," trumpeter Thomas "Papa Mutt" Carey (1886–1948) said, "the man who started the big noise in jazz was Buddy Bolden." Another contemporary trumpeter, Willie Gary "Bunk" Johnson (1879–1948), remembered, "Bolden was the first man that began playing jazz in the city of New Orleans, and his band had the whole of New Orleans real crazy and running wild behind it."

Bolden's gift was this: While he could probably not read music well, he could play almost anything by ear, carry dozens of tunes in his head, improvise across each one, teach the parts to his bandmates, and find new and different sounds that could dazzle his audience. Without a word yet to describe the music he was inventing ("jazz" would first be used in 1912), Bolden was said to play "blues slow and mean and the rags fast and dirty . . . that raggedy uptown stuff." Jazz historian Charles Edward Smith envisioned "a whacky horn playing an uptown rag, way out and way off, filling out the tune." Another wrote that, while Bolden's band knew quadrilles, polkas, and other traditional dances, it was "of the rough-and-ready school, without the polish of note readers." Yet another referred to Bolden's music as "new ragtime." It was, in Schumpeterian terms, a combination of styles so novel that it defied easy description.

From the start, writes biographer Marquis, Buddy drew upon all these musical resources unlike anyone else: "The ideas in his head had to come out, had to be expressed, and Buddy's way of expressing them was, it seems, different from what had been heard before." The fact that his music was distinctive and pushed the limits in a city famous for its trained, talented, and competitive musicians was an indication of his genius.

"TOO GOOD FOR HIS TIME"

Three things conspired against Buddy Bolden the entrepreneur. First, a lack of formal training, set against his desire to improvise, caused Buddy to "hear" things that he could not play. Combined with the need to out-perform other bands for both pride and commercial success, King Bolden could wilt under the pressure of retaining his title. Like software developers a century later, constant innovation was necessary in the New Orleans music community because good ideas were impossible to patent, and "theft" between practitioners was an accepted way of doing business.

The second strike against Bolden was his weakness for hard drinking. And the third challenge Buddy faced, clear in retrospect, was the presence of some underlying mental illness made worse by his musical frustrations, drinking, and lack of proper medical care. By March 1906, Bolden was experiencing severe headaches, followed by depression and paranoia. The act of playing seemed to cause him anguish. He became violent and was arrested and booked for insanity on several occasions that year. Bolden played his last job on Labor Day 1906, when he broke down and was thrown in a jail cell without receiving adequate medical attention.

On June 5, 1907, Buddy Bolden was committed to the State Insane Asylum at Jackson, Louisiana, never to return home. While there were times over the years when his family and friends thought he might be released, by the 1920s he no longer recognized his family. In 1925, Bolden was given a routine examination by his doctor, who found an incoherent, tortured soul and diagnosed "dementia praecox, paranoid type."

Buddy died at age fifty-four in 1931, leaving behind no interviews or recordings. Not until two years after his death did jazz historians even begin to recover his name and legacy. In so doing, they realized that what Bolden created between 1900 and 1906 was novel and striking enough to his contemporaries that they believed they were hearing something entirely new. Don Marquis resolved that, if Buddy was not the first to play jazz, "he was the first to popularize it and give the music a base from which to grow." Another shining product of the New Orleans jazz community, Louis Armstrong (1901–1971), concluded that

Bolden "was just a one-man genius that was ahead of 'em all . . . too good for his time."

In an America where aspiring black entrepreneurs had few opportunities to innovate, and in a city filled with stellar musicians, Buddy Bolden stood out as creating something entirely new. He launched an art form that confounded those who expected original "American music" to somehow emerge from the classical traditions of Europe. Bolden "did not just stumble across a new sound or style," Marquis wrote. "He was consciously striving for something new." As tragically as his story ends, Buddy Bolden also serves as a poignant reminder that even marginalized entrepreneurs can flourish where community thrives and where race and class are second to innovation and talent.

BACK AT THE BAR

By now, the barroom guests were beginning to understand that they were hearing two different kinds of entrepreneurial stories. One was focused on mechanization and mass production, themes of the Industrial Revolution in America. Other stories, like Bolden's, were about social and cultural innovation. And both kinds of stories were happening at once, jazz and razor blades, oyster bars and shovels, spilling into the economy of the nation and the lives of its consumers.

"If I have this right," said Willis Carrier, leaning over to speak with John Merrick, "about the time I was designing the air-conditioning system in Brooklyn, Mr. Bolden was helping to invent jazz in New Orleans, Mr. Gillette was almost ready to launch his razor blades in Boston, Mrs. Sharpe was starting her candy empire in Syracuse, and you were beginning to build a giant insurance business in North Carolina. It's impossible to tell all those stories at once, but there's no denying they happened at the same time."

Elizabeth Arden had been chatting with Mary Elizabeth Sharpe about the difficulties of operating a business in New York City. Now, she stood to speak, a wisp of a woman but clearly used to command. "What's interesting, Dr. Carrier, was what yours and some of the other stories have hinted at. It was a problem I faced almost from the start of my career."

Heads turned. What did she mean?

"I started selling 'beauty' before many women in America thought they were *allowed* to be beautiful," she added. "I could manufacture new cosmetics almost as fast I could invent them. But making new customers—that was the real challenge."

Part Three

CONSUMERISM

Chapter 9

ELIZABETH ARDEN:
A RIGHT TO BE BEAUTIFUL

Observers of American life in the early twentieth century found a nation that had become expert at producing and delivering goods to its citizens. Automated factories were booming. A dazzling supply of new products flew off assembly lines.

By 1900, some sixty thousand traveling salesmen such as King Camp Gillette crisscrossed America. Aaron Montgomery Ward created the first national mail-order firm, followed by Sears, Roebuck and Company, whose catalog carried one hundred thousand items. The railroad, Rural Free Delivery (in 1896), and parcel post (in 1913) delivered goods to small towns and farms throughout America.

With the growth of cities came the rise of the department store and the growth of chain stores. Americans living thousands of miles apart were being joined together by magazines, the telephone, Hollywood, the radio, and the automobile. A journalist traveling cross-country in the early twentieth century found Americans from New York to California "are more and more coming to be molded on something of the same outward pattern." This included their clothing, their homes, and the novels they read. A "mass market" was rising implausibly from a nation that was once a loose collection of regions and not long before at war with itself.

Having mastered mechanization and mass production, industry was suddenly faced with a new crisis. "The problem before us today is not how to produce the goods," journalist Samuel Strauss (1870–1953) wrote in 1924, "but how to produce the customers." The function of *marketing management* arose in the twentieth century. "To find markets rather than to supply those already active is in general the more difficult problem of business today," wrote Arch Wilkinson Shaw (1876–1962), the first lecturer on business policy at the Harvard Business School. Sometimes this meant discovering what people already wanted, and sometimes it meant creating new demand.

CONSUMER PULL OR PRODUCER PUSH?

The concept of "style" arose as an important attribute of a product, and style could be manipulated. "This new influence . . . is largely used to make people dissatisfied with what they have of the old order," advertising executive Earnest Calkins (1868–1964) wrote, "still good and useful and efficient, but lacking the newest touch." People purchase new furniture for their home, he added, "not because the old furniture is unable to perform its duties as furniture, but because it is out of date, out of style, no longer the thing."

Academics disagreed about who was responsible for this phenomenon of consumerism. Some saw its birth as the result of a generation of high-quality, low-cost product being available in the market. Americans had come to expect the newest and best, all at an affordable price. "This is our proudest boast," Strauss added: "The American citizen has more comforts and conveniences than kings had two hundred years ago." For Strauss, consumerism was the result of a ceaseless *pull* from consumers.

Others believed that business was more responsible, more manipulative, having found ways through clever marketing to create new demand. A 1925 advertisement by Crane Company asked, "Has Your Family Outgrown One Bathroom?" while another from the Washington Automotive Trade Association wondered if "Every motorist who plans the construction of a new home should figure on erecting a three-car garage." The journalist Mark Sullivan (1874–1952) believed that new demand was created by businessmen who realized that "if the old could be made to seem passé . . . the new could be sold in profitable quantities." For Sullivan, consumerism was the result of a calculated *push* from producers.

Pull or push, consumer or producer, the transformation was real. When Robert and Helen Lynd took a detailed look at attitudes in the town of Muncie, Indiana, in 1929, they found residents being informed by their local paper that the "citizen's first importance to his country is no longer that of citizen but that of consumer. Consumption is the new necessity." Consumer credit soared among young people. So did a signature cultural innovation of the age: planned obsolescence. "We are urged deliberately to waste material," one commentator wrote. "Throw away your razor blades, abandon your motor car, and purchase new."

Style over function, credit, and obsolescence had all become virtues—a way to keep the giant factories of automation humming along, but a complete about-face from the frugal world of the previous century.

Today's entrepreneurs are at home in this land of desire. Accelerators and business schools spend as much time teaching their students how to find, satisfy, or create customers as they do teaching how to create products. In the early twentieth century, however, consumerism was a new cultural force, and one that entrepreneurs were just learning to understand and exploit.

Elizabeth Arden was one such pioneer, eventually constructing a billion-dollar empire and living an American entrepreneurial experience described as a "sociological and historical" phenomenon.

FREEDOM, BEAUTY, AND SEX APPEAL

Born in Canada, Florence Nightingale Graham (1884–1966) dropped out of high school to seek employment after her mother's untimely death. Graham lasted just three weeks as a nurse and had equally unfulfilling experiences in Toronto as a stenographer, bank teller, and dental assistant.

Graham moved to New York City in 1908, taking a position in Eleanor

Adair's beauty salon, where wealthy women paid high prices for massages and facial treatments. This was the first work that appealed to Graham, and after developing a clientele and learning the rudiments of cosmetics, she left Adair in 1910 to open a beauty salon on Fifth Avenue with partner Elizabeth Hubbard. Both strong-willed, Graham and Hubbard soon parted ways. Seeking a new name for her salon, Florence decided to keep her partner's first name but replace "Hubbard" with "Arden" from her favorite poem, "Enoch Arden," by Alfred Lord Tennyson.

With funds borrowed from her brother, the new "Elizabeth Arden" created a luxurious salon, establishing pink as her color of choice behind a trademark red door. From there her business model evolved to focus on America's "New Woman" who, in the opening decades of the twentieth century, was becoming better educated, more independent, and who desired "freedom, beauty and sex appeal."

Arden's marketing genius led her to target two specific segments: middle-aged women who wanted to recapture their youth, and plain-looking or unattractive women who hoped to find "beauty in a bottle." At a time when cosmetics were often associated with prostitutes trying to conceal signs of disease, and respectable women used only talcum powder, rose water, and glycerin (all in moderation), Arden offered new creams, lotions, and oils in an ever-expanding variety of products designed to enhance beauty. Her salon business flourished.

In 1915, Arden launched a wholesale business to distribute her products to upscale department stores around the country. That same year she married Thomas Jenkins Lewis, a banker, who successfully ran the wholesale business until their divorce in 1934. Lewis never owned stock and was never admitted to the partnership, suggesting the marriage—which also made Arden a US citizen—was one of friendship, convenience, and marketing: Arden believed her clientele would trust a married woman more than a single woman. By 1935, the wholesale business served five thousand drug and department stores.

Arden's slogan, "Every woman has a right to be beautiful," resonated with customers in her growing cosmetics and salon empire, from

Boston to San Francisco and Palm Beach, and from London to Paris and Berlin. Her business model was so robust and her marketing so effective, she ran one of the few US businesses immune to the Great Depression.

Arden's greatest insight, and perhaps greatest piece of luck, was building a business in beauty at a moment of fundamental change in America's perception of the human form, driven by the experience of World War I. Before the war, being plump was a sign of good health. Actress Lillian Russell, said to be the most beautiful woman in 1880s America, tipped the scales at 200 pounds. Nearly one-third of all World War I draftees were rejected as physically unfit, many because they were overweight.

But with the war came rationing—addressed in special cookbooks by women such as Mary Elizabeth Evans—which forced Americans to rethink portions, variety, and the quality of food they consumed. Within a decade, Americans were eating a more varied diet, trading starches for fruits and vegetables. Knowledge of nutrition became more common. Borden and Sealtest promoted safe, pasteurized milk. Clarence Birdseye offered frozen foods. Cereal makers encouraged a change from meat and potatoes for breakfast. In all, post–World War I America ate less but ate better. Girth was no longer a sign of good health.

Just as the revolution in transportation represented an opportunity for Oliver Ames and his shovel factory, this change in the perception of health and beauty represented a rising tide for Elizabeth Arden. Her business grossed a phenomenal $2 million a week in 1925. Arden rejected a $15 million offer to sell at the start of the Depression and continued her expansion. Her sister, Gladys, oversaw a direct sales effort by which account executives could earn up to $8,000 annually.

If loyal and generous with good performers, Arden was also a tough and demanding boss, saying, "I only want people around me who can do the impossible." With employees, she could be mercurial, as journalist Margaret Case Harriman wrote:

She is tyrannical and exacting or affectionate and lavish, by turns. Her employees, seldom knowing from one hour to the next whether to expect a calling down or a champagne party, have learned to take what comes with a good deal of serenity.

These mood swings might have been explained at least partially by the occasional hip pain resulting from an injury suffered as a youth. Arden struggled with this pain for thirty years, sometimes taking to bed for as long as six months. But beneath these bouts there clearly lurked an autocrat and perfectionist, legendary in her need to manage her empire to the last detail, and famous for the certainty that she was always right.

A true innovator, Arden launched a steady stream of new products. When told that production of a "fluffy" face cream was impossible, she vehemently disagreed until she found a chemist who would create Cream Amoretta. She launched the "Vienna Youth Mask" of papier-mâché and tinfoil, which applied heat via an electric current. She created cosmetics to complement clothing, not just skin color, and encouraged the everyday use of mascara and eye shadow. In her first twenty-five years, Arden developed more than a hundred items. She tried each new cosmetic on herself—and often on her staff—and had the final say on all product development decisions, brand names, and advertising.

Did her treatments really work? A 1935 profile of the entrepreneur suggested that there was some snake oil in Arden's approach. For example, a bottle of her Ardena skin tonic retailed for eighty-five cents but had just three cents' worth of water, grain alcohol, boric acid, and perfume in it. Her conviction that electricity generated by the Vienna Face Mask replenished skin cells was met by a skeptical medical establishment. No matter. Women willingly paid $200 for thirty-two treatments. "In one day recently, between the hours of nine and six," Harriman's profile noted, "three hundred and ninety-four women went through the little red door of Elizabeth Arden's New York salon at 691 Fifth Avenue to be rolled, massaged, baked, bathed, and otherwise persuaded into beauty." Persuasion was the key to the new consumer economy; no matter the client, one of Arden's staff noted, there was always *some* treatment.

Described as "comely, fragile, fluttery and ageless," this former farm girl from Canada was, like many driven entrepreneurs, not to be trifled with, her obituary noting:

> *Although she stood only a little over 5 feet tall and was slender, she was about as fragile as a football tackle; and anyone who mistook her wispiness for indecision quickly discovered that she had a will of steel and the power to execute it.*

Arden retained a lifelong passion for improving women's looks, sometimes noting the flaws of a visitor to her company and recommending lotions and creams on the spot. She worked until the day she died. Her only distraction was horse racing, where her Thoroughbred Jet Pilot won the Kentucky Derby in 1947. Arden's horses received the same pampering as her customers, with music piped into their decorated stalls, and regular massages and treatments with Elizabeth Arden products.

She was also her own best advertisement. Blessed with beautiful skin, she appeared twenty years younger than her actual age and seemed to be living proof that her products worked. Arden had an immutable formula for beauty: Clear skin, natural makeup, a slim waistline, and a simple hairdo—though not too short. "If you read the papers, you will notice that no girl with short hair has made an advantageous marriage lately," she said in 1950.

When Arden died in 1966, she left bequests totaling $11 million and a total estate valued at as much as $40 million, including fifty beauty salons, a stable of racing horses, and a twelfth-century gothic castle (with an interior suffused in pink) outside Dublin. She generously left gifts to family and friends and large sums that were divided among employees. In a final act of loyalty and kindness, she also directed that, when her racehorses were sold, mares and foals must be sold together.

BACK AT THE BAR

"Interesting," King Gillette mused. "Mrs. Sharpe appealed to consumers by emphasizing traditional values. Mrs. Arden appealed to consumers by emphasizing the 'New Woman'—who was anything but traditional. And both worked!"

"While you, Mr. Gillette, appealed to both traditional shavers tired of cutting themselves," Joseph Knowles Milliken chuckled, remembering his own experience with a heavy, forged razor, "and to the 'New Man' who believed 'looking sharp' was an important part of his image and needed to shave every day."

"Imagine telling our grandfathers they'd be throwing out their razors every few weeks," Gillette said with a smile.

As waitstaff cleared dishes and checked on refills, "J. K." Milliken strode to the middle of the barroom. Arden's story and Gillette's comments had resonated with him. "I saw this same transformation from traditional thinking to new values happen—but on the floor of my factory," Milliken said. He paused in thought for a moment. "Because," he added, "the American consumer was also the new American employee who brought their new ideas to work every day."

The barroom of entrepreneurs settled back, wondering what lessons this new story would hold.

"It all started long ago with a train ride to a forgotten little town," Milliken said, "a place I never thought I'd call home for the rest of my life."

Chapter 10

J. K. MILLIKEN:
COMMUNITY IN A MODEL VILLAGE

On a mild January morning in 1901, twenty-six-year-old J. K. Milliken (1875–1961) and his uncle, J. Frank Knowles, stepped off the train in Taunton, Massachusetts, and walked along a muddy road into the shabby village of North Dighton. There they found an abandoned, dilapidated, ninety-year-old cotton mill on the bank of the Three Mile River.

Knowles was one of the country's leading textile industrialists, visiting North Dighton on behalf of other prominent mill owners in nearby New Bedford seeking to establish new capacity to finish raw, or "gray," fabric being produced at their mills. Advanced technology introduced in the late nineteenth century had turned finishing—which might include bleaching, dyeing, and printing colors on gray cloth—into a high-volume, mechanized process requiring chemists and copious amounts of clean water. Attracting skilled labor from England, where cloth finishing had been invented and perfected, would be especially important to the plant's success.

Born in Salem, Massachusetts, Joseph Knowles Milliken was raised in New Bedford and graduated from Harvard in 1896. His passport described a man five feet five and a half inches tall with blue eyes and a strong chin. He was employed at the Dunnell Mill in Pawtucket, Rhode

Island, until 1899, when he took a position with the Hathaway Mill in New Bedford, where his uncle was a director. Knowles and his nephew were both part of a New Bedford textile community that had grown from the profits of the older whaling industry; owners and their families had long-standing relationships and interlocking business interests. It was a tight-knit community that would provide a steady supply of customers and ensure the younger entrepreneur's success for nearly a half century.

The two men measured the abandoned mill and explored the nearby water supply, concluding that this was a superb location in an otherwise backwater town.

Mount Hope Finishing Company was incorporated in June 1901 and capitalized at $125,000. Knowles invested $50,000 and was joined by several of his wealthy New Bedford associates. Milliken was the smallest shareholder, investing $5,000. He began turning out finished cloth by December while simultaneously refurbishing the old facility.

Knowles had advised his nephew that "success meant an infinite care and attention to detail," something that could only be done by focusing on a single business opportunity, "with the boss constantly on the job." Milliken embraced this concept, holding a meeting every workday morning with superintendents and foremen that included a full discussion of the day's orders. He knew every detail of the plant, and he seemed always to be on site, completely absorbed in the business even on Sundays, when he brought along his two sons, destined to join the business in the 1920s.

The twenty-seven-acre plant became a model of technology and efficiency. Materials were moved with electrically operated tractors. A "huge vacuum cleaner" visited every room weekly to remove dust from the floor, walls, and ceilings. The company boasted several labs under the direction of expert chemists who were constantly seeking exclusive finishes for customers.

IN A CLASS BY ITSELF

Revenue grew from $175,000 in 1903 to $430,000 in 1907. Milliken avoided debt and reinvested earnings. In 1907, he brought a spur of the New York, New Haven and Hartford Railroad to Mount Hope, eliminating the need for teamsters. Sensing war in 1913, he bought up huge quantities of the best German dyes and shipped them home, providing a steady profit stream during World War I. In 1914, Milliken played a leading role in the founding of the National Association of Finishers of Textile Fabric. By 1916, Mount Hope revenues grew to $1.7 million, giving the company a sizable 5 percent share of a fragmented industry. When the market crashed in 1929, Mount Hope was debt free and remained profitable. Over time the company added a branch office in Norfolk, Virginia, to be closer to its sources of raw material, and a selling office on Broadway in New York City to be nearer its customers.

Despite the regular introduction of new technology into the plant, and a steady stream of new products, the singular achievement of J. K. Milliken in the fifty-year history of Mount Hope in North Dighton was the reimagination of North Dighton itself. The need to attract skilled labor had, in 1901, encouraged the company to purchase and refurbish thirteen old tenement homes. Redecorated and outfitted with new plumbing, the homes were made available at modest rental fees to new employees. Over the next fifty years the company acquired, built, and rented nearly two hundred homes in what would come to be called a model village.

Mount Hope mowed lawns, trimmed trees, raked leaves, and cleared snow for its tenants. All houses were repainted and repapered every three years. By the early 1920s, new homes included steam heat, hot and cold water, baths, electric lights, gas, and sewer connections. If a worker became sick or could not work, the company guaranteed that any "occupant with an honest heart and good intentions" would be well cared for. If the worker died, provisions were made for the family.

Mount Hope paid to construct and maintain a number of paved roads throughout the town and financed the village's power system, water, and street lighting. Workers' phones were connected to the local system free of charge. Mount Hope established a town park and hosted employee clambakes and lobster boils. It also sponsored ski trains to New Hampshire and excursions to Cape Cod for its workers.

The company converted an old homestead into a fifteen-bed hospital, including an operating room, for its employees and their families. For a fifty-cent annual fee, employees had access to a clubhouse with bowling alleys, billiard and card rooms, a gym, and a nearby baseball field. There was a movie theater, cooperative bank, glee club, and baseball team good enough to win the Eastern Industrial League in 1920. The company subsidized fire and police services and several churches. It operated a 150-acre model dairy, poultry, and vegetable farm, providing inexpensive fresh food to employees. Workers planting home gardens also received free seed and fertilizer.

In 1924, an article in the *Fall River Globe* painted a rosy picture of life in North Dighton. It was a beehive of industry, a modern New England village of rare beauty and "in a class by itself." The article noted that Milliken often ate lunch and dinner in the company restaurant with workers, "coming and going just as the fireman or the chauffeur would." The restaurant's chef had even been attracted from "a certain high-toned club in a neighboring city." Many employees in the town owned their own automobiles and had pianos, Victrolas, and radios. Milliken himself lived in an unpretentious two-story house: "He lives and works among his people, and his whole life is devoted to the fullest possible development of the happy community which he has organized and established."

J. K. Milliken seemed to understand intuitively the power of community in creating and retaining a skilled and productive workforce. And, there seemed nothing forced or artificial about his participation in it.

The company's *Mount Hope News* made regular attempts to impart a set of values to employees. The March 1920 edition noted that the Permanent Safety Committee had held a meeting with about a hundred employees who watched a movie designed to help rid the workplace of "King Carelessness." An article entitled "Produce or Perish" encouraged workers to be efficient and productive or face the ruthless lessons of Mother Nature. Several items selected by J. K. Milliken appeared, including "Collective Responsibility" (in favor of group productivity bonuses over individual bonuses), "Let's Clean Up" (about factory orderliness), and "Clearing The Air of Rumors" (on the importance of good communication). One feature highlighted a class on "Americanization" being offered at the local school, while another asked employees to voluntarily return extra pay if placed inadvertently in their weekly envelopes.

TENSE AND "SEALED OFF"

The relationship between Milliken and his employees created an enormous reservoir of goodwill. Mount Hope was untouched by the Fall River textile strike of 1904, or by the "Bread and Roses" labor strike in 1912 in Lawrence, Massachusetts. In 1922, New England's textile industry suffered its largest and longest strike to date, lasting nine months and involving as many as eighty thousand workers. Six years later, twenty-seven thousand workers in fifty-six mills struck for six months in New Bedford. Through it all, Mount Hope remained immune from labor discontent.

The textile workers' strike of 1934, which involved four hundred thousand textile workers from New England, the Mid-Atlantic states, and the South, turned out to be more threatening. While Fall River and New Bedford felt the brunt of it, Mount Hope was singled out by the United Textile Workers as the only large nonunion plant in the region. Milliken responded aggressively when he heard that strikers planned to visit the village, bolstering the town's three-man police force by deputizing some fifty employees armed with clubs and pistols. Every street leading into town was barricaded with piles of sandbags. Every plant entrance was manned by armed guards, including twenty recruited from New York and New Jersey.

In September, a convoy of forty automobiles and two trucks left Fall River headed for North Dighton but was turned back twice from entering the town. The convoy was unarmed, but its leaders threatened to return with tear gas and other weapons. "A virtual state of martial law existed within a half mile radius of the Mount Hope Finishing Company," the local paper reported. "Guns bristled on every highway leading to the mill and every person approaching within a half mile of the plant was challenged." Dighton resident Patrick Menges recalled that North Dighton "was sealed off during those days. Anyone wishing to proceed into the village by Lincoln Avenue or Spring Street had to be vouchsafed. Their automobile was stopped, and a guard in a temporary shack telephoned the plant for a decision whether or not the person could proceed up the street. If not, the car was turned back."

Fortunately, the crisis passed in a few weeks. As resident Harry Corr remembered, "The people of North Dighton did more to turn back the mob of strikers than the New York goons. All the help was on J. K. Milliken's side. They wanted no part of unions in those days." One of the union leaders later admitted, "If all bosses were like him maybe there wouldn't be a strike." In the wake of the threat, Milliken made a $10,000 gift to the town, increasing the police force to include twenty-three special police and eighty-six reserves. The members of this force drilled with rifles and bayonets for a few months before the town returned to fighting its more typical criminal activity, such as dogs invading chicken coops.

By World War II, the plant, farm, and village of North Dighton had become a single entity. Milliken had been successful in establishing a system that gave him nearly as much control over workers as over any of his other raw inputs. The floors of his factory were, employees said, clean enough to eat off. This cleanliness and order extended to the neighborhood, where Milliken was known to stop his car on the way to work to retrieve a bit of trash along the side of the road. The entire village had become an extension of the bleachery.

After forty years in business, Milliken had become one of the best-known industrialists in New England, a tough and fearless competitor, "dean of the finishing business," and the patriarch of North Dighton who knew each of his workers by name. Even in hard times he could be counted on. When business was off in the first quarter of 1936, for example, the company reduced production time but workers remained fully employed at their current pay by painting, mowing lawns, or scrubbing floors.

THE STING OF ABUNDANCE

Such largesse came at a price, however—one that an English immigrant worker in 1910 might have accepted but the new second- and third-generation American living in an increasingly affluent and mobile society found less agreeable. For example, the Mount Hope–sponsored cooperative bank did not grant loans because Milliken believed debt instilled bad habits. Any employee needing to borrow money could come directly to the company and present his case, often receiving funds debt-free. Employees knew, however, that Milliken disapproved of borrowing for pianos, phonographs, and other "luxury" items, and that he was the final arbiter.

Workers had no say in how their homes were repainted and repapered. Employees wishing to build in the village were sent to a company-approved architect, and Milliken insisted all home mortgages be cleared in twelve years. For the majority of workers who continued to rent, a so-called "village visitor" made regular calls to provide advice on diets, sanitation, and other household matters. Workers approaching retirement had no formal pension program. Instead, Milliken met with each to construct a confidential plan thought to be generous but uncomfortably arbitrary.

The residents of Dighton's other sections felt the sting of North Dighton's abundance and Milliken's power. In 1929, an angry audience filled the South Dighton School, opposing the move of its eighth-grade class to North Dighton, believing "Mayor Milliken" was behind it. By mid-century, even those who admired Milliken and benefited from his benevolence came to see his power in a new, more conflicted way. One person, for instance, said of Milliken that he was "never a tyrant—more of an autocrat . . . People did things his way." There were mounting tensions over schools, the water supply, and road construction. To cross J. K. over an issue in public could spell the end of a career or the loss of a home.

Residents recall the moment he rose at a town meeting in 1951 after the vote to approve a new elementary school went against his wishes, saying, "I'll stop the sale of the bonds!" Many of Dighton's younger or newer residents, untouched by Milliken's largesse, did not hear "benevolent father" in such a threat.

Disenchantment with Milliken's paternalism swelled while New England's textile industry felt increasing pressure to relocate to the New South. In 1880 there were just 561,000 active cotton spindles in the South competing for business with 8.6 million in New England alone. By 1933, Southern mills produced more than 70 percent of cotton and woolen textiles in facilities usually more modern than those found in the North, drawing on a labor pool willing to work for roughly 40 percent less than their Northern counterparts. Southern states were less likely to restrict work hours for women, supporting fifty-five to sixty hours per week versus forty-eight in Massachusetts. Southern mills and finishing plants boasted shorter distances from the growing fields, cheap hydroelectric power (versus coal in the North), and lower taxes. One cotton producer with factories in Massachusetts and Georgia testified in 1928, "I can make anything at all in my Georgia mill that I can make here, make it just as well and make it cheaper."

In addition, new technologies were invading the industry. By 1931, for example, synthetic rayon was growing at 20 percent annually, already having replaced 2.5 million cotton spindles.

Despite these ominous trends, the Milliken family hung on, always ready to adapt to new products and new customers. In 1949, the family bought out its coinvestors and gained the flexibility to make whatever moves necessary to meet market demands and protect the business.

"THEY BROUGHT GUNS WITH THEM"

The final collapse of Mount Hope's community in North Dighton came in the early 1950s amid a general slowdown in textile production, made worse by the Korean War (1950–1953). Running at 50 percent capacity, the plant was losing money, and the Milliken family felt pressure to investigate Southern locations. Meanwhile, the company's New York sales team encouraged J. K. Milliken to host a huge, fiftieth-anniversary celebration to attract potential buyers and reenergize Mount Hope's sales. According to the company, the decision to hold the celebration might, if successful, eliminate the need to dismiss hundreds of workers.

On June 13, 1951, fourteen Pullman cars arrived at Mount Hope from New York City. Passengers included textile converters handling half the volume in America. After meetings and a tour, employees and some seven hundred guests were treated to a gigantic clam and lobster bake in the park in front of the facility. Massachusetts Congressman Joseph Martin served as toastmaster. A crowd of 2,300 people rose as one to cheer their beloved J. K. Milliken, described as "the backbone of the industrial and civic life of North Dighton, and the strong right arm of the neighboring city of Taunton, where its payrolls over the last 50 years have in no small measure been a life-giving shot in the arm." It was, however, the last time management and employees of Mount Hope would find reason to celebrate together.

Later that month, rumors of a layoff prompted several employees to obtain union cards from the Textile Workers Union of America and begin a membership drive. Milliken and his two sons were divided over the response, J. K. wanting to work through difficulties with the existing employee base, while his older son pushed to relocate to a facility that had been identified in Butner, North Carolina. On July 31, the company laid off 190 of its 615 workers. Milliken invited the plant's remaining employees to his home, where many assembled on the front lawn. He described to them the current challenges faced by the company, the threat from Southern finishers, and the logic for the layoff. He made a personal appeal for understanding, saying, "North Dighton is my life. North Dighton is my home. Here my roots are deeply established, and here in North Dighton, God willing, I expect to die."

Milliken's heartfelt plea was not enough to stop employees from walking off the job on August 13. Some saw duplicity, interpreting the

July layoffs as an underhanded attempt to end the union's organizing efforts; 53 percent of all employees had signed cards seeking a union election, but of those laid off, 69 percent had signed cards—magically tipping the balance back to 53 percent in the company's favor. Milliken made a second plea by letter just days before the union election in September 1951 that reinforced Mount Hope's fifty years of "happy association with fellow employees" and reminded workers that "the violence, the vicious actions, the name calling, the hatreds and bad feeling created are entirely foreign to this community and have never occurred before." It was too little to turn the tide. On September 17, the union won a National Labor Relations Board election by a count of 369 to 210.

Younger workers, including the children of longtime Milliken loyalists, had turned against J. K. Older workers were upset by the cancellation of bonuses in light of the expensive fiftieth-anniversary celebration. Workers formed picket lines, disrupted operations, and damaged automobiles, with the increasing presence of guns adding to the sense of menace. A day after the vote, a crowd of between four and five hundred men and women gathered in front of the plant. Angry workers threw stones at homes and the factory. Employees loyal to Mount Hope sat on their front porches with shotguns ready. One worried resident said, "It was just like Minute Men. There were about 15 or 20 of us against this mob. They ran like rats when they heard the guns go off." The governor of Massachusetts refused to intervene.

The Millikens made the final decision to close the North Dighton plant when strikers halted the shipment of goods outside factory doors, freezing as much as $5 million worth of inventory. "When we located here, we were in the heart of the textile industry, but since it's all gone south, we've been fading away," J. K. said. "A finishing plant is only a glorified laundry, and we must be near the origin of the wash." After September 19, 1951, all gray goods were returned or sent elsewhere for finishing; by October, North Carolina attorneys had paved the way for a smaller "Mount Hope," called the Creedmore Company, to move to Butner, North Carolina.

It was time for J. K. Milliken to retire, leaving his oldest son to guide the company in its new home. Despite turmoil at the end, it had been an enormously successful, fifty-year run in North Dighton. Throughout, J. K. had ensured that Mount Hope was competitive, profitable, and maintained the newest technology and a skilled workforce, even as the New England textile industry imploded all around it. And it was not lost on the Milliken family that acceptance of mandatory union terms in exchange for a reduction in Mount Hope's generous and voluntary benefits might have saved the company millions of dollars. What was less clear until the final union vote, however, was that a younger workforce was unwilling to tolerate the price of "community" and its associated paternalism, no matter how benevolent or magnanimous.

BACK AT THE BAR

"What benefits!" one of the younger entrepreneurs exclaimed. "I worked for a tech company in Silicon Valley and I had a gourmet cafeteria, free babysitting, and even someone to clean my apartment—but that was nothing compared to the benefits of living in your village."

"Apparently," Milliken replied, "the benefits I offered at Mount Hope came at too high a cost, at least for my younger workers. Perhaps too much community can be as bad as not enough?"

That's when a tall, slender man in a dark double-breasted suit, starched collar, and spats spoke up. His Brooklyn accent was unmistakable. "You lived through a revolution, Mr. Milliken," he said. "A real revolution. I feel sure we saw more change, more progress and advancement, in the world from 1900 to 1950 than any generation in history."

This was Alfred Sloan, a giant even among the successful entrepreneurs gathered in the barroom that evening. "And if consumers came to expect the latest and newest thing, it's no wonder they grew impatient at work with the old style of management. You did your best, Mr. Milliken," he added, "and it worked well for a long time."

"As for my story," Sloan continued, "I grew up in a land where Henry

Ford had perfected mass production and ruled the industrial world. But the changes you saw in the workforce, Mr. Milliken, and those that Mrs. Arden saw in the marketplace—well, we saw in spades in the automobile industry. Mass production was necessary but insufficient to compete in the modern world."

Someone slid a stool up for Sloan, who settled back, perched on its edge. "Let me explain."

Chapter 11

ALFRED SLOAN: AMERICA'S MOST SUCCESSFUL ENTREPRENEUR?

orn in New Haven, Connecticut, Alfred Sloan (1875–1966) moved with his family to Brooklyn, New York, where he attended Brooklyn Polytechnic Institute, showing an early talent for engineering. Enrolling in the Massachusetts Institute of Technology at age seventeen, he studied tirelessly, graduating in three years. It was a work ethic that would define his career.

Sloan was an introvert who lacked the bluster often associated with successful entrepreneurs. "I was thin as a rail, young and unimpressive," he wrote. "Asking favors and pushing myself into places where I am a stranger always did go against my grain." Despite these reservations, the young graduate landed his first job at the Hyatt Roller Bearing Company in Harrison, New Jersey, working alongside owner John Wesley Hyatt. Sloan earned fifty dollars a month serving as draftsman, salesman, and general assistant. He came to appreciate the inventiveness of his new boss, but, unhappy with a firm that was perpetually strapped for cash, Sloan left Hyatt for a brief and unsuccessful entrepreneurial fling trying to market a mechanical icebox. "It is astonishing what you can do when you have a lot of energy, ambition and plenty of ignorance," he concluded.

Learning that his former boss was preparing to retire, Sloan persuaded his father to invest $5,000 to acquire and recapitalize Hyatt Roller Bearing. Now in charge, he reorganized the business, turning a profit in the first six months.

In 1899, Sloan received a request for information from a manufacturer of a horseless carriage, seeking to upgrade from traditional greased wagon axles. While his interest was piqued by the emergence of this new industry, he had no desire to pursue dozens of shops all over the East and Midwest. "I looked upon these people more or less as adventurers," Sloan wrote, and not "as potential pioneers in the development of an industry that was to advance the economic and social status of humanity more than any other."

This perspective changed, however, when the Olds Motor Works in Detroit placed a trial order with Hyatt. Already known for manufacturing a quality gasoline engine, Olds had recently built a vehicle robust enough to travel from Detroit to New York in only seven and a half days. Soon, another fledgling automaker, Henry Ford, requested samples. Hyatt's business grew, as did Sloan's reputation as a talented executive.

Early interactions with Henry Ford were memorable. Ford "had the vision to see that lower prices would increase volume up to the point that would justify such lower prices through reduced costs," Sloan wrote. This framework for producing affordable vehicles was made possible by Ford's genius in combining a continuous flow of parts with a continuous system of production—the moving assembly line. "Right there lies Mr. Ford's outstanding contribution to industrial progress," Sloan concluded. It was the pinnacle of mass production, a system dependent on suppliers never missing a delivery promise. "Humanity never had wanted any machine as much as it desired this one," Sloan remarked about growing consumer demand for the automobile, "and it was a capital offense to hold up a production line."

A SURPRISING COMMUNITY OF INNOVATION

The automobile was conceived in Europe and migrated to America, premiering in New England, the nation's traditional center of mechanical excellence. Frank Duryea drove the country's first successful gasoline-powered vehicle in Springfield, Massachusetts, in 1893. Four years later, the Pope Manufacturing Company in nearby Hartford, Connecticut, produced more than five hundred electric vehicles. New England seemed a logical place for the automobile to take root and thrive.

Other locations around the country such as Chicago, Cleveland, Buffalo, Toledo, Indianapolis, Kenosha, Kalamazoo, and Charlotte also showed early promise. In 1900, Detroit was considered a beautiful city with a long tradition of stove manufacturing but an otherwise lackluster economic outlook.

Four years later, the city had become America's leader in automotive manufacture. By 1920, Detroit accounted for more than 70 percent of US production and employed hundreds of thousands of workers, 80 percent of all rubber, 75 percent of all plate glass, and 20 percent of all steel production. Road construction, advertising, suburbanization, shopping, dining, crime, romance—the automobile changed everything. How had Detroit, a city of less than 250,000 people in 1900, become the epicenter for this transformation and the most important community of innovation in America for the first seventy-five years of the twentieth century?

In part, the city was blessed with a combination of commercial and natural advantages. In 1895, 125 firms in Detroit and throughout Michigan manufactured horse-drawn vehicles, many of which would use their know-how and profits to experiment with the horseless carriage. Detroit also had a thriving railroad car works, access to iron ore, and good connections to the rest of the country by water and rail. Still, compared to Cleveland, Buffalo, Chicago, and other larger cities, none of these regional advantages was unique or decisive.

What Detroit had that other locations lacked was the aforementioned entrepreneur Ransom Eli Olds (1864–1950). Olds had received his first patent for a gasoline-powered car in 1886 and was, a decade later, ready to produce vehicles commercially, founding the Olds Motor Vehicle Company in Lansing before reorganizing as Olds Motor Works and relocating to Detroit.

Even then, the selection of Detroit had been chance. In need of capital, Olds had been in contact with Eastern investors; some $400 million had been raised in New York, Boston, and elsewhere to back the new horseless carriage industry. He had settled on relocating to Newark, New Jersey, visiting in 1899 to choose a site for a new plant before his promised financing fell through. Olds then sought funding locally, settling on a group of Detroit-based investors and opening his new plant there in 1900, the same year he called Sloan to sample Hyatt ball bearings.

In 1901, Olds produced eleven prototype vehicles, including steam, electric, and gasoline powered. When his factory burned to the ground, however, just one model survived, a gasoline-powered, "curved dash" runabout. In retrospect, this small fire—measured against even the great fires of Rome, London, and Chicago—may have been the most consequential in history. The Curved Dash Oldsmobile became the first automobile in the United States to be mass-produced on an assembly line. It was gasoline powered and, at $650 per vehicle, designed to appeal to the middle class. Olds built 425 cars in 1901, nearly 2,500 in 1902, and became America's largest auto company by 1903.

Detroit's emergence as America's most formidable industrial cluster was helped, of course, by the fact that Henry Ford and General Motors' William Durant decided to locate their companies there—but the city was a thriving innovation community before either began producing automobiles in quantity. Some combination of Ransom Olds's vision and a factory fire helped to invent the future: Gasoline would win out over electric and steam, and the automobile became a middle-class necessity, not simply a toy for wealthy thrill seekers. The fire also forced Olds to outsource key components of his vehicles, including purchasing transmissions from the Dodge brothers, helping to establish a flourishing ecosystem for parts that would support the formation of Buick, Ford, and Cadillac.

Olds's outsourced business model, which spread wealth and knowhow regionally, was indicative of his generous personality. Like Willis

Carrier and the formation of the air-conditioning industry, Ransom Olds was a teacher and a mentor. He had an outsize influence on the future leaders of the automobile industry, being called by one biographer "the schoolmaster of motordom."

However, the decisive factor in Detroit's emergence as America's premier innovation community was, economist Steven Klepper believes, a function of *spin-offs*—when founders leave established firms to launch their own. Spin-offs tend to locate near their parents (forty-nine of fifty-four remained in Detroit through 1924) and survive longer than start-ups. And leading firms tend to create spin-offs at the highest rates, not because of dysfunction, but because the parent company has an abundance of ideas or technologies that cannot all be readily absorbed into its existing business model. This phenomenon is the real impact of Ransom Olds's organization, whose seven spin-offs in seven years (before its acquisition in 1908 by General Motors) included three of the industry's leaders and provided the foundational ecosystem for the Motor City.

So, why Detroit? Ransom Olds and his company established a flourishing innovation community from which Henry Ford, William Durant, and Alfred Sloan all would benefit. It was not the result of regional advantage—factors such as access to iron ore or legacy carriage manufacturers—but a geographic clustering propelled by the formation of new companies spinning off from the industry's first established leader.

Decades later, Silicon Valley would be formed in a similar fashion when Fairchild Semiconductor, the early success story, would spin off twenty-four "Fairchildren," including Intel.

Ransom Olds's early years in Detroit reflect the frenzied automotive world into which Alfred Sloan's Hyatt Roller Bearing made its first sales. From 1895 to 1900, some twelve firms entered the industry annually, and almost thirty-seven per year from 1901 to 1905. By 1909 there were 272 automobile firms in America, before that number collapsed to fifty-one in 1925 and just nine in 1941. When Alfred Sloan visited his customers in Detroit, he found a city full of "original, forceful, strong characters, ambitious fellows." And he recognized the mobility of talent in this open-shop, nonunion city, saying, "In those years the American mechanic was a restless wanderer ... They were seeking growth and opportunity, not merely searching for a living."

Often the search for opportunity brought these wanderers to the Pontchartrain Hotel, one of those essential "third places" where motorcar gossip was exchanged, and "when the crowd thinned out of the dining room, the tablecloths would be covered with sketches: crankshafts, chassis, details of motors, wheels, and all sorts of mechanisms. Partnerships were made and ended there. New projects were launched." It was the barbershop of Durham and New Orleans, the future coffee shop of Silicon Valley, and a place by 1915 where a visitor "soon falls into line with the rest of the folk and sets his watch a half-hour ahead of standard time"—just one more way in which Detroit sustained its commanding if surprising community of innovation that would lead the automotive world for seventy-five years.

OUT ON A LIMB

With orders placed and lessons learned from entrepreneurs such as Olds and Ford, Sloan soon found himself under pressure from another of the great Detroit automotive patriarchs, William Durant, once the country's largest manufacturer of horse-drawn carriages and now General Motors' colorful chief. Sloan had watched GM become Hyatt's largest customer and an uncomfortable percentage of total revenue. Durant and GM were known to be active acquirers, and Sloan grew nervous that GM might purchase a competitor and begin making its own bearings. "I was, I feared, out on a limb," Sloan wrote. With four thousand employees, a daily capacity of forty thousand bearings, and $10 million in annual revenue by 1915, the forty-year-old Sloan saw his life's work at risk.

Consequently, when Durant called, Sloan listened, selling his business to GM for $13.5 million. Durant recognized Sloan's management and engineering talents, installing him as president of United Motors Corporation, an affiliate of GM that produced bearings, rims, and horns.

Alfred Sloan prospered at the helm of his first multi-product-line company. When United Motors was consolidated into GM in 1918, he was made a vice president and director. Under Durant, he found a new boss with integrity, a prodigious work ethic, imagination, generous human qualities, and a contagious optimism in the future. Despite all these positive qualities, however, Sloan did not see himself as "a Durant man," finding him to be impulsive, overextended, and too casual an administrator. Cronyism was rampant. Nearly every division overran its budget. "If General Motors were to capitalize its wonderful opportunity," Sloan wrote, "it would have to be guided by an organization of intellects. A great industrial organization requires the best of many minds." From this, he would build an entire management philosophy.

When business fell abruptly in 1920, Durant was unable to shed bloated inventories. General Motors stock plummeted in November of that year, pushing the company to the brink of bankruptcy. The du Pont family stepped into the crisis, assuming Durant's personal obligations and 2.5 million shares of General Motors. The founder was forced to resign, which "shook the enterprise to its foundation," wrote Sloan, adding, "in short, there was just about as much crisis, inside and outside, as you could wish for, if you liked that sort of thing." Eventually, however, these events redefined General Motors as a disciplined, modern corporation.

NO GREATER OPPORTUNITY EVER

Alfred Sloan was brought into the inner circle of GM management under Pierre S. du Pont (1870–1954), who stepped down a few years later, in May 1923, and made Sloan GM's president. Du Pont's role in steadying the company during a turbulent time was pivotal, and his selection of Sloan was one of the masterstrokes of twentieth-century business. A giant of modern management himself, Pierre du Pont "came to have a greater respect for Sloan than for any other businessman he had ever known."

At that time the company was doing $698 million in revenue. Six years later, under Sloan's leadership, GM had grown to $1.5 billion, its stock price quintupled, and the company's Chevrolet had displaced Ford as the leader in low-priced automobiles. This brilliant yet humble entrepreneur never lost sight of the luck involved in finding himself where he

did, when he did. "I believe it is reasonable to say that no greater opportunity for accomplishment ever was given to any individual in industry,"
Sloan wrote of those first years leading GM. "I determined right then
and there that everything I had was to be given to the cause. No sacrifice
of time, effort, or my own convenience was to be too great. There were
to be no reservations and no alibis."

Sloan cut a striking figure as he traveled North America, visiting as
many as ten dealers in a single day. Six feet tall and just 130 pounds, General Motors' CEO invariably dressed in a dark, double-breasted suit with
a breast-pocket handkerchief, a high starched collar with conservative tie
and pearly stickpin, and spats. He listened in meetings "with the extra
intentness of the deaf," and sometimes made his audience smile when
he chimed in with the Brooklyn accent he never entirely lost. He did not
smoke, rarely drank or read for pleasure, and considered golf and other
sports a waste of time. Relaxation for Alfred Sloan was limited to an
occasional evening of watching television. Associates described him as a
"functional, frill-less man."

Sloan never shook his introverted nature, seldom flashed his ego, and
relied on those around him for ideas and consensus. "I never give orders,"
he said. "I sell my ideas to my associates if I can, I accept their judgment
if they convince me, as they frequently do, that I am wrong." Sloan once
described his method for tackling problems in this way: Get the facts.
Analyze them completely. Decide the course. Don't rely on hunches. Leave
"all the glory of that kind of thinking to such men as liked to be labeled
'genius.'" It was a modesty that belied his powerful impact on shaping
the largest and most successful American enterprise in the first half of the
twentieth century.

THE FAMOUS "ORGANIZATIONAL STUDY"

Sloan's most famous contribution to organizational management would be
an abrupt departure from tradition, originating in the form of a memo to
Durant, who sat atop a General Motors in 1920 that was so decentralized

as to be chaotic. What Sloan concluded in his famous "Organizational Study" memo to his boss was that a company the size and complexity of GM required a kind of decentralization that still allowed for central coordination. It was a paradox, a tension that required autonomous leaders to yield some of their power to a central office for the common good.

Sloan was addressing a problem faced by American business leaders who had harnessed the power of mass production to construct enormous companies such as General Motors, often with multiple product lines. Organizational theory was lagging. The autocratic rule of a single individual, practiced by more traditional leaders like Henry Ford, had become a bottleneck to progress. Likewise, the decentralized rule of a CEO like William Durant led to bedlam. There had to be some middle ground.

Sloan's "Organizational Study" became a kind of best seller during the 1920s, reprinted for executives around the world. And Sloan put these ideas into practice, shaping GM into a decentralized-centralized organization that became the template for American industry. He would soon divide the company "into as many parts as consistently can be done, place in charge of each part the most capable executive that can be found, [and] develop a system of co-ordination so that each part may strengthen and support each other part." One result, for example, was that by 1924, all of GM's autonomous operating divisions shared a five-thousand-acre proving ground, a vast outdoor product laboratory where cars were tested twenty-four hours a day.

Sloan's organizational ideas were foundational to the company's success. Between 1920 and 1940, GM built nearly $19 billion worth of new cars. In no year, even during the Great Depression, did the company fail to make a profit or pay a dividend.

EMBRACING CONSUMERISM

There was more, however, for Alfred Sloan had a gift for looking both inward at company needs and outward at market demands. His second extraordinary contribution to the modern corporation recognized that something called the "American consumer" had emerged with a new set of demands from his or her nineteenth-century parents. Because of this, Sloan believed by 1920 that GM required a new business model, a novel "concept of the automobile business."

At one end of the market, Henry Ford offered a standard model at the lowest price, with another twenty automobile makers competing for this position. At the other end of the market, manufacturers offered high-priced vehicles, selling only modest volumes. GM itself had seven lines; of these, Sloan believed, only Buick and Cadillac had clear concepts. Chevrolet was trying to compete with Ford on price and quality, failing at both. "The hard fact was," Sloan said, "that all of the cars in the General Motors line, except Buick and Cadillac, were losing money in 1921."

In retrospect, Sloan described two watershed periods in the opening decades of the automotive industry. The first had been ushered in by Ford when his Model T stormed the nation in 1908, turning what had been a playground of expensive toys for the rich into a mass market. The second was in the mid-1920s and went unheeded by Ford, eventually costing him market leadership. It was the result, Sloan believed, of five great market trends that would define consumerism.

First was installment selling: By 1925, 65 percent of new cars were sold on credit, a sign that American income was rising and was expected to keep rising. Buying on installment meant that consumers could focus on features, not just price. Second, a vibrant market for used cars had evolved as second-time buyers created a high-volume, low-price market that competed effectively with brand-new Model Ts. Third, by 1927, 85 percent of all new cars had closed bodies, a design that created comfortable, year-round transportation for any family. Fourth, these factors were all supported by the construction of thousands of miles—692,000 by 1929—of smooth, paved roads.

The fifth great market trend, a product of Alfred Sloan's individual genius, was the creation of the annual model. "Middle-income buyers, assisted by the trade-in and the installment financing, created the demand," Sloan explained, "not for basic transportation, but for progress in new cars, for comfort, convenience, power, and style. This was the actual trend of American life, and those who adapted to it prospered."

NO CONCEIVABLE AMOUNT
OF CAPITAL COULD WIN

Sloan and his teams segmented demand to produce a car in each price range, with no overlap. In retrospect, he wrote, this segmentation seemed as simple as a shoemaker saying he would make different sizes of shoes. But at the time it was not simple at all, with Ford dominating the market, and a slew of powerful companies—Dodge, Maxwell (Chrysler), Hudson, Studebaker, and Nash—all in active competition.

Sloan and his executive committee set pricing so that GM would compete at the top of each segment and tempt customers—those who might have intended to pay a little less—to stretch for a car with better quality, features, and styling. Particularly important to GM was its Chevrolet, which was going head-to-head with Ford's Model T. "No conceivable amount of capital short of the United States Treasury could have sustained the losses required to take volume from [Ford] at his own game," Sloan wrote. "The strategy we devised was to take a bite from the top of his position, conceived as a price class."

Change did not happen at once, Sloan recalled. Even by 1924, Chevrolet still had not established a successful competitive niche against the Model T. But GM had created a plan that spoke to consumers, relying on improved features that transcended basic transportation, the concept of annual upgrades, and marketing plans to encourage buying. Chevrolet would soon prove that mass production and variety could be reconciled—the opposite of the Ford concept. Sloan wrote of Ford, "The old master had failed to master change. Don't ask me why. There is a legend cultivated by sentimentalists that Mr. Ford left behind a great car expressive of the pure concept of cheap, basic transportation. The fact is that he left behind a car that no longer offered the best buy, even as raw, basic transportation."

Caught flat-footed, Ford shut down his great River Rouge plant in 1927 to retool, leaving the field to Chevrolet. The Model A launched in 1928 was a superb car but was intended, like the Model T, to be a static model. Ford had again failed to grasp the realities of the new consumer market. Alfred Sloan's General Motors had become proof that a capital intensive industrial giant could still be versatile and nimble enough to offer benefits beyond low price. Companies could flourish if they replaced perfectly good items on a regular basis with something perceived as new and better. The annual model was driven by the understanding that regular improvement and periodically discontented buyers were necessary to growth. "One of the fundamental purposes of research is to foster a healthy dissatisfaction," Sloan's R&D chief, Charles F. Kettering, concluded.

Economist Joseph Schumpeter found General Motors' innovations in financing, marketing, and organization were as significant to consumerism as Ford's assembly line had been to mass production. GM and its elite management "all but buried Ford in a blizzard of innovations." In 1927, Cadillac stunned the public, for example, when it offered a choice of five hundred color and upholstery options. One GM executive wrote, "The question was no longer 'can I afford an automobile,'" but—thanks to the marketing brilliance of GM and its leader, "'can I afford to be without an automobile?'"

THE MOST SUCCESSFUL ENTREPRENEUR IN AMERICA EVER?

Alfred Sloan built the largest, most innovative, and arguably most important company in the world—one that fundamentally transformed the century. In 1918, he joined a General Motors that was disjointed and nearly bankrupt, with just 12.7 percent market share behind Ford's 55 percent. He faced America's greatest industrialist at the top of his game in a fluid and hypercompetitive market.

By 1929, when nearly 4.6 million vehicles were sold, GM's 32.3 percent share topped Ford's 31.3 percent. When Sloan retired as chairman in 1956, GM held a 52 percent market share and was one of the world's most profitable, admired, and best-run companies. Its annual revenues surpassed the GNP of half the world's countries.

Sloan is credited with not just saving General Motors, but with being the father of the modern corporation, a genius of consumer marketing, and the most effective CEO ever. An internal memo he wrote became a sought-after best seller in the 1920s, and his book, *My Years with General Motors* (1963), was the bible for a generation of managers who aspired to lead like America's most famous CEO. Sloan is known for creating effective public relations, implementing long-term forecasting, hiring professional designers to spearhead GM's parade of annual models, and funding both a series of technological breakthroughs and long-term, visionary research and development. Historian Daniel Boorstin writes that when Sloan asked his staff to look out five years into the future to envision something new and better, he helped invent the modern world.

Sloan is known for other accomplishments as well. He encouraged his best friend, Walter P. Chrysler, to launch his own company when Ford was failing in the 1920s. "GM, in its own interest," Sloan believed (unlike many of America's most famous entrepreneurs bent on monopoly), "needed a strong competitor." And when the automobile market slowed, General Motors introduced a gas-powered diesel engine for trains that, almost overnight, destroyed an American icon, Baldwin Locomotive Works.

Above all, Alfred Sloan innovated in two essential areas: the effective organization of a complex institution (what he would call "centralized administration with decentralized operations"), and the brilliant segmentation of consumer brands designed to *create* endless demand. The German philosopher Arthur Schopenhauer (1788–1860) wrote that talent achieves what others cannot achieve, a fitting tribute to the legendary work of Henry Ford. But, Schopenhauer added, genius achieves what others *cannot imagine*. That was the contribution of Alfred Sloan.

BACK AT THE BAR

One of the entrepreneurs sitting at the bar asked, "Why Detroit?" And then, grinning, he answered his own question: "Ransom Olds, William Durant, Henry Ford, and Alfred Sloan all did business there. That's 'why Detroit.' It would be like having Bach, Haydn, Mozart, and Beethoven sharing the same apartment and then asking, 'Why is the music so good around here?'" The bar erupted in laughter.

Even Sloan smiled. "It all looks obvious now, I suppose, but there were 272 entrepreneurs thinking they could make automobiles, I almost lost my $10 million business to Mr. Durant, and then he almost lost General Motors to bankruptcy." The tall, slender man in the starched collar began walking back to his spot near the door.

The entrepreneurs along the bar didn't want to let go of a good joke, though. "Al Pacino, Jack Nicholson, Robert DeNiro, and Meryl Streep are all in the cast. Why is that movie so good?" Another round of laughter.

"Yep," said another. "Ty Cobb, Babe Ruth, Joe DiMaggio, and Willie Mays all in the same dugout—hey, why is my baseball team so good?" More laughter.

"How about Jackie Robinson?" This was a new voice, belonging to a man who seemed as rumpled as Sloan was starched. "I say, how about adding Jackie Robinson to the lineup?" Branch Rickey stood from his stool. "He may not have had Cobb's batting average or Ruth's home runs, but Jackie did something just as remarkable—maybe more remarkable."

Though the jokes might have gone on for another few minutes, the barroom quieted.

"Mr. Sloan knew the American consumer when he wanted a new car. Miss Arden knew the American consumer when she wanted to be beautiful. Mr. Milliken knew the American consumer when he worked on the factory floor. But I knew the American consumer in a whole different way," Rickey added, "when he was sitting in the grandstand of a big-league ballpark on a hot summer day—and, let me tell you, it wasn't all about batting averages and home runs."

Chapter 12

BRANCH RICKEY: PROPHET OR PROFIT?

Born in Stockdale, Ohio, Wesley Branch Rickey (1881–1965) was another young American who fled life on the farm in search of opportunity. He worked first as a country schoolteacher before enrolling at Ohio Wesleyan University, where he excelled at baseball, graduating with a bachelor's degree in literature in 1904.

Intent on a career in the growing world of professional baseball, Rickey entered the University of Michigan as much to coach the baseball team as study law. After graduation he tinkered in a law practice, but in 1913 found a way back to his passion, becoming a talent scout for the St. Louis Browns baseball team under owner Robert Lee Hedges (1869–1932). From that inauspicious start he was promoted to club secretary, manager, and by 1917, vice president and general manager. It was with the Browns that Rickey let it be known, because of his devout Methodist upbringing, that he refused to work on the Sabbath, handing over management responsibilities to an assistant any time the team played on Sunday.

Robert Hedges turned out to be an important role model for Rickey. Hedges had been a successful horse-and-buggy carriage manufacturer but recognized the coming of the automobile before others did and sold his company at peak value. Then, seeing the potential of baseball, he purchased a Milwaukee minor league franchise, moving it to St. Louis in 1902. He was a shrewd innovator who banned the sale of alcohol in the park and hired security guards at a time when an afternoon in the stands of a professional baseball game could be a rollicking affair. By bringing a sense of decorum to the ballpark, he was able to host the first "Ladies Days," attracting a new audience segment.

Innovative, gentlemanly, and with a talent for spotting the newest trend, Hedges modeled the traits that would come to define Rickey throughout his long career.

A LIFETIME OF INNOVATION

After working in the Chemical Warfare Service during World War I, Branch Rickey joined the St. Louis Cardinals, where he convinced the team to take partial ownership in the Houston club of the Texas League. This new "farm team" system—sometimes described as Rickey's "chain-store idea"—was so effective in uncovering inexpensive talent that the Cardinals soon controlled two minor-league teams and had interests in several others. Rickey was practicing a kind of "vertical integration," not unlike Andrew Carnegie acquiring coal mines to ensure the steady output of steel. It was an industrial innovation applied to human talent, so effective and quickly copied by other Major League teams that baseball commissioner Judge Kenesaw Mountain Landis (1866–1944) limited each organization to only one affiliation in each minor league. Rickey's innovation altered baseball's business model, turning the minor leagues into what baseball historian Bill James called "boot camp."

Described as owlish, rumpled, and cigar-chomping, Branch Rickey was a study in contrasts. In a game full of colorful language and hard drinking, he never swore and gave lectures on temperance. He was gentlemanly and refined but unabashedly competitive, focused throughout his adult life on a single goal: constructing baseball teams good enough to win the World Series.

Perhaps Rickey's most endearing if frustrating trait was his habit with reporters of making voluminous, convoluted pronouncements. One fan described him as "a man of many faucets, all running at once." He could overwhelm, misdirect, and evade simultaneously, using language as a weapon. However, careful observers saw in Rickey's verbal acrobatics an underlying brilliance. "The Rickey brain is a most versatile instrument," wrote Roy Stockton of *The Saturday Evening Post*. Indeed, one of the affectionate nicknames bestowed on Rickey during his career was "the Brain."

This was an especially appropriate nickname when applied to another of Rickey's game-changing innovations, the application of data to player performance. He was perhaps the first proponent of "moneyball," the practice of using special, often hidden metrics to gauge a player's value. Rickey first hired a young reporter to sit behind home plate and keep track of each batter's "base and out efficiency," a system he devised to assess talent beyond conventional statistics. Later, he hired a traveling statistician whose job it was to catalog every pitch and hit. "Theoretically," one sportswriter said, "he could tell you where any batter in the league was most likely to hit when facing any given pitcher."

This reliance on analytics gave Rickey insight into the performance of individual players that competitors and fans sometimes found baffling. Did a hitter still have the strength and reflexes to pull a ball? Could a pitcher still hit the corners of the plate late in a game? Rickey generated insights that made him willing to part with popular star players when his analysis determined that they had passed their years of peak performance. In St. Louis, he sold future Hall of Famer Dizzy Dean to the Chicago Cubs and willingly traded Rogers Hornsby, considered among the best second basemen of all time.

Rickey's data mining was widely admired, though often at odds with fans' wishes. What Rickey understood, however, was that "you have two years to stay ahead of your competition when you come up with a new idea in baseball." This was Schumpeter's emphasis on perpetual "creative destruction" applied brilliantly by Rickey to America's pastime.

Rickey managed in St. Louis until 1925 but remained as vice president and business manager until 1942, when the Cardinals beat the defending champion New York Yankees in a five-game World Series. All but one member of the championship St. Louis team was a product of the club's farm system. His next stop was as president of the Brooklyn Dodgers, where his reputation for innovation preceded him. One sportswriter suggested that "those who know believe he'll find a way, and baseball will experience another revolutionary innovation of some kind."

Little did he know.

THE GREAT AMERICAN PASTIME, SEGREGATED

From its beginnings after the Civil War, professional baseball in America was a segregated sport. The Negro Leagues evolved separately to include dozens of celebrated teams. Formed and re-formed, the leagues weathered the Great Depression, catering primarily to an urban, Northern black population. Despite hard times, oppressive laws, lack of access to capital, and a relatively small fan base, Negro League teams "barnstormed" across the country, often beating their white opponents and providing revenue windfalls to white ballpark owners.

An important goal of the men who formed the Negro Leagues in the 1920s was to eventually integrate baseball. A black newspaper reported in 1930 that "Colored ballplayers in the big leagues are inevitable." White sportswriters were beginning to take up the cause of integration in the mid-1930s, and by the latter part of the decade it was not uncommon to read a column railing against the organized racism that excluded so many talented black players. Important voices in the game, from Babe Ruth to Stan Musial, seemed supportive of their talented brethren. By the early 1940s the stars were beginning to align.

In 1941, the outspoken manager of the Brooklyn Dodgers, Leo Durocher, answered a reporter's question about hiring stars from the Negro Leagues by saying, "Hell, yes! I'd sign them in a minute if I got permission from the big shots." With black Americans fighting overseas against a foe that championed the Aryan race, an "End Jim Crow in Baseball" committee picketed parks with photographs of dead black soldiers and the caption, "Good enough to die for their country but not good enough to play for organized baseball."

Controlling the game with an iron fist, Commissioner Landis responded to Leo Durocher's enthusiasm with one of the more disingenuous statements in the history of the game, saying, "Negroes are not barred from organized baseball by the commissioner and never had been during the twenty-one years I have served." In reality, Landis not only opposed integration, but he worked to minimize the popular integrated barnstorming games that created so much revenue for white owners. Consequently, his death in late 1944 was a tipping point.

Baseball tapped Kentuckian Albert Benjamin "Happy" Chandler (1898–1991) from the United States Senate to become its new commissioner. Chandler had been the chairman of the military affairs subcommittee and had just returned from a battlefield tour. When asked about blacks in baseball, he said, "If they can fight and die on Okinawa, Guadalcanal, (and) in the South Pacific, they can play ball in America." When it came to baseball integration, Chandler showed a combination of inevitability and courage: "I wasn't running for anything, and I wasn't running away from anything either."

The stage was set. Branch Rickey was sixty-five years old when he signed twenty-five-year-old Jackie Robinson to the Brooklyn Dodgers in 1947. It is an oft-told story, a supremely courageous act for both. It helped enormously that Robinson was a gifted ballplayer, leading the International League in batting and his Montreal team to a pennant in his only year in the minor leagues. Then, in a professional sport where players were sometimes more abusive to Robinson than the fans, he was named Rookie of the Year. Everywhere he went, the ballparks were filled. Nothing quieted ignorant racism like talent, courage, and profit.

DOING GOOD OR DOING WELL: DO WE CARE?

There is a story that Branch Rickey rarely told before his signing of Jackie Robinson but afterward told often, saying it haunted him. In 1903, the Ohio Wesleyan baseball team, which Rickey coached, set out on a road trip to play Notre Dame. Upon reaching South Bend, Indiana, the team's catcher and only black player, Charles "Tommy" Thomas (1881–1970), was denied hotel accommodations. Only when Rickey asked if Thomas could sleep on a cot in his room, implying a subservient relationship, did the hotel clerk oblige. Thomas was inconsolable. Rickey remained positive, saying, "We'll lick this one day, but we can't if you feel sorry for yourself."

In Branch Rickey's authorized biography, Arthur Mann wrote that the decision to sign Robinson in 1942 was not complex, nor was it a crusade. Rickey was trained as a lawyer and "found not a shred of law or reason to prevent Negroes from providing the playing skill which he needed desperately." Rickey himself said, "I want players to help me win a pennant in Brooklyn." This was the businessman in Rickey, reinforced by the popular ditty, "Jackie's nimble, Jackie's quick, Jackie makes the turnstiles click."

At another time, Rickey was more emphatic about the competitive nature of the move. "I'd play an elephant with pink horns if he could win the pennant," he said. Bill James agreed, describing Rickey's motive as wanting "to establish an organization that would give him control of, and first crack at, the pool of black talent, should the integration of the major leagues occur." This was the competitor in Rickey, always seeking an edge.

However, Jackie Robinson himself had a different interpretation of his Major League signing, saying, "I will always believe [Rickey] had reasons purely democratic in nature." And at certain times Rickey agreed, saying, "I couldn't face my God any longer knowing that his black children were held separate and distinct from his white children in a game that has given me all I own." This was Rickey the devout Methodist, the man who would not coach on Sunday, shaped by a long-ago moment in South Bend, Indiana.

So, was he a prophet, or was it profit?

Clearly there are conflicting narratives. Even Rickey was inconsistent in describing his motivations. There seems to have come a moment when capitalism and social progress aligned, when being competitive could also mean being virtuous, and when "doing well" and "doing good" met. Rickey's gift was in sensing that moment and acting on it, and Robinson's was in having the courage and resilience to respond to the call. The result was a Brooklyn Dodgers team better able to compete for the pennant and more likely to make its ownership wealthy, and the American national pastime finally and irrevocably open to people of color.

These moments of social entrepreneurship, when capitalism and profit align with social progress and people's better natures, tend to be controversial, groundbreaking—and filled with positive consequences. Branch Rickey's farm system and his innovations in analytics changed the business model of Major League Baseball. But it was his and Jackie Robinson's social entrepreneurship that had the greatest impact, fundamentally expanding the community of Major League Baseball—and changing forever the American consumers who came to watch the game.

BACK AT THE BAR

"So you can see," Rickey finished up his story, "when you talk about this 'American consumer,' you're dealing with an awfully complicated subject. Sometimes people see and know immediately what they want, like Mr. Whitney found with cotton gins, and Mr. Gillette found with his razor blades. Then, you must work as hard as you can just to meet their demands. And other times, like Mr. Sloan and his model year, you have to show them what they want and make them just a little bit unhappy until they get it."

To many of the younger entrepreneurs in the barroom, this idea of finding new customers and creating demand seemed second nature. It was eye-opening that the age of consumerism was only about a century old.

"But then," Rickey added, "in the case of my friend Jackie Robinson and the American consumer, you sometimes must show them *what they should want,* even if *they don't want to want it.*" There was a brief silence as Rickey's audience tried to absorb his words. Elizabeth Arden leaned over to Mary Elizabeth Sharpe and whispered, "It sounds like one of Mr. Rickey's many faucets might be running again."

Stephen Mather took a last sip of his beer and stood, seeing a good moment to intervene. "I can tell you about another complication, Mr. Rickey, one that you haven't yet mentioned." The baseball legend was ready to yield the floor, afraid he might launch into a speech on temperance, and ready for a hot cup of coffee. "My own tale involves this same fickle American consumer, but the new idea," Mather said with a twinkle in his eye, "is that sometimes you have to talk them *into wanting something,* and then, when you are successful, talk them *out of wanting so much of it.*"

Part Four

SUSTAINABILITY

Chapter 13

STEPHEN MATHER: MACHINE IN THE GARDEN

As the twentieth century progressed, Americans found themselves enjoying the highest standard of living ever, anywhere, in a nation that produced about half of the world's iron, steel, and coal, two-thirds of its petroleum, and four-fifths of its automobiles. The country's reputation for embracing the "newest thing" included everything from industrial processes to consumer products and fashions. The journalist Edwin E. Slosson (1865–1929) reminded his countrymen that even God tossed away obsolete work, including the megalosaurus and pterodactyl, "in favor of more modern designs." Likewise, common wisdom held, American progress "could be measured by the size of its scrap-heaps"—waste being proof that the nation was stepping boldly into the future.

However, a growing number of Americans began to wonder if there was a problem with all those scrap heaps. Was the nation's economic strength part illusion, built on dirty water, foul air, ruinous obsolescence, and the exploitation of forests, minerals, and grazing lands? For example, coal smoke plagued residents of Chicago, St. Louis, Pittsburgh, and other urban areas. Sewage and industrial waste spilled into waterways. In the country's Southern Plains, mechanized plowing of topsoil coupled with drought brought about a decade of choking dust that left one hundred million acres of farmland degraded. Americans recognized that thirty million buffalo roaming the Plains in 1800 had been reduced to less than one thousand by 1900. Filthy cities, barren wastelands, and the decline of once abundant species were among the more ominous signs that material progress might be extracting a terrible price.

While the term *sustainability* would not become common until the 1970s, the need to balance growth with resource conservation is the fourth important entrepreneurial theme in America. Sustainability would come to address pollution, overconsumption, and climate change, but its roots were set in the conservation movement that sprang up in the early twentieth century. Among the entrepreneurs who helped to shape this movement, Stephen Tyng Mather (1867–1930) left his lasting imprint in the creation of America's national parks, what novelist and environmentalist Wallace Stegner would call "America's best idea."

To understand Mather's work as a pioneering entrepreneur of sustainability, it helps first to meet Francis Marion Smith (1846–1931), a Wisconsin native who headed west in 1867 to prospect for minerals. By 1872, Smith had established a flourishing works near Marietta, Nevada, to mine borax, or sodium borate, sometimes called "the miracle mineral" for its many uses. Smith's Pacific Coast Borax Company was the first to popularize borax as a household detergent.

That same year, the US Congress designated America's first national park at Yellowstone, an act designed to preserve undeveloped land in perpetuity. The act was not without controversy. Some congressmen believed that creation of national parks exceeded federal powers under the Constitution. Other officials felt that national parks put the federal government in the business of raising wild animals. Senator George Graham Vest of Missouri expressed a more practical point of view, saying, "There are no votes in Yellowstone Park for the Republican or Democratic Party."

Francis Smith's activity in Nevada, mining the land for profit, was a more common practice in nineteenth-century America than preserving land undisturbed for the enjoyment of future generations. And the newly dubbed "Borax King" was growing rich, hauling great quantities of the mineral by mule teams from mines around Marietta for distribution to homes throughout the United States.

Stephen Mather likely thought little about borax when he graduated in 1887 from the University of California, Berkeley. Moving east, he spent five years as a reporter for the *New York Sun* before joining his father, Joseph, who worked as the administrator of Francis Smith's operations in New York City. When Joseph helped his son become advertising manager for Pacific Coast Borax Company, the futures of Francis Smith, Stephen Mather—and Yellowstone Park—became inextricably linked.

20 MULE TEAM BORAX

Pacific Coast was mining borax faster than it was selling and needed to increase demand. Mather had heard his father and Smith reminisce about the days of mule skinners and wagon trains, and he came to believe that mining borax should have the same romance associated with it as America's rush for gold. He set out to take a nondescript mineral and create an emotive consumer brand.

Mather thought big, with his first campaign designed to put a package of borax on every kitchen shelf in the United States. Smith was skeptical and refused to fund the program. Undeterred, Mather wrote letters to fifteen women's publications "describing how borax had come to the rescue at some decisive moment in the kitchen."

Miraculously, every letter was printed. He next offered consumers a dollar for every published letter about borax, a ploy so popular that Smith grew panicky as the reward money grew. Finally, Mather gathered all the free press he had generated, mailing booklets to consumers with free samples of Borax. In the process, he created a national brand and made Smith an even richer man.

Mather's crowning achievement was the company's "20 Mule Team Borax" advertising identity. It glamorized the history of the Pacific Coast Borax Company through an unlikely mix of mule trains, Death Valley, and a commodity mineral that worked as a laundry detergent. Borax became one of the best-known household brands in America, while profits soared.

Placed in charge of the firm's Chicago office, Mather became friends with Thomas Thorkildsen (1869–1950). In 1898, Thorkildsen resigned, heading to Ventura, California, where he invested in his own borax mine. Mather secretly became president of his friend's new company, helping to support its launch.

A VISIT TO EUROPE

In 1903, Stephen Mather was institutionalized for nervous exhaustion. Prone throughout his career to bouts of frenzied activity followed by deep melancholy, Mather probably suffered from manic depression. The episodes came unannounced and were uncontrollable. Few people knew of Mather's condition, and his closest associates were careful to guard his privacy.

What Mather came to discover, however, was that time spent in nature helped to relieve his anxiety. He began making annual visits to Western parks, including his favorite, Yosemite, designated a national park in 1890. The benefits he experienced from these wilderness excursions are now better understood, as modern research shows that regular contact with nature can improve mood and fight depression.

While convalescing in 1904, Mather and his wife traveled to Europe, where they visited outdoor parks in a half-dozen countries. He was inspired by the careful preservation and accessibility of Europe's public lands, conditions often in stark contrast to those created by grazing, mining, and lumber interests operating in America's public spaces. Upon his return to the United States, Mather joined the Sierra Club, where he was introduced to the thinking of founder John Muir (1838–1914), an inspirational Scottish-American preservationist and philosopher.

When Mather returned to work in Chicago, he found that Smith had cut him from the payroll. Mather resigned, publicly announcing the Thorkildsen-Mather Borax Company. Thanks to rich borax deposits and Thorkildsen's management skill, Mather became a millionaire. This wealth freed him from stressful employment and provided the resources to pursue his next professional venture.

"WE ARE NOT WILLING TO DIE FOR THEIR POCKETS"

In 1912, Mather met John Muir on a hike in the Kern River Canyon in California's southern Sierra Nevada. In this meeting of charismatics, Muir conveyed a passion for preservation that would fuel Mather for the rest of his career.

Muir's most pressing battle involved preserving Hetch Hetchy, which had become a flashpoint for the preservation movement in America. Its name derived from the Native American Miwok word *hetchetci*, a species of grass that the Tuolumne Indians used for food. Hetch Hetchy was one of the most breathtaking landscapes in Yosemite, a glacier-formed valley with cliffs and waterfalls. Its admirers found it transcendent. It was also the perfect spot, thanks to its bowl shape, to build a reservoir and create a new, sorely needed water supply for San Francisco. A plan to develop Hetch Hetchy was underway even though the valley had been protected in perpetuity under the act that created Yosemite as a national park in 1890.

The battle over Hetch Hetchy generated fierce national debate, illustrating the contrast between conservation, which employed science and engineering to responsibly develop natural resources, and preservation, which emphasized the aesthetic and spiritual virtues of unspoiled wilderness. California senator James Duval Phelan (1861–1930) represented his state's conservationists, saying:

> To provide for the little children, men, and women of the 800,000 population who swarm the shores of San Francisco Bay is a matter of much greater importance than encouraging the few who, in solitary loneliness, will sit on the peak of the Sierras loafing around the throne of the God of nature and singing His praise.

Phelan was answered by diplomat Robert Underwood Johnson (1853–1937), who had partnered with Muir to protect Yosemite. The records show, Johnson wrote, that San Francisco "could get water anywhere along Sierra if she would pay for it." The issue, he added, was that city leaders wanted a bargain. Hetch Hetchy was not the only available resource—it was simply the cheapest. If the great parks of the United States were given over to every local interest, he wrote, then sooner or later they would all be lost. "We hold that while we are willing to die for the lives or the health of the citizens of San Francisco," he finished, "we are not willing to die for their pockets."

Stirred by this indignation, Mather traveled to Washington to attend congressional hearings on the Hetch Hetchy proposal. He witnessed a debate, historian Paul Sutter believes, that has framed conservation history ever since. Those who saw nature as a thing to be developed won the battle. Woodrow Wilson signed the Raker Act in December 1913, and Hetch Hetchy was dammed and flooded. This victory of developers would turn out to be Pyrrhic, however, and Muir spotted the silver lining. "The conscience of the whole country has been aroused from sleep," he wrote, "and from outrageous evil compensating good in some form must surely come."

That compensating good was the fire kindled in Stephen Mather, whose next move—a surprise even to himself—was to create the most powerful preservationist organization in America.

TRAVELS TO WASHINGTON

In 1914, Mather was forty-seven years old and a millionaire. His future was secure, and he need never work again or subject himself to debilitating stress. But a visit to Sequoia and Yosemite National Parks that year was a turning point. Angered by the neglect and commercial exploitation of these areas, Mather fired off an angry letter to Franklin K. Lane (1864–1921), Woodrow Wilson's new secretary of the interior. Lane was a native of San Francisco, a fellow Berkeley alumnus, and a kindred spirit of Mather.

The new secretary supported the idea of a national parks system, especially in response to a vocal segment of the American public that sought to ensure there would be no more travesties like Hetch Hetchy. Lane also recognized that this evolving national impulse to preserve land for future generations had met an even stronger impulse—the love affair Americans were having with the newest wonder of the Industrial Revolution, the automobile. With both the auto and rail industries squarely behind a "See America First" campaign, and a looming war that was threatening to close Europe to tourism, Lane saw an opportunity to reclaim some of the $400 million a year Americans spent touring Europe. In his view, vacationers simply needed to be provided with attractive destinations in their own country.

Lane invited Mather to Washington and offered him the role of assistant secretary, his only job to lobby Congress for a national parks bureau. Mather agreed to stay for a single year, worried that his freewheeling entrepreneurial style might not play well in the nation's capital. "I have never been under restrictions or a lot of regulations and I'm just not temperamentally fitted for this type of work in Washington," he said. "I'll probably get into trouble before the job is an hour old."

Mather's solution was to hire a young legal assistant, Horace Albright (1890–1987), another native Californian who had been in Washington for a year—some of that time spent responding diplomatically to angry letters about Hetch Hetchy. Mather and Albright were a strong match and formed a lifelong bond, one a visionary thinker and the other a thoughtful, talented administrator. Mather supplemented Albright's government salary of $1,600 annually with another $1,000 from his own pocket.

Young enough to be Mather's son, Albright had to run hard to keep up with his new, entrepreneurial boss.

> *With plans and ideas popping from Mather's head every minute, I was frantically busy trying to carry them out . . . From the very beginning, he said that he hated office work, administrative minutiae, what he called chores. With his nervous*

energy, he simply couldn't sit still at a desk and handle details. He preferred to conduct business with people he felt were important to his plans over long lunches, or at elegant dinner and theater parties.

Albright learned that Mather solved problems by talking them through, scheduling a constant string of meetings to test new ideas. "'Talking over' an idea," Albright remembered, "meant listening while he restlessly paced around the room, gesturing to make his points, his words barely keeping up with his mile-a-minute brain."

But Mather was always gracious and charming, and he soon became well liked in Washington's political circles. "He was an experienced public relations man," Albright wrote, who "created instant rapport with strangers, had a personality that radiated poise, friendliness, and charm, could talk easily with anyone he met, confidently instilling perfect strangers with his enthusiasm."

In his first year as assistant secretary, Mather traveled thirty thousand miles. His young assistant often remained in Washington, becoming an effective lobbyist himself. "I thanked my stars I was young, strong, and healthy," Albright wrote, saying Mather's "energy would have killed someone who wasn't."

Another important member of Mather's team was Robert Sterling Yard (1861–1945), hired away from the *New York Herald*. Yard and Mather met during Mather's reporting stint in New York. Mather paid the talented Yard $5,000 a year to run publicity, and Mather also underwrote the cost of a personal secretary to assist him. Yard was a prolific writer who launched a barrage of persuasive material in support of Mather's efforts.

Mather, Albright, and Yard were attempting to create a framework for thirteen national parks and eighteen national monuments. These parks and landmarks "were orphans," Albright wrote, "split among three departments—War, Agriculture, and Interior. They were anybody's business and therefore nobody's business." There were no uniform standards of operation and no plans to rescue other precious lands at risk to development. "Not many knew the parks were even plural," reporter Herbert Corey wrote. "Yellowstone was the national park. All by itself."

Mather now faced a puzzling chicken-and-egg situation: To succeed, he first had to get Congress interested in national parks. To do that, he had to get voters interested, and to do that, he had to make the parks accessible and attractive. But without funding from Congress, he had little means to improve the parks or entice the public to visit them.

Mather had faced a similar challenge years before when he was asked to build a national brand from a base mineral but was provided no funding to do it. His tutelage under the miserly Francis Smith was the perfect apprenticeship needed to succeed among conservative federal officials. Mather also understood—in a country that rail, telegraph, telephone, magazines, and now automobiles were knitting into a national market—the best ways to generate free publicity, and the power it had to influence consumers.

THE MATHER MOUNTAIN PARTY

Mather's approach to the creation of a national park bureau was counterintuitive. He chose to fight his first and signature battle in his favorite park, Yosemite. It was as far from the red tape of Washington, DC, as he could get, and it placed him in an environment where he could be most effective.

Yosemite's only western access was via Tioga Road, a poorly kept private mining road that would require substantial upgrades to accommodate automobiles. Congress could not appropriate funds to repair a private road, so Mather decided that he, along with his still unsuspecting friends, would purchase the road and donate it to the government. This idea was novel; the federal government was not a charity, Mather's friends told him. "Giving things to the government," Mather's biographer Robert

Shankland wrote, "was almost as suspect as making bank deposits to the account of a Cabinet officer." Mather remained unfazed.

He arranged a luncheon at the Bohemian Club in San Francisco with friends and members of the Sierra Club. He told the assembled group about the wonders of Yosemite, his enthusiasm growing the longer he spoke. Then Mather told his audience that he had negotiated an option to purchase rights to Tioga Road for $15,000 from a mining company. He would put up $1,000 and had already raised another $7,000. "Needless to say," Albright wrote, "he had his money right then and there. He went on to close the deal, acquired the Tioga Road, and thus opened a new entrance to Yosemite Park . . . This was my first real experience with Mather's mesmerizing power of enthusiasm and persuasion," Albright added, but not his last.

Mather then moved to the second act in his unusual lobbying effort, this one focused on creating the entrepreneurial community that was to ensure his success.

The so-called Mather Mountain Party that gathered in July 1915 in Visalia, California, did not know what to expect from their host. The group included Mather and Albright, renowned world traveler Elias Burton Holmes (1870–1958), Western novelist Emerson Hough (1857–1923), and Gilbert H. Grosvenor (1875–1966), director of the National Geographic Society and editor of its magazine. Government and business were also represented, including the ranking Republican on the House appropriations committee, a vice president of the Southern Pacific Railroad, the paleontologist for the Canadian and US Geological Surveys, and a number of other political and corporate dignitaries. In all, the group numbered nineteen, not counting packers and cooks. For some, the Western wilderness was home; for others, like Grosvenor, it would be his first trip ever west of Ohio. For all of them, the Mather Mountain Party would be the event of a lifetime.

The group's route was carefully chosen by Mather to include a national park (Sequoia), private holdings within a park (the Giant Forest, which Mather was already negotiating to purchase), and public domain ready for park status (Kern River Canyon). The route also ran to Mount

Whitney country, and most of the party would climb Whitney's nearly fifteen thousand feet. It was the highest point in the United States and allowed visitors to gaze at a distant Death Valley—perhaps a nostalgic moment for Mather.

Mather spent $4,000 for equipment and food from his own funds. The Geological Survey lent the party their trail cook, Ty Sing, who was both culinary craftsman and artist. Sing made fresh bread and rolls each day (utilizing the heat of a mule to make the dough rise). One of his signature wilderness dinners included fried chicken, venison and gravy, and English plum pudding with brandy sauce. Despite daily exertions, nobody in the group lost weight.

The party took autos, hiked, and rode horseback. They stopped at a new site every evening. If they passed through a disorderly camp, they picked it up and left a note encouraging the campers to respect the woods. The men in the party became fast friends. Mather was indefatigable, stopping at the occasional waterfall so he could lead a skinny-dip into the icy stream. The men chose nicknames for each other and competed for best facial hair. "By July 26," Albright wrote, "everyone in the party looked like a caveman."

The kinetic executive that Albright raced after in Washington was on full display in the Sierras. It was the first glimpse for many of the man who was to become the poster child for the American preservationist movement. Grosvenor said, "His vitality was amazing. He seemed immune to fatigue." To others, who might even have sensed Mather's underlying illness, "he gave the impression of being carbonated."

Most of all, however, Mather was effective at assembling a passionate and loyal community through sheer force of personality. His friend Francis Farquhar said, "If he was out to make a convert, the subject never knew what hit him." From valley to mountain, Albright added, Mather's "personality and enthusiastic energy carried everything before him as he charmed one important person after another."

The results of the Mather Mountain Party were both immediate and long lasting. Mather arranged the purchase of the Giant Forest in

Sequoia with $50,000 from the federal government and $20,000 from the National Geographic Society. Hough fought the enemies of the national parks from the pages of the *Saturday Evening Post*. Grosvenor's April 1916 issue of *National Geographic Magazine*, titled "The Land of the Best," appeared just as the hearings on the bill to establish a national park service were going on before the House public lands committee. Every member of the committee received a free copy.

It took Mather, Albright, Yard, and their new friends a year of steady lobbying and publicity to enlist the support of Congress, but on August 25, 1916, President Wilson signed into law an act creating the National Park Service. Mather became its first director, with Albright second in command. Mather's one year in Washington would turn into an entire second career.

Over his thirteen-year tenure, Mather added Zion, Grand Canyon, Rocky Mountain, Bryce Canyon, Mount McKinley, Grand Teton, and Hawaii to the national park system. He expanded Yosemite and Yellowstone. He also advanced the idea of national parks east of the Mississippi, helping to create Shenandoah and the Great Smoky Mountains national parks in 1926. Mather, and Albright after him, turned the park ranger into a symbol of integrity, one of the most admired of public employees. He also made it not just possible but admirable for private individuals to donate land and money to the national parks.

The journalist Herbert Corey estimated that Stephen Mather donated a quarter of a million dollars to the government, not including his time. "He has been the most successful publicity agent the Government has had in its employ. He started out to sell the parks to the people. And he did." Most of all, he took a disorganized group of preservationists around America and knit together a national community capable of real impact.

Mather died in 1930 but is remembered today by areas of natural beauty named in his honor, including Mather Point in Grand Canyon National Park, Mather Gorge of the Potomac River, and in the Stephen T. Mather Training Center in Harpers Ferry National Historical Park.

Bronze plaques placed in America's national parks after his death say, "There will never come an end to the good that he has done."

HEROIC FEATS OF HIGHWAY ENGINEERING

An entrepreneur's legacy is measured not in bronze plaques, however, but by how much success his new combinations have in disrupting economic flows and creating new customers. By this measure, Mather's impact can be measured along several different but related dimensions.

First, the National Park Service was a unique American innovation, as different in its conceptualization of land use as Buddy Bolden's jazz was to traditional classical and dance music. The preservation of public lands reflected a profound cultural change that was responsive to the unbridled consumerism that emerged in the twentieth century. Mather's contribution to this remarkable innovation was to appeal first to the American consumer and then work to ensure that the political process followed. From the beginning, Albright wrote, Mather emphasized road improvements, concessions, and increased tourism—not the creation of a national park bureau per se. His success came from the insight that in a modern, consumer economy, grassroots efforts and swelling consumer demand could have a dramatic political impact. Stephen Mather and Branch Rickey might each have had a similar epiphany, a moment when they realized that "doing good" and "doing well" were perfectly aligned.

Between 1915 and 1920, annual national park visitation tripled to 919,504 people. This growing popularity was a direct result of Mather's most astute of all innovations, the embrace of the automobile into the American wilderness. Yellowstone, whose amenities included a collection of horses and wagons in 1915, was entirely motorized by 1917. The Park Service report from that year showed the distribution of eighty-three thousand auto map guides. By 1919, representatives of twelve states had formed the National Parks Touring Association.

"Mather and his successors initiated some of the most heroic feats of highway engineering of the twentieth century," writes environmental historian Paul Sutter. "By pushing strips of concrete and asphalt ever deeper into some of the nation's most remote and scenic landscapes, the Park Service created some of the most exhilarating driving experiences to be found anywhere on the planet." In 1955, 56 million Americans visited a national park, and in 2017 some 330 million, more than the entire US population.

Today, America's sixty national parks are being loved to death by automobile and bus congestion, visitor wear and tear, and climate change. Stephen Mather purchased Tioga Road as a way for automobiles to gain access into Yosemite; today, park visitors can sit in traffic for three hours. Officials speak of "greenlock" when visitors bump wildlife from their habitat, wash diapers in park rivers, have fistfights over parking spots, mob scenic vistas to take selfies, and fly unauthorized drones. Zion has twenty-five miles of developed trails but some six hundred miles of visitor-made paths. The disposal of human waste alone can ruin a visitor experience or upset a park's budget.

And these are the more manageable threats in the overconsumption of Stephen Mather's beloved parks. The impact of climate change is pervasive and unpredictable. An environmental assessment published in 2012 urged the Park Service to act boldly to address the rise of "biodiversity loss . . . habitat fragmentation, land use change, groundwater removal, invasive species, overdevelopment, and air, noise, and light pollution." Even rock, the most permanent feature of the global landscape, is subject to deterioration from acid rain.

The national park system is an American crucible, facing the irreconcilable mandates of providing a world-class experience to every visitor who enters while leaving the park and its resources unimpaired. The American consumer experience appears to have reached its limit in places like Yellowstone and Yosemite. "These are irreplaceable resources," says retired park superintendent Joan Anzelmo. "We have to protect them by putting some strategic limits on numbers, or there won't be anything left."

In the summer of 2018, Muir Woods, the 560-acre forest in northern California named for Mather's inspiration, John Muir, introduced a new parking reservation system designed to improve visitor safety and preserve the serenity of the woods. Success will come when the system has *reduced* annual visitation by two hundred thousand people.

BACK AT THE BAR

Mather's story had thrown an interesting twist into the evening's narratives.

Stories of mechanization, mass production, and consumerism were first about supply meeting demand, and then about demand pushing supply. This formula, which turned Americans from citizens to consumers, had been accompanied by rising prosperity and optimism. Everyone could live in an air-conditioned home or drive an attractive, affordable automobile. Every man could shave his way to success. Any woman could choose to be beautiful.

But what would happen, as Mather's story of America's national parks suggested, if consumer demand overwhelmed the system? What would happen if the technology upon which prosperity relied was now creating its own set of bewildering problems?

"What if," one of the guests wondered aloud, "creative destruction suddenly turned more destructive than creative?"

As Mather concluded his story, it seemed a good time to hear from the barroom's newest entrepreneurs, those men and women forced to address this issue head-on.

Chapter 14

EMILY ROCHON: GIVING VOICE TO THE ENVIRONMENT

*F*ortune magazine's 1976 list of the largest US corporations showed Exxon first, followed by General Motors, Texaco, Ford Motor, Mobil Oil, and Standard Oil of California. While International Business Machines and General Electric held positions seven and nine, Gulf Oil and Chrysler rounded out the top ten. The largest enterprises in America's bicentennial year painted the unmistakable portrait of a fossil-fuel economy.

US corporations ushered consumers into America's third century in other ways, as well. Of 107 million US households in 2001, 106 million had color televisions, 96 million had VCRs or DVD players, 92 million had microwave ovens, and 81 million were air-conditioned. Credit card debt was at an all-time high.

With less than 5 percent of the world's population, Americans in the opening decades of the twenty-first century created half of all global waste. And Americans each consumed the equivalent of 9.7 hectares of productive land on a planet estimated to have 1.9 hectares per person. In a fight between capitalism and the planet, author and activist Naomi Klein wrote, "Capitalism is winning hands down."

"NO ONE IS COMING TO SAVE US"

If signs that Americans needed to balance economic growth with conservation had become obvious to entrepreneurs such as Stephen Mather in the early years of the twentieth century, signs of resource exploitation and overconsumption had become unmistakable by its close. In June 1988, NASA's Jim Hansen told the US Senate Committee on Energy and Natural Resources, "It is time to stop waffling so much and say that the evidence is pretty strong that the greenhouse effect is here." The "greenhouse effect" referred to heat trapped in the earth's atmosphere by "greenhouse gases," a natural phenomenon being destabilized by human activity. The Worldwatch Institute followed Hansen's warning with their "State of the World 1989" report, envisioning a future in which climate change, ozone depletion, soil erosion, and deforestation would all be inevitable. "Time is not on our side," the report concluded.

In 2009, the UN climate summit in Copenhagen collapsed. "It was the moment," Klein writes, "when the realization truly sank in that no one was coming to save us." The nonbinding pledge to keep global temperatures from increasing by more than 2°C—the so-called safe limit of climate change—was undermined by the fact that governments were free to ignore their pledges.

In 2014, academics Naomi Oreskes and Erik Conway offered one possible future, describing the collapse of Western civilization as early as 2041, when a heat wave would destroy food crops around the world. With a mean global warming of 3.9°C, the authors wrote, governments would fall, the Black Plague would return, the Indian monsoon would shut down, and the West Antarctica Ice Sheet would break down. Seventy percent of species would become extinct. Wealthier and better protected than most countries, the US would still see great swaths of its farmland become desert.

In 2018, the World Meteorological Organization warned that global temperatures could easily rise beyond what Oreskes and Conway projected, to as much as 5°C by 2100. Against this foreboding backdrop, entrepreneurs in the twenty-first century scrambled to address sustainability in a world becoming hotter and deadlier every day.

"I CHOSE THE ENVIRONMENT"

Few innovations demonstrate Schumpeter's "creative destruction" more convincingly than renewable energy. The burning of fossil fuels to produce electricity, heat, and power contributes 52 percent of global greenhouse gas emissions. The business of harnessing resources like the sun and wind means the disruption of massive, entrenched industries.

It also means the creation of new technologies and business models, a process that attracted some $280 billion in 2017. Both government and industry drive this investment, which has created a thriving entrepreneurial community in the US. One essential if unsung player in advancing renewable energy is the activist lawyer, an entrepreneur often able to frame options and remove obstacles in the construction of new, innovative business models. Emily Rochon (b. 1979) is one such lawyer.

Raised in Rhode Island, Rochon grew up in "a somewhat broken home," she says, "and through that dynamic learned what it's like to be powerless and have no one to speak on your behalf." In high school she took an ecology class and fell in love with the subject. "It was really just a matter for me of finding who I could give my voice to," she adds, "and I chose the environment."

Rochon earned her bachelor's degree in environmental studies at Providence College but struggled to get a job in her chosen field. "I wasn't sure how I was going to save the planet," she deadpans, but she concluded she needed more science training. She earned her second bachelor's, this one in biology, in 2003. She then accepted an internship in Washington, DC, for Earthjustice, the nation's largest nonprofit environmental law organization, a position that would prove transformative.

When a bill came up in the Senate, the organization needed a Rhode Islander to lobby the Ocean State's senator, Lincoln Chaffee. "I was the only Rhode Islander that they could find," Rochon recalls. "They dragged me up to the Capitol, the first time I had ever been there and the first time I had ever lobbied. The moment I walked into that building, tears filled my eyes," she laughs, "and I thought, 'This is the work I need to do for the rest of my life.'" With knees shaking, she met with Senator Chaffee, "who was lovely to me, such a nice guy. So I thought, 'OK, I know what I want to do now: I want to be a policy person, and I want to be an advocate.'"

Rochon's experience at Earthjustice helped her get a job with Clean Water Action, an organization founded in 1972 to help pass the landmark Clean Water Act and now committed to protecting the environment through grassroots groups and political action. This experience convinced Rochon that her passion was in advocacy but that she also needed more education to be effective. After a year and a half, she moved to New York state to earn her master's degree in environmental toxicology from Cornell. The original intent was to pursue a PhD, Rochon admits, "but being in a lab measuring how much zinc and cadmium were in the leaves of willow trees drove me absolutely insane."

At graduation in 2007, with an advanced degree in hand and the nation's environmental agenda under assault by the Bush administration, she was ready for a change. "I just couldn't envision continuing to rail against his administration. We were just losing left and right, and I was tired of being angry. I had always wanted to live in Europe," she adds. "All I had was a cat and a car to worry about, so I sold my car and gave my cat to my sister and got a job working for Greenpeace International in Amsterdam."

Founded in 1971, Greenpeace is a nonprofit global environmental organization active in thirty-nine countries. Rochon was placed in charge of the organization's global campaign against coal, a huge leap in responsibility from doing renewable energy work in the US's smallest state. As she recalls, "I was completely unqualified for that job but managed to do something good, I think." Her signature achievement was to lead the drafting of a report on a technology called carbon capture and storage (CCS), designed to capture carbon dioxide (CO_2) from power station smokestacks and dispose of it underground. "At the time," she says, "it was being peddled as the solution for coal, and nobody was standing up to say, 'This is a bunch of baloney.'"

CCS is one example of what is sometimes called a techno-miracle, the lead element in a philosophy that says humankind can continue its harmful practices because some advanced technology will arrive to save the day. Bill Gates's optimism around "energy miracles" has come under special scrutiny given his high public profile. The billionaire's "energy-miracle-centered strategy," physicist and climate expert Joe Romm writes, "is the exact opposite of the deployment-driven innovation strategy Gates himself used to make Microsoft a software giant." Such rhetoric, Romm adds, "can disempower people and policymakers and pundits into thinking that individual or even government action is not the central weapon needed to win the climate fight and that our only hope is some long-term *deus ex machina* strategy to avoid catastrophic warming."

In many entrepreneurial ecosystems, undying faith in advanced technologies can provide inspiration and motivation. For climate change entrepreneurs already armed with a host of practical renewable-energy alternatives, techno-miracles can be distracting and destructive.

Thanks to Rochon's 2008 report "False Hope," Greenpeace became the first organization to publish a comprehensive critique of CCS, work still cited today in academic literature. "False Hope" concludes that CCS would not reach utility scale in time to avoid dangerous climate change, would itself use enough energy to erase fifty years of coal power efficiency gains, and could not guarantee safe and permanent underground storage of CO_2. "Investment in CCS risks locking the world into an energy future that fails to save the climate," the report concludes. In short, CCS was a faux innovation that did nothing to create but potentially much to destroy.

THE URGE TO CREATE

Rochon found the work at Greenpeace, known publicly as a highly effective campaigning organization, to be rewarding but often grueling. "I love Greenpeace, and I love the people who work there," she says, but "it's a large global organization with multiple levels of management and staff. To get something moving through the various chains of command is as much of a job as it is to campaign once it's out the door." In addition, the organization's aggressive, sometimes confrontational public style could also seep into its internal dynamics. "Greenpeace is not a job, it's a way of life," Rochon adds. "It's a very demanding job and very difficult emotionally, and I just don't have the energy to do that all the time."

Rochon also worked at Greenpeace during "Copenhagen," shorthand for the 2009 United Nations climate summit that ended without a new global agreement on climate change—the moment, Naomi Klein had written, when it became clear that "no one was coming to save us." This event had a greater impact on Rochon's career than 9/11 or the 2008 recession. "We had staked all of our hopes and dreams on Copenhagen solving the climate change problem, and there was no way the politics would ever lead to anything meaningful. I kept warning all of my European colleagues, because they kept saying, 'Obama is president, it's all going to be fine,' and I said, 'No, it's not. The Senate will never ratify a treaty.'"

She was correct. Copenhagen yielded no new agreement, and many climate activists within and outside Greenpeace were devastated.

Rochon had also begun to appreciate that she could be a more successful advocate if she understood the law better. Once again, she got "that university itch," returning to the US where she earned her law degree at Northeastern University. Upon graduation in 2013, she took a job with Boston Community Capital (BCC), a nonprofit community development financial institution that invests in projects to provide affordable housing, good jobs, and new opportunities in low-income communities. The organization's solar initiative, BCC Solar, represented an innovative business model designed to address the main obstacles that low-income customers face when adopting clean technology, including the need to provide up-front capital, the ability to capture solar tax credit incentives, and the expertise to ensure systems are built to maximize solar electricity generation.

"This role is where innovation and entrepreneurship really started to come into play," says Rochon. "Prior to BCC, my career was very much focused on shutting things down—let's close down this coal plant, for example. It was emotionally satisfying, it's important work, but it's fundamentally different than actually trying to build something, which is what the solar and the renewable energy work that I'm doing now is."

The urge to create, however, has not lessened the need to disrupt. "And that's where you come straight up against the vested utility business interests, the energy company interests, the fossil fuel interests, the inertia—the entire energy system is up against you," Rochon adds. "And you're trying to carve out a space for a fleet of technologies that are going to, in theory, democratize the energy system and bring a whole range of benefits to the forefront that nobody has seen yet." This is the work of a lawyer-as-activist attempting to introduce new technologies and business models that disrupt a powerful existing economic cycle.

One of Rochon's skills is storytelling, strengthened by her background in science, law, practical project development, and advocacy. And one of her most compelling stories is the impact that small-scale distributed renewables can have on a large utility system. "The predominant narrative that you hear when somebody puts solar on their rooftop is, 'If you've gone solar and I haven't, you're free-riding on the system, and you're shipping costs to me.' You hear that here in the US, in Europe, in Australia. It's a common refrain," Rochon says, promoted by utility companies. "It's black and white and very persuasive: You're not paying utility bills so you are cheating the system."

Her counternarrative redefines those who adopt solar as responsible stewards of the grid. People who invest in their homes, adding solar panels, air-source heat pumps, and insulation have, Rochon says, "prepaid their electricity bill for the next ten years. When the sun is shining and everybody has turned on their air-conditioning, their house is not part of the problem. We need these people to participate." They spend private dollars at no risk to others, generate clean local power, support the economy, and create jobs. "I'm not a finance or technical person," she says, "but what I can do is provide the framing, story, and arguments required to do the good work that needs to be done. That's how I engage in things."

"WE'RE TOTALLY WINNING"

In 2018 Rochon accepted a position with Vineyard Wind, a Massachusetts-based company on track to build the country's first commercial-scale offshore wind farm. "It's a tremendous opportunity," she says, "and I absolutely love the work." She also remains active with BCC. "I have my toes in so many different pools because there's so much to learn. Developing projects makes me a much better advocate than I would otherwise be. I know how the market is working and not working." In that way, she says, she can create compelling legal interventions.

Fundamental to Rochon's work in both Europe and the United States is the creation of new entrepreneurial opportunities and attractive business models, and helping to spread best practices. "If you give renewable energy developers in the US the right framework and right incentives, they can solve almost any problem. You don't see that same level of creativity in Europe," she says. "It doesn't have the same capitalist roots. But the story that I tell is that you just need to give the market the right framework and let the forces innovate. Renewable energy developers everywhere can be extraordinarily clever, creative people if you give them the space within which to do that stuff, and the guidance to ensure it happens responsibly."

Despite setbacks, Rochon believes that energy markets are moving in the right direction. "We're totally winning. From an economic perspective, the cost of solar in most parts of the world is lower than coal and coming down below natural gas. We used to say, 'You should do it for the climate.' Now we say, 'You should do it because it's cheaper.'" Renewables have become a compelling story—a powerful alignment of "doing good" and "doing well"—though the clock is ticking on global warming and there is much work to be done.

BACK AT THE BAR

The key, Rochon concluded, is to follow the science and to be bold. "What I can lend to these discussions is the ambition that sometimes is lacking. That's a key role for an environmentalist to play—keeping the bar high."

Greenhouse gases? Climate change? Sustainability? Giving voice to the environment? Keeping the bar high? The older entrepreneurs in the barroom, many of whom associated progress with dark smoke spewing from factories and industrial waste flowing into rivers, were not sure they liked these stories. The idea that growth was not an end unto itself complicated commercial life considerably.

"And the stakes couldn't be any higher," one of the entrepreneurs along the back wall noted, "but so too is the energy and optimism for creating sustainable businesses."

It was the kind of energy that encouraged entrepreneurs such as Emily Rochon to take on enormous, entrenched industries by using entrepreneurship as a tool—providing new business models and profit incentives to achieve sustainability. This same approach is also fundamental to the story of Rochon's peer, Kate Cincotta, who chose to tackle another problem central to the health of the planet: Will there be enough clean water?

Chapter 15

KATE CINCOTTA:
CREATING CLIMATE
ENTREPRENEURS

K ate Cincotta (b. 1984) was an undergraduate engineering student at the University of Virginia (UVA) expecting to board a plane heading to Cancun for spring break in 2003. When her week in the sun fell through at the last minute, she says, "I had another friend who was going on this service trip to Nicaragua, so I just tagged along." It was done on a whim, the first time Cincotta had ever ventured to Central America.

"I wasn't particularly inspired before I departed the States," she recalls, "but when I arrived in Nicaragua, it was eye-opening." The team she accompanied had volunteered at an orphanage. "I remember coming back from that week feeling really good that we'd made those kids happy." But then she thought, was that all? "I could have left behind something that would have had much more of a lasting impact."

It took time for this sense of missed opportunity to sort itself out. After all, Cincotta had been inspired to become an aerospace engineer by the movie *Apollo 13*, about NASA's successful rescue of a badly damaged spaceship and its three astronauts. At eighteen, she'd committed to one day work for NASA. "Being the typical type-A, overachieving oldest child in my family . . . I set a goal and I went for it. Full speed ahead. NASA, here I come."

But her experience in Nicaragua continued to exert its own pull. Cincotta looked up UVA's Engineering Students Without Borders club. She proposed another trip to the country, but this time to use some of her newly acquired engineering skills. "That was probably the first moment when I thought, 'If I'm going to go back, I want to actually take what I've learned in school and do something with it.'" Cincotta and her team partnered with a Nicaraguan bakery seeking to expand its business. "They had to meet all of these sanitation codes to be able to start selling their product in grocery stores," she says. "So it ended up being a water and sanitation project, helping this bakery get off the ground."

By the time graduation rolled around in 2006, Cincotta's degree was still in aerospace engineering—but her passport told a different story. "I had been back to Nicaragua five times. I went to Cameroon. I joined Engineers Without Borders. I started learning about the global water crisis. And I was interested, intrigued, and excited. And I almost turned off that road to NASA. Almost."

Cincotta stuck with her childhood dream, taking a job as an aerospace engineer, one with "a great salary, benefits, and my own office." She still loved math and physics, and she could see the positive impact senior managers at her company were having on their industry. But she felt bogged down by bureaucracy, unable to make her own contribution. After a year of being "totally miserable at that job, I got the courage to let go . . . and changed the course I was on, even though I wasn't really sure where I was going to end up."

"PLENTY OF FILTERS THAT WORKED"

In 2007 Cincotta began work on her MS degree in technology and policy at the Massachusetts Institute of Technology. She studied under thesis advisor Susan Murcott, who was leading a graduate research program on household water treatment in Northern Ghana. Cincotta examined treatment and storage technologies, focusing on solutions that were practical, safe, and sustainable. During her research she met Vanessa Green, a fellow MIT student who was studying consumer preferences of household water products.

Murcott, Cincotta, and Green were focused on sustainable clean water for a good reason—many nations were already facing extreme conditions of water scarcity. Global demand has increased by six times in the last century, continues to grow at 1 percent annually, and is complicated by climate change, which makes wet regions wetter and dry regions drier. Michel Jarraud, secretary-general of the World Meteorological Society, warns that scarce water is the greatest threat from our warming environment, more than intense storms or rising sea levels Some 3.6 billion people live in areas already facing water scarcity, estimated to climb as high as 5.7 billion by 2050.

Murcott, Cincotta, and Green were focused on Ghana, also with good reason. Located in West Africa, the country faces intense drought conditions in the hot, dry north that have led to deforestation, overgrazing, soil erosion, habitat destruction, and inadequate supplies of drinking water. The three million Ghanaians who suffer from insufficient potable water are a microcosm of the stress felt around the world.

"When I first started," Cincotta says, "my goal was to provide clean drinking water to a rural community in the Northern Region of Ghana. The mission was clear, specific, and solely focused on water. Vanessa and I came up with the idea for a locally run community water business and thought that it would probably be best for women to manage the businesses. In Ghana, women knew water. Women collected water, managed the water in the home, and made all water-related decisions for their families."

The wrinkle in Cincotta and Green's business plan was their decision not to focus on high-tech solutions but to address issues of community and empowerment. "It was frustrating for me to meet with people who were doing small iterations on a water filter. We already had plenty of filters that worked, but no one was using them," Cincotta said. She and Green studied behavior and usage, trying to understand why some products were adopted in a community and others were not. Cincotta viewed this work "as part of the engineering problem, not the job of someone else. It was exciting for me. That got me out of bed in the morning, trying to figure out those types of questions."

The technology Cincotta and Green eventually chose was tried and true, a coagulant called aluminum sulfate, or alum. "It's a little ball that looks like salt crystals," she says. "You swirl it around in water and it makes all the particles flock together, and they become denser than the water and settle at the bottom of a tank." Once the water is clear, it's moved to a different tank and treated with chlorine, which disinfects it. The process looked to be teachable, affordable, and repeatable. The cofounders secured funding for their idea from the Public Service Center at MIT and headed to Ghana in June 2008. An enormous, complex global problem was now being addressed by a simple, local solution. Cincotta and Green's business model would turn not on some exotic technology, but on human behavior.

CLEAN WATER, NEW ENTREPRENEURS

Soon their new nonprofit organization, Saha Global, implemented its first project in the community of Kasaligu. A local woman named Fati was taught to treat contaminated water from her village's source. Cincotta and Green's solution was "a great success," says Cincotta. "The entire village of Kasaligu (about a thousand people) gained access to safe drinking water, and we went back to the States confident in Fati's ability to run the business."

When Cincotta returned to Kasaligu six months later, she found that Fati had used the income from her clean-water business to send her two youngest children to school, the first in her family. "When she told me about her children going to school, that's when it clicked. I realized these businesses could be so much more than just about providing clean drinking water," Cincotta says. "They could provide opportunities for a portion of the population that is often marginalized in northern Ghana—and that's women—in an area where they were already experts—and that was in water."

The word "Saha" means *opportunity* in Dagbani, the local language spoken in Ghana's Northern Region. The training, water tanks, and alum given to aspiring female entrepreneurs were important, but it was the opportunity to participate in a market economy that Cincotta and Green's new organization provided. Over the next nine years, Saha Global launched 134 clean-water businesses serving more than sixty thousand people at a fraction of the cost of drilling a borehole or well. One hundred percent of these businesses remain in operation today.

While Cincotta's entrepreneurial story is inspirational, so too are those of the Ghanaian women that Saha Global has encouraged to become entrepreneurs. In one village, a woman named Azara farms groundnuts and okra while selling clean drinking water to her community. "Anytime I treat water and make announcements," she says, "people come to buy clean water from the center, and that makes me glad. I am happy to make sales!" Saha's first entrepreneur, Fati, says, "Kids used to complain of stomach pains in the mornings, and many people used to have runny stomachs. But after the water treatment center was opened, all those complaints have stopped. I am happy to make sales and thankful for the opportunity given me."

Each village is different, and each entrepreneur brings her own talents to bear. "Sometimes the women are super entrepreneurial. They'll have a lot of ideas and try them out. Sometimes they just feel honored to fulfill the job and do everything right. The ones who have more creative ideas are definitely more successful," Cincotta says.

"And the entrepreneurial impulse is about the same as in America," she adds. "We have one business that four women run, and it's so interesting to see their different personalities when they each take a week doing it. One is more of the money woman who manages all the finances. One is more the techie person who knows how to fix things when they break. One is super feisty and kind of the saleswoman. That's the same anywhere, I think."

GROWING THE BUSINESS

Some three-quarters of Saha Global's funding comes from foundation grants that provide seed capital for the launch of each independent business. After that, it's the responsibility of the newly minted entrepreneurs to maintain their operations' financial sustainability. This business model is attractive and scalable. "Our goal," Cincotta says, "is to reach everyone in Northern Ghana without clean water, approximately 800,000 people, by 2023."

In the United States, Cincotta has worked hard to ensure that Saha Global itself is financially solid, most notably through a strong board of directors. They act as both community and inspiration. "At least once a year there's a dark point," she says. "There'll be a major donor we thought we were going to land and didn't. Or we have a good partnership for years and something happens outside our control and they're no longer a partner. It almost always has to do with funding. There have been so many times when I've sat down with the board and said, 'Our cash flow is going negative in three months and we need to figure out what we're going to do.' But Vanessa, my cofounder, will always remind us: 'Remember, we were in a much worse position than this three years ago, and we'll figure it out.' And it always ends up working out."

As Saha grows, Cincotta has been able to identify her own strengths, and the role in which she can be most effective. "I'm best at thinking through programs," she says, "looking at problems that we have, making really quick decisions, not dwelling on them, and being able to say, 'That didn't work' and making a pivot. I can be really flexible while still having our general mission in mind." These were skills learned in the field, when Cincotta first lived in Ghana and "things were going wrong all of the time. And now, so much more of my job is thinking about the bigger organization as a whole—funding sources, hiring, and what country will we expand to—instead of worrying about what we're going to do in this one village. I'm very used to big disasters happening, and I'm very confident that it's going to be fine. We're going to figure it out. If we have to change everything we're doing tomorrow, we'll just do it. And it's going to be OK. I'm very calm under pressure. It takes a lot to get me flustered. And I try to set that example for our whole team."

The need is growing for sustainable clean water and for entrepreneurial models like Saha Global. "We see climate change every day with our water sources in Ghana," Cincotta says. "All of our communities have surface water sources. Many are man-made ponds where they just collect rainwater during the rainy season, which lasts about three months. So a lot of our communities are seeing their sources dry up—and they have never dried up before. The rains aren't coming as soon. The rainy season is getting shorter. A lot of the farmers are telling us—sometimes they can get two harvests during the rainy season—that they're totally missing the first one now. They don't know when to plant."

Cincotta adds, "I've really noticed the difference in the weather pattern. I've just been amazed in the huge difference I've seen in just the short period of time I've been traveling there."

Climate change. Clean water. New entrepreneurs. It's all a long way from an office at NASA. But Cincotta, who found herself doing entrepreneurial things before she recognized she was an entrepreneur, has no regrets. "I feel very lucky," she says. "I didn't have student loans when I graduated from school. I had very supportive parents, so I was able to not take a salary and move to Ghana for a year. If I had been in a different position, I might not have been able to do that—and I don't discount that at all."

BACK AT THE BAR

Cincotta's supportive community and innovative, low-tech business model were both essential to her success, but there was no discounting chance.

"It's hard to say what might have happened if the trip to Mexico had gone off as planned," Cincotta recalled. "So there was skill, but also a lot of luck and good circumstances that allowed me to do this work. I'm thankful every day."

Gratefulness is a sentiment that resonated with others gathered at the bar. Eli Whitney recalled how lucky he had been to have his first tutoring job fall through and to have been befriended by Catharine Greene. Willis Carrier thought back to the first, unanticipated order that his fledgling business won at the start of World War I. King Gillette considered his luck in being introduced to inventor William Emery Nickerson after years of failing to manufacture steel-sheet razors. Mary Elizabeth Sharpe remembered the day when her neighbors had unexpectedly provided the first piece of mechanized equipment to her struggling family business. There wasn't an entrepreneur in the barroom who couldn't think back to at least one event when, in retrospect, their future hung in the balance—and luck smiled on them.

"I was trying to figure out if graduate school made sense," climate entrepreneur Viraj Puri began, "when I took a job at a small sustainable-engineering firm in New York. They happened to assign me to a floating hydroponic greenhouse." He smiled, as if he had just missed his flight to Cancun. "That experience changed everything."

Chapter 16

VIRAJ PURI:
PLANTS ARE NOT WIDGETS

66 I grew up in a family that valued the natural world," Viraj Puri (b. 1981) says. "We enjoyed a lot of outdoor recreation in places like the national parks, and on safaris, and my parents often took us to India, where my family is from. We would visit the Himalayas and the jungles. I developed an early affinity for wildlife and outdoor sports and from there an interest in the environment and conservation issues."

Puri is the cofounder and CEO of Gotham Greens, a pioneer in the field of urban agriculture, focused on producing hyperlocal, premium-quality, greenhouse-grown vegetables and herbs. "I don't come from an entrepreneurial family," Puri says. "My parents were professionals, and I don't have siblings or grandparents who were entrepreneurs. I think one contributing factor to my wanting to be an entrepreneur and launching a unique business in Gotham Greens was that I'd always had an independent streak. I traveled extensively during summer breaks, did study-abroad programs in high school and college, and have always had a sense of wanderlust. If there had been such a category in high school, I might have been voted 'Most Likely to Be a *National Geographic* Photographer,'" he says with a laugh.

Puri has an easygoing and engaging way and an optimistic outlook on the future, but he and his cofounders, Eric Haley and Jennifer Nelkin Frymark, have chosen to tackle one of the more sobering issues on the planet. Agriculture is humankind's largest employer, with 575 million farms around the world providing food for seven billion people. Together, these farms use more land and water than any industry, generate the most pollution, and are the source of some 15 percent of global greenhouse gases—spewing more carbon equivalents annually than all of civilization's autos, trucks, trains, and airplanes combined.

In addition, some 40 percent of the land currently being farmed around the world has been degraded by the extremes of climate change, pollution, and destructive farming practices such as deforestation and monoculture, the intensive growing of single crops and varieties. These many interrelated factors put pressure on yields as the global population climbs toward ten billion by 2050.

As agricultural supply struggles to keep pace with demand, people are flocking to cities at an unprecedented rate. In 2008, for the first time in history, more than half of humankind lived in urban areas, with 69 percent expected by 2050. Urbanization has helped to reduce poverty, but it has also separated people from their food production, creating long, complex, and fragile supply chains linking farm and city. In response, about 800 million people today practice some form of urban agriculture (or "urban farming"), embedding new and sometimes unconventional farming practices in the urban ecosystem to supply up to 20 percent of the world's food.

In the United States, the opening decades of the twenty-first century witnessed the introduction of a powerful set of tools dedicated to indoor agriculture, a specialized, rapidly growing segment of urban farming. Participants in indoor agriculture range from small, container-based vertical farms (which grow product vertically to optimize square footage) to large hydroponic greenhouses that forgo soil for liquid nutrients, and control for light, heat, humidity, water, and nutrients through a set of sophisticated sensors and data analysis. In Sweden, for example, Plantagon CityFarm grows greens hydroponically beneath a twenty-six-story office tower in Stockholm, sending warmth from its LED grow lights to a heat-storage system for the office building. Plantagon sells its harvest to two restaurants in the high-rise and local grocery stores. In France, Cycloponics grows mushrooms, herbs, and lettuce in a subterranean garage beneath a three-hundred-unit affordable housing complex in Paris, while in Japan, subway operators have designed an urban garden of lettuce and herbs beneath the elevated train tracks of the Tokyo Metro Tozai Line.

"AN AMAZING WAY TO GROW FOOD"

Puri's introduction to these new agricultural practices happened by chance. He studied liberal arts at Colgate University, intent on "doing something in the environmental field"—perhaps environmental law, finance, or entrepreneurship. By his senior year he had grown interested in renewable energy and cleantech. After graduation he spent several months testing the world of corporate environmental law, but, he says, "ended up pivoting away from that to try my hand at a couple of grassroots projects overseas. I spent a year in Africa and a year in India each, doing a variety of projects around renewable energy, environmental design, and sustainable development."

One project involved fuel-efficient cookstoves in Africa, and the other green building and solar photovoltaic cells (PV) in the Himalayas. "Those experiences took me to twenty-four or twenty-five years old," Puri says, "and I decided I wanted to pursue a career in clean technology. I applied to graduate schools to do a joint MBA and MS in environmental management."

While Puri was plotting his path into graduate school, he worked at a small sustainable-engineering firm in New York that placed him, in 2007 and 2008, on the "Science Barge," a 1,200-square-foot floating hydroponic greenhouse and education center launched on the Manhattan waterfront and now docked in Yonkers, New York. That experience changed everything. By 2009, Puri was deep into due diligence around sustainable food production, inviting Haley and eventually Frymark to help him sort out the opportunities in hydroponics and high-tech urban agriculture.

"My original conclusion had been that buildings were the largest consumer of energy on the planet, so if we're serious about climate change, if we're serious about making a difference, we need to be looking at energy efficiency and the built environment. But then I switched gears," Puri says. "As I did my research on the global food system, I was alarmed to learn that agriculture is a significant contributor of carbon emissions, the largest consumer of land and freshwater on the planet, and the largest contributor of global water pollution. And full of waste and inequities. It seemed like there was an urgent need to develop better strategies, technologies, and supply chains for sustainable food production."

One solution seemed to be hydroponic farming. "I thought," Puri concludes, "that it was an amazing way to grow food using far fewer resources. And deploying hydroponics in cities was a way to combine those interests and simultaneously address both macro issues."

"NOT NECESSARILY APPROPRIATE FOR TYPICAL VC FINANCING"

Puri, Haley, and Frymark are entrepreneurs, technologists, and "foodies." They had watched as the "farm-to-table" movement arose in America's cities in the early 2000s, emphasizing fresh, local food and low carbon footprints. "Let's create an urban-agricultural setup," Puri thought, "that could disrupt the conventional supply chain and provide New Yorkers with really high-quality, really tasty and delicious produce consistently and reliably year-round." Their company, Gotham Greens, was founded in 2009 and launched in 2011 in Greenpoint, Brooklyn. The trio's novel combination was seeing the intersection of existing hydroponic technology with New York City's acres and acres of rooftops and brownfield sites—underutilized, undervalued real estate assets that landlords were anxious to rent. "We were in the right place at the right time, wanting to do something entrepreneurial in the cleantech/sustainability field," Puri recalls.

But rooftops were just the start, the first step forward. "Our vision was to bring food production into the urban and built environment. Rooftops were an enabling factor because we started looking at real estate and found that it was too difficult to come by, especially in a very expensive market like New York City. So, rooftops became a compelling option, a way to turn dead space into something valuable and productive." It helped, too, that Frymark had worked on a project at the University of Arizona where she proposed a rooftop greenhouse on a department building on campus. Her experience only illustrated the complementary nature of the partners' skills.

"As a practical matter," Puri says, "we have very different skill sets. Jenn is a plant scientist and hydroponics expert. Eric is a financial professional with high quantitative and financial skills. And I have sustainability, project management, vision, and strategy development experience. We complement one another, and collaborative decision making has served us very well." He adds, "There's also a good mix of risk tolerance among us. The three of us bring to any decision different perspectives in terms of how aggressive or conservative to be."

The first year and a half turned out to be a lesson in real estate development, zoning, ordinance, and occupancy laws; an investigation into the science and practical applications of hydroponics; and a lot of hard work, on a shoestring budget. But in 2011, Gotham Greens launched its flagship greenhouse in the Greenpoint section of Brooklyn, the first commercial-scale rooftop greenhouse in the United States. The fifteen-thousand-square-foot enclosure produces over one hundred thousand pounds of leafy greens annually.

"After we built the first greenhouse, we had VCs knocking on the door saying this is brilliant and we should go build a hundred of them," Puri says. "But we were wary. As a practical matter, farming is not like assembly-line manufacturing, and plants are not widgets. You can build a beautiful box for them with a lot of technology, bells and whistles, sensors, robotics, and automation, but the plants still need a lot of human care and operational expertise to thrive. There's a unique combination of horticultural science and engineering techniques that allow the plants to grow. Indoor farming technology is evolving rapidly—cameras, sensors, machine learning, artificial intelligence, Big Data, yes—but, that's not there yet. And it certainly wasn't there when we launched. Basically, we wanted to walk before we ran."

Gotham Greens' first greenhouse might have been a one-off project. "We wanted it to be financially sustainable," Puri says, "and we wanted to be sure it could be successful before we made a decision to scale. And there was still a lot to figure out."

Rather than taking a slug of money from venture investors looking for rapid growth and a quick return, Puri and his partners thought, "Let's have more thoughtful, patient growth. Let's try to fund this sustainably using appropriate, longer-term financing structures. Literally and figuratively speaking," Puri says, "we're building brick-and-mortar manufacturing facilities that are capital-, operationally-, and real estate–intensive. We're not an ecommerce business nor a consumer packaged-goods company that can outsource its production to third-party manufacturers and distributors. We're a vertically integrated real estate developer, agribusiness, ag-technology, marketing, and distribution company. There wasn't any precedent. We're really pioneering in the field. It's a unique business in that regard, and not necessarily appropriate for typical VC financing."

A MORE AGGRESSIVE GROWTH PATH

Meanwhile, demand for the company's produce was outstripping supply. Gotham Greens received broad exposure and great press. "The chefs love it; the supermarket buyer loves it; the end-consumer loves it. This is working. Forget grad school." Puri laughs. "So we decided to expand beyond this first project. One of our large customers, Whole Foods Market, was working on a new store in Brooklyn. They wanted the store to feature cutting-edge green building design and innovation. We developed a relationship with their executives and real estate development team, and we started talking about a rooftop greenhouse at the store. That became our second project," the nation's first commercial-scale greenhouse farm—twenty thousand square feet—integrated within a retail grocery space.

"We had one greenhouse, and now we'd doubled that," Puri says, "and now we needed to know if we could run a profitable, sustainable business and continue to grow high-quality product. We ran both greenhouse sites for a year, and demand was still outstripping supply. We'd proven our model twice. The next step in our evolution was to try to triple the size of the greenhouse to see if that worked."

Gotham Greens built its third greenhouse in the Hollis section of Queens, New York, on the rooftop of a former toy factory. At sixty thousand square feet, it produces more than five million heads of leafy greens annually. The model continued to work. "Three different rooftops, three very different projects, all very successful," he says. "Now let's see if we can replicate this in another city."

Gotham Greens turned to Chicago. "It's a great city," Puri says. "It's a cold-weather place. They don't have reliable produce availability year-round. It has a thriving urban agriculture scene, and is just a great food town. A lot of things were aligned. We pursued a really unique and innovative urban revitalization project in partnership with a sustainable cleaning products company, Method." Gotham Greens' 75,000-square-foot greenhouse, located on Chicago's south side, opened in 2015 and produces ten million heads of greens and herbs annually.

"Now we've proven to ourselves that we can run multiple facilities well in two different cities," Puri says. "We've validated the margins and the business to ourselves." In June 2018, the company closed a $29 million Series C round to help support five hundred thousand square feet of hydroponic gardens under development in five states. Investors share the company's long-term perspective. "Now there's a more aggressive growth path on our horizon," Puri adds.

In its opening chapter, the company constructed four greenhouses across two cities with more than 140 employees growing fourteen varieties of produce, including lettuce, mustard greens, basil, kale, and tomatoes. From 2015 to 2016, revenue grew 270 percent. The company has announced the development of a 100,000-square-foot hydroponic greenhouse at a former steel mill in Baltimore County and another

100,000-square-foot greenhouse on the south side of Chicago, also on the grounds of a former steel mill. The team is clicking. Gotham Greens' hydroponic farming and advanced growing methods yield twenty to thirty times more product per acre than field production and eliminate the need for new arable land.

"We use 100 percent renewable electricity to power these green-houses. We recycle 100 percent of our irrigation water, and all the produce is non-GMO and pesticide-free," Puri says. "Our 170,000 square feet of greenhouses across the four facilities produce yields equivalent to over 100 acres of conventional field farming. This makes us the largest urban agriculture company in the world."

Puri is realistic and knows that Gotham Greens won't be able to feed the entire world. "But I believe in the mission, and I believe this solution will have a positive impact on food supply and sustainability," he says. "All the projects we'll be doing going forward will be urban, but not all will be on rooftops. Our real DNA is urban farming—revitalizing urban areas that are underserved and distressed, disrupting the food supply chain, growing fresher, nutritious food and focusing on sustainability."

BACK AT THE BAR

The barroom crowd had now heard stories about food, water, and renew-able energy, innovations led by entrepreneurs who took as their mission the creation of business models that emphasized the smart use of resources. A powerful community of eco-investors, green funds, and climate entre-preneurs had emerged in twenty-first-century America to support these new models.

Like mechanization, mass production, and consumerism before it, sustainability had become the fourth great theme of American entrepre-neurship—but not the last. And, as the evening was growing later, there was one more group of entrepreneurs that had yet to tell their stories.

For many at the bar, this last set of tales would sound less like inno-vation or creative destruction and more like science fiction.

Part Five

DIGITIZATION

Chapter 17

BRENNA BERMAN:
BUILDING A SMARTER CITY

The same 1976 *Fortune* magazine that illustrated America's fossil-fuel economy also offered a glimpse into the technology that powered the nation in its bicentennial year. "We make discs of people," EMI advertised, touting its leadership in recorded music. Likewise, Olivetti seemed to merge human and machine when it advertised distributed data processing that "speaks your language." And RCA highlighted the microprocessor, saying, "Never before have we crammed so much thinking power into so small a space."

For most Americans, digitization—the conversion of analog signals into a digital format—seemed less flesh-and-blood and more about rudimentary word processors and computers that were useful if uninspiring, best left in the office with the filing cabinets at the end of the workday. This ambivalent relationship with technology would change in 1976, however, when Steve Jobs and Steve Wozniak incorporated Apple Computer. Three years later, Apple and its competitors sold 724,000 personal computers. In 1982, *Time* magazine named the computer its "Person of the Year," explaining that Americans had begun welcoming screens as new members of their households.

When computers linked to the Internet in the 1990s, growth in home computing was unstoppable. By the close of the century, forty million Americans had purchased a product online, and nearly half of all users already agreed that, like a close friend, they would miss the Web "a lot" if denied its company.

Machines began amassing data at a staggering rate. By 2016, the storage capacity of the Internet was approaching 10^{24} bytes, growing at 30 to 40 percent annually. More important, science historian George Dyson writes, was the moment when computers allowed numbers that *mean* things to become numbers that *do* things. Machines in the form of robots and artificial intelligence that might harm or even replace human-kind became a fearful narrative that grew alongside more optimistic entre-preneurial visions of smart cities full of clean, self-driving cars, factories without unsafe or repetitive labor, digital health care, robotic compan-ions, improved farm yields, and dazzling new forms of entertainment and community. Digitization inspired a wholesale disruption of traditional, analog business models. The great themes of entrepreneurship—mechani-zation, mass production, consumerism, and sustainability—had found a fifth and equal partner.

The pace of digital development in the twenty-first century remains unclear. A consensus forecast in 2017 hypothesized that AI would out-perform human beings in translating language by 2024, driving a truck by 2027, working in retail by 2031, writing a best-selling book by 2049, and working as a surgeon by 2053. These same researchers believed that there is a 50 percent chance that AI would outperform humans in all tasks by 2062.

In the moments when machines best human beings, the impact can be startling. When chess grandmaster Garry Kasparov played IBM's Deep Blue supercomputer, he "sensed something new, something unsettling. Perhaps you will experience a similar feeling the first time you ride in a driverless car," he wrote, "or the first time your new computer boss issues an order at work." When Ke Jie, the world's strongest player of the game Go, was defeated by a Google algorithm, he said, "It became like a god."

These experiences confirm science fiction author Arthur C. Clarke's

(1917–2008) belief that any sufficiently advanced technology is indistinguishable from magic. This was undoubtedly true when the first plantation owner witnessed Eli Whitney's cotton gin clean fifty pounds of cotton in the time it had taken a person to process a single pound, or when the Memorial Day 1925 audience at Broadway's Rivoli Theatre felt the first cool breeze of Willis Carrier's "manufactured air." What Whitney, Carrier, and the modern entrepreneurs of digitization understand is that, as disruptive as a technology might be, the real magic comes in the building of community and in the successful launch of new business models that make the technology accessible to the marketplace.

CITIES HAVE TO WORK

Brenna Berman (b. 1976), executive director of the City Tech Collaborative in Chicago, doesn't consider herself an entrepreneur. And she doesn't work in a function—city government—renowned for the delivery of leading-edge innovation. Yet her personal story is undeniably entrepreneurial, and the results achieved by her teams have disrupted traditional service delivery and enhanced the lives of millions of people. Her territory is the modern city, arguably the most important center of community in the twenty-first century.

By 2050, the earth's urban population is expected to grow to perhaps two-thirds of all human beings and account for 80 percent of wealth creation. Harvard economist Edward Glaeser calls cities "our species' greatest invention," tracing a "near-perfect correlation between urbanization and prosperity across nations." However, urban areas that grow haphazardly can result in poverty, slums, pollution, and congestion. More than 80 percent of people living in cities that monitor air pollution are exposed to air-quality levels that exceed World Health Organization limits, for example. By 2050, cities will account for 60 percent of total energy consumption, and, if managed poorly, a greater share of global greenhouse gas emissions.

"The trend of people moving into cities is undeniable," Berman says, "but cities have to work, or I'm not sure humanity will continue to work." This is a consensus view. The Rockefeller Foundation's 100 Resilient Cities organization, for example, believes that the world's future depends on how cities manage their challenges. "I'm not sure I get up every morning and think about the gravity of this work," Berman says, laughing. "It might keep me in bed. But even if cities stopped growing today, we still have plenty of problems to tackle."

"SEE A MOUNTAIN, CLIMB A MOUNTAIN"

Raised in New England, Brenna Berman was daughter to a mother who worked "high-level customer service for the phone company," modeling how to balance the demands of life, and how to keep the customer—"or resident, in the case of my work—front and center. My father was a social worker," Berman continues, "so I grew up with a really strong example that if you have more than the person next to you, then you have a responsibility to give back and to serve."

Berman was exposed to computers at an early age. One of her uncles was an astrophysicist at Cornell, another a pioneering computer science professor who passed down his old personal computers to Berman and her sister. "So I had a PC when I was five years old, and I was emailing my uncles, when most of my age group didn't have PCs until college. I grew up with folks in my life who were science and technology geeks who opened up that world to me."

Moving to the Midwest after high school, Berman earned her bachelor's degree and master's in public policy (2000) from the University of Chicago. "In graduate school I knew I wanted to work in government," she says, "and knew I wanted to exercise this passion that I have for trying to solve big, hairy problems. Probably the most defining characteristic of my personality is what I call 'Mount Everest syndrome': See a mountain, climb a mountain. When you're done, find the next one." Berman would find that government, and specifically city government, was a geography dotted with Mount Everests.

Berman's energies were directed at government modernization and transformation, not technology. "For me, technology was always a tool and a means to an end, to help solve big-government and big-city problems—rather than getting a big thrill from technology itself." She recognized, however, that there were few solutions in government that did not involve technology, and she took her first job with IBM, "one of the best places to apply technology to government."

At IBM, Berman was able to work on a variety of big-government problems, often in an international setting—and often with a twist. "When you think about veterans' affairs, and how to deliver better services to veterans in the US, for example, we know who our veterans are. You enlist or are drafted, and there is a record of your service. But I worked on building a new veterans' system in South Africa," she says, "where the country had just come out of apartheid, and where their veterans were rebels. We needed to create a system to catalog people who said they were veterans and may or may not have been—a very different model."

Berman was working for IBM as 9/11 unfolded. The company's response to this national tragedy, and the way it cultivated a personal level of responsibility in its executives, have become part of her leadership style. "On the morning of 9/11, there were something like 110,000 US IBMers on assignment," she says. "The very first thing IBM did—and it took three days—was to locate every single employee and make sure that he or she was OK. We lost one person that day, an IBMer on the Pentagon plane, but we had 122 customers impacted. IBM did all of the repair, restoration, and document replacement work that they could do as a huge pro bono effort by the entire company. And they never said anything about that." This kind of people-centered, principled leadership, Berman concludes, "shaped the kind of executive and leader that I hope that I am."

Berman's projects at IBM focused on the use of analytics, best practices in delivering services, and an acceleration of modernization efforts—all initiatives that would play a role in her career. "It was a fascinating process," she says. "I did that for twelve years, almost entirely outside of the US, and then had the opportunity to come back to Chicago to work for Mayor Rahm Emanuel. He was the first new mayor that Chicago had had in twenty-five years. He was part of this new crop of mayors like Mayor Bloomberg in New York who are not parochial leaders but global city leaders." He was, Berman explains, "a caliber of leader that you rarely had at the city level. So that was a huge opportunity to come home and ply my craft where I lived and was beginning to raise children—to be part of the transition we are seeing in the urban space of cities being at the forefront of solving global problems, and to use technology to solve those problems."

Berman joined the Emanuel administration in 2011 as deputy budget director. After a year, she became the first deputy commissioner of the Department of Innovation and Technology (DoIT)—the city's chief information officer (CIO)—supporting the mayor's commitment to an open and data-driven government. This position cast her as one of the leaders of the "smart city" movement, defined as those cities seeking to adopt digitization technologies—including cloud computing, machine learning, sensors and asset tagging, geo-spatial information, Big Data management, and smartphones, all connected through the Internet of Things—to gather data, mine historical trends, and use predictive analytics to deploy city services more effectively.

While she is a leader in this smart city movement, Berman is careful to avoid jargon and to place problem solving and people ahead of technology. "In Chicago, for example, you'd never walk into the mayor's office and ask to see his 'smart city strategy,'" she says. "That's not a term he's focused on. We're focused on reducing crime rates and improving schools and fostering economic development—making life in Chicago better. And I was focused on ways that technology could support or fix those problems. If calling something 'smart cities' helped me get the right partners to the table to invest in those opportunities, I was happy to do it. But for me, I wanted to cultivate a strategy that was problem driven, and where the outcomes could be quantitatively evaluated."

NOT AN ENTREPRENEUR?

As CIO of Chicago, Berman worked on a variety of urban innovations using analytics—essentially, a series of new business models—to improve service delivery. Her team helped introduce an open portal to provide data to city residents that helped them understand how the city was performing—and how efficiently the city employed their tax dollars. This open data program has become one of the largest in the country. She led a rat-baiting project that involved analyzing data from the city's 311 nonemergency phone service to help predict infestation problems. By sharing this data with the Department of Streets and Sanitation, the city discovered the largest infestation on record.

Berman's DoIT also tackled the issue of food inspection, which fell to thirty inspectors responsible for overseeing fifteen thousand establishments. The DoIT developed an algorithm with variables including prior violations, weather, and age of business. The result for the city's inspectors, Berman says, is that "we improved their ability to identify potential food-borne problems by seven and a half days.

"We also have a project around flooding," she adds, "where we've integrated sensors and green infrastructure to divert water out of our traditional sewer system because it becomes overwhelmed when we have intense rainstorms."

After Berman's nearly seven years as CIO of the city, Chicago offered more than six hundred data sets in its open data portal. These sets support the initiatives around rodent baiting, restaurant inspections, and, Berman says, everything from "detecting levels of West Nile virus in the lake and the river to elevator inspections." These varied projects speak to the nature of the city as a huge laboratory full of "Everests" waiting to be climbed and suggest the kinds of entrepreneurs Berman needs to attract.

"Cities are such a complex system of systems—there are so many lines of business, which is what I've always loved about it," she says. "When we were recruiting for the city we didn't pay the highest salaries, but we were going after the same talent as Google and Microsoft. We saw ourselves a little bit like the Peace Corps without living in a mud hut." She smiles and says their pitch was, "Now is your chance to give back. If you're the kind of person who loves working on new problems all the time, there are not a lot of places where you can work on public safety one day, waste management the next day, and health and human services the next day. But you can in cities."

Ask Berman if she thinks of herself as an entrepreneur, and she'll say no. "I think of an entrepreneur as someone who starts their own business, which is something I've never done and never had the desire to do. The type of work I do fits much better in established organizations," she explains, "while my skill set as an executive is much more suited to and most challenged by the growth that occurs in mid-level organizations." But if an entrepreneur's task is to deliver innovation that improves a process or disrupts an economic flow, Berman is a lifelong entrepreneur. She has practiced this craft within enormous organizations such as IBM and the city of Chicago. Her efforts reflect the fact that large-scale innovation—meant to redesign massive government infrastructure and impact millions of people—is often beyond the reach of start-ups.

Talented individuals like Berman may work in offices instead of garages and may be part of wide-ranging, multidisciplinary groups, but the impressive results they achieve are a reminder that innovation in America flows from sources well beyond the latest high-tech start-up.

A FITNESS TRACKER FOR THE CITY

Berman's move in May 2017 from CIO of the city of Chicago to executive director of City Tech (part of UI Labs) was made specifically to support innovation initiatives in Chicago. "The city wanted to work on new projects that required strong public–private partnerships," Berman says. As CIO, she had helped create City Tech, a foundation designed to build these partnerships while creating new investment vehicles to promote innovation. The move to City Tech was encouraged by the mayor, but it also suited Berman personally. "In any job, there are things you really like that you look for in your next job and things that you don't like that you look to avoid."

One of those things Berman would not miss, for example, was sleeping with her phone, required in her role overseeing the city's 24/7 operational IT team. "In this new job," she says, "I'm doing all of those things I liked. For example, I really love product development, understanding what the problem is and finding the solution, and then building it and getting it into the market. We did that at the city, but because I was CIO, it was my job to get the obstacles out of the way for my team to do that—which is important, but I was not doing as much hands-on work, and I missed that. In essence, that is what my new organization does. I kept all the good parts of my old job."

City Tech's products include low-cost and consumer-friendly solutions to manage traffic and crowds during Cubs night games, virtual mapping of underground structures to coordinate design and permitting and reduce accidental disruption of utility services, a public portal to compare health-related data over time and across city communities, a public portal to help parents applying for early learning programs, and a Wcb map to help residents take advantage of forest preserves in Cook County.

Perhaps the most exciting project is a joint program sponsored by the University of Chicago, Argonne National Laboratory, and the City of Chicago called the Array of Things (AoT). Designed to collect real-time data on Chicago's environment, infrastructure, and activity, AoT will allow the public, researchers, and scientists to view the city in new ways. Berman's City Tech supports a part of the program focused on resident engagement. "There's this belief that cities are already awash in data," Berman says, "but it's not true. The question is, how do we build a Fitbit for the city and collect the level of data that we can know for a person, say, as [with] a highly sensored athlete."

AoT envisions this city-fitness tracker as a kind of cabinet of sensors, and plans to hang five hundred of them from streetlight traffic-signal poles all around Chicago. The initial collection of sensors measures temperature, barometric pressure, light, vibration, carbon monoxide, nitrogen dioxide, sulfur dioxide, ozone, ambient sound intensity, pedestrian and vehicle traffic, and surface temperature. More sensors can be added in the future. "What if the light pole told you to watch out for an ice patch of sidewalk ahead," the AoT website asks, "or told you the safest route for a late-night walk to the El station, or could provide weather and air quality on a block-by-block basis?" The system is designed to be secure from hackers and to specifically minimize any potential collection of data about individuals.

Berman sees AoT as a game-changer. "Cities have been using sensors for a long time—sensors on bridges to tell you when they freeze, sensors in water to measure water-quality elements. But the challenge has been that those sensors were siloed and often disconnected," she says, "and they weren't purpose-built for the urban environment. You'd put sensors in Lake Michigan, they'd work fine for a little while, but then they'd begin to degrade. There'd be no maintenance plan. And eventually they would become space trash. That's not an enterprise-level urban solution."

Instead, she outlines a contrasting goal: "Providing the kind of data necessary to drive either good operational decision making or, more importantly, urban research to actually improve how the city or the lake (in that case) is managed. It was perfectly fine to get a one-off reading of *E. coli* levels, but that is not going to increase the city's understanding of Lake Michigan as a key feature and element of our urban environment."

By creating this enormous cache of open source urban data, AoT will become a resource for researchers all over the world. Its hardware is being developed to withstand climate extremes, allowing for eventual deployment in other cities and leveraging globally the work now being done in Chicago.

Mobility and air quality are two urban problems especially import-ant to Berman. "Mobility is such a long-term problem," she says. "There are fixes today, small solutions you can put in place to help cities better utilize their current transportation infrastructure. But what really matters is coming up with planning models so that we don't make decisions today that have bad outcomes fifty years from now."

Air quality is an issue that consistently rises as a top problem in cities. "Bad air quality can't be stopped with a wall," Berman adds. "There's no amount of healthy diet or exercise that saves your lungs from bad smog. Air quality is one of the most challenging problems because sometimes it's viewed as an inverse problem to economic growth, which isn't necessarily true. It can be hard to get people to focus on it. There's a behavioral change associated with it that I find fascinating."

BROADENING THE APERTURE

While only midway through her career, Berman is already a veteran of the smart-city space. "I've been a committed leader to that space for ten years now," Berman says, "and it's fair to say I've been frustrated with two things in particular. One was how slowly, even for government, the industry was maturing. There is a 'tyranny of the pilot.' There are thousands of smart-cities pilots around the US, many of which worked well, that never scaled because there was never any planning about how to scale it from a technical, business model, or an IP management and marketability perspective."

In other words, smart cities require smart business models. "All the standard blocking and tackling that companies do," she says, "were just not happening. At City Tech, while we do pilots, we also define the go-to-market model. We are looking to create market-viable solutions with near-term ROI. The point is to make this marketplace mature faster than it is."

Berman also finds a smart city needs to be supported by an inclusive community, part of the reason she made the move to lead City Tech. "Everything in smart cities has been defined as a product or solution targeting city government. This is narrow and puts the city in the position of having to be the 'solver' all the time. But cities are made up of a whole bunch of important institutions that are not city government. Universities matter," she says. "Hospital systems. Other large institutions. And then there are the people who live in a city. And none of those organizations or individuals had voices. City government is only 20 percent of the footprint of any Western city," she adds. "So if smart cities were going to just keep focusing on city government, it's just too narrow for a market to be sustainable or the impact to be broad enough. Our solution portfolio is about 50 percent government and 50 percent other urban customers and issues. My new position has given me the ability to broaden the aperture of the solutions we were developing."

Like many entrepreneurs who have come of age in the twenty-first century, Berman's work is a mix of professional ambition alongside some very personal goals. "I'd like my kids to live in a city that works," she says. "And I'd like that to be true for every kid. I want my kids to have the benefit of the diversity that comes from every kid having the same opportunities. Technology has a lot to do with that," she concludes. "If cities aren't killing themselves to clear the basics, they can turn to higher-level needs. If we really begin to focus on equality from basic health needs, like air quality, and provide access to resources in an equitable way, that's how things really start to change."

BACK AT THE BAR

"A smart city?" Some of the older entrepreneurs found the idea of an inanimate object having intelligence to be baffling—and uncomfortable.

In fact, there wasn't a *young* entrepreneur in the barroom who had not had a moment of apprehension when pondering the future of a digital world. Computers could already pick stocks and diagnose illnesses. Many contemporary entrepreneurs relied on the digital magic of algorithms to help them choose the next movie they would watch or the next item they might purchase online. More than a few had smart robotic vacuum cleaners. And most could expect to see 2050 and beyond, the period when machines might overtake human intelligence.

One modern narrative feared this moment; physicist Stephen Hawking believed that artificial intelligence might mean the end of humanity. But a competing storyline held that a digital world could really be about humans and machines working together, with smart machines shouldering the tedium of life so that humans could be more human.

This was a barroom, though, and it was getting late. Nobody was ready to leave just yet, but nobody was in the mood for an existential philosophical discussion about the future of humankind. "Maybe," a helpful voice rose above the din, "another story might help explain?"

Chapter 18

JEAN BROWNHILL:
A COMMUNITY OF TRUST

If building community is an entrepreneur's indispensable skill, Jean Virginia Brownhill (b. 1977) is an expert. Her network of support is expansive, including parents, teachers, and supervisors, an unexpected lift from a stranger, and an even less likely message from Warren Buffett. But it also includes three departed industrialists, men she never met—Peter Cooper (1791–1883), John Loeb (1902–1996), and Henry Crown (1896–1990)—who all figure prominently in her successful entrepreneurial journey.

What's more remarkable, however, is that there was nothing in Jean Brownhill's upbringing in New London, Connecticut, to suggest that she would one day become an entrepreneur at all.

REWIRING HER BRAIN

"My parents are an interracial couple who had a child pretty early on." Brownhill refers to a US Supreme Court case that had invalidated laws prohibiting interracial marriage just ten years earlier. Her father was black, from Hobe Sound, Florida. His mother had been a domestic worker in the upscale neighborhoods of nearby Jupiter. He ran away from home when he was thirteen and, through a series of adventures and jobs, made his way up the East Coast, eventually settling in New London.

"It was during President Johnson's Model Cities program," Brownhill says, referencing an opportunity for US cities to experiment with alternative forms of municipal government. "They wanted more people of color to be policing. My dad signed up. They gave him everything except a gun." Brownhill laughs. Meanwhile, Brownhill's mother had graduated from Connecticut College in New London and joined the program as an administrator. The two met, both dedicated to improving urban life, including building and architecture. "All the things," Brownhill says, "that came to be really important in my life."

From her mother, she received a love of books and education. Her father provided her with a passion for technology and problem solving. "He had this Commodore 64," she recalls. "He was so excited. He would sit there in front of that green screen. He didn't have a lot of formal education, but his mind is so mechanically and technically sharp. He built and rebuilt all his cars, all his computers. He's really a genius with that stuff."

Brownhill's mother, with whom she lived after her parents separated, provided stability and fostered her daughter's education in a turbulent neighborhood. "We were surrounded inside by books, but there were riots right down the street. There was a house nearby that sold crack [cocaine]. I was terrified and felt totally unsafe. I would never walk around my neighborhood at night." And yet, thanks to her mother's commitment to education, "I put my uniform on each day and went off to Catholic school. It was never questioned if I was going to graduate from high school and attend college."

Brownhill believes that "this very complicated childhood gave me some of the strength and the ability to internalize many different worlds and perspectives." It is a special talent that would come to serve her well throughout her life.

As a student, she loved math and art but struggled with reading. It wasn't until college that Brownhill was diagnosed with dyslexia. "I always felt like I had weights on my back," she says. Because of these struggles, however, there were moments when she was able, as she describes it, to "rewire" her brain out of necessity. Around the time she got her driver's license, for example, she remembers visiting the library in nearby Waterford. Describing a moment of epiphany there, she says, "They had this oversized book section with all these art books. I opened one up and lost my mind. I remember looking around the library wanting someone to witness: 'Did you know these were here? This is so amazing! Did you know these were here?' I was so excited."

Later, in college, Brownhill visited the Metropolitan Museum of Art for the first time and, she says, "The same thing happened. I was standing in front of the art in those oversized books. I couldn't believe that I had classes where I had to go to the museum and look at the artwork and say what I thought about it." She explains that it was not the art *per se* that sparked her interest, but the creativity it represented. "It encourages me to think about all the possibilities and then try to construct and reconstruct them into reality. That's so much of what artists think and do. Anybody doing their job at a high level is doing that." These moments of "rewiring," a function of dyslexia, curiosity, surprise, and motivation, have helped her to see, Brownhill says, "patterns in things, a framework for organizing stuff."

Her high school guidance counselor recognized her talent for math and art and suggested she look at architecture. It was an inspired choice. "My mom got really excited about the idea. I had no clue what architecture was," she laughs, "and we had no money saved for college. But my mom found Cooper Union, and it was free," a legacy of Peter Cooper. His idea of a free, nonsectarian institute offering practical education to adults in New York opened in 1859. Brownhill poured her heart into the school's take-home admissions test, "which was like a puzzle that really played to my curiosity—all theoretical problems that you answered with art projects. I didn't have stellar grades or SATs. I just think my enthusiasm for that home test must have really come through. Thank God," she concludes, "because tuition was completely free, I got a bunch of Pell Grants, and my mom took out some loans so that I could live in New York City."

Brownhill's story is marked throughout by a sense of gratitude. "I think about my parents and how lucky I am to get all of the breaks that they did not get," she says. "And Peter Cooper probably didn't have me in mind when he set up the school [in 1859], but I am so thankful. Getting in was so exciting, like somebody had cracked my head open. I couldn't sleep."

SITTING IN A STEEL TUBE

For the first few months at Cooper Union, Brownhill believed that there must have been a mistake and she would be dragged out of school. The work was hard, but she persevered. "I got a great education in architecture," she says, graduating with her bachelor's degree in 2000. "My instructor, Elizabeth O'Donnell, offered me a job, my first office job. I worked for her for the last two years of school." From 1998 to 2001, Brownhill served as project manager for Elizabeth O'Donnell Architect, a boutique design practice focused on high-end projects in New York City. "I graduated on a Monday and started full time on Tuesday. It was so incredibly fortunate for me. It was a small office. I got a ton of exposure to business. I was doing everything."

Then came the terrorist attack on 9/11. "It really freaked me out, which is the understatement of my life. It was another moment when my brain rewired," Brownhill recalls. "I was coming across the Manhattan Bridge on the train, and we could see the first building on fire. Then we watched the second plane hit. And we just sat there on the bridge. Someone had a beeper. They said, 'I think it's a terrorist attack.' And I'm sitting in a steel tube that I can't get out of, on a bridge. It was so frightening." At a loss for what to do, Brownhill went through the motions of going to work, sitting at her desk, and then having the surreal experience of walking home over the bridge, alongside people covered in ash.

"Over the course of the next few months," she says, "I started thinking to myself, 'Oh my God, you just spent five years of your life completely focused on learning how to build buildings. You have no idea why anybody would want to take them down. You have no idea the kind of economics or political conditions that brought this attack about.' And so, I decided that I needed to understand about money and power." This quest would mean reading every book she could find about money, trying to understand economic and social drivers. It was a self-education that would eventually lead her away from a traditional career path in architecture.

From 2001 to 2004, Brownhill served as a senior designer with Andrew Pollock Architect, a high-end residential design firm specializing in single-family residences in New York City and the Hamptons. In 2004 she joined Coach Inc., a company specializing in handbags and luxury accessories, as senior manager of global architecture. "I specifically wanted to work in a company that wasn't just an architecture company. I wanted to have a broader, more global perspective of the world. I had been so focused. I wanted to break out," she says. "With architects, we all know the same twenty books. We all know the same hundred buildings. I wanted to be with people who had different educations, different everything."

Shortly after joining Coach, she decided that the work flow in her department could be improved. "And remember," she explains, "I wanted to understand how the rest of the company worked. I pitched my boss about building a website for the architecture and construction group to help us be more efficient. I really had no idea what that meant. 'You know—a website! Everyone's doing it. Cool!'" Brownhill was sent by her boss to speak with the COO of Coach, who embraced the idea. The company sent her to school for certification in information architecture. "I designed the platform, got all the stakeholders, became the system owner. I had no clue what I was doing, but I figured it out." It was wildly successful—so successful that Brownhill won the Chairman's Award in 2005.

The next year, as part of her ongoing self-education in economics, Brownhill read Roger Lowenstein's *Buffett: The Making of an American Capitalist.* "I was so inspired by Warren Buffett and the example he set that I wrote him a letter," she says. "When I got a response from him, that was the next moment my brain rewired again. Impossible things might be possible. This incredibly important person wrote me back." She adds, "The letter back from Warren Buffett was the moment that ignited the belief in my entrepreneurial vision, that I could shape my own life. It all clicked in."

THE LAUNCH OF SWEETEN

Brownhill left her job at Coach in 2008. "I did an exercise when I was there and thought, 'OK, everybody talks about climbing the corporate ladder. Where are you climbing to?' And I realized I didn't want any of the jobs at the top." She adored Coach, which had strong management and leadership training. "It was the best environment of that type for me," she says, but it was no longer right. "When I left Coach, it was because I finally realized it was time to start my own thing."

Brownhill dabbled in launching a company, unsure of what it might be. She had an interest in the impact of the Web on her field of architecture. One night in 2010 she was asked to give a talk outlining her thoughts. "The Web has destroyed other hierarchical creative enterprises like journalism and music," she recalls saying. "At some point the Internet will come for architecture. I care about architecture, I care about our built environment, and I want people who also care about these things to be the 'architects' of the actual platforms that are going to be on the Internet."

When the lecture ended, Brownhill headed for home. "This woman whom I had never met before caught me in the subway, and she said, 'The Loeb Fellowship at Harvard is incredible, and I want to nominate you for it—I think you'd be great.'" Brownhill's angel that evening was Reese Fayde, an expert in urban planning and affordable housing, and CEO of Living Cities, a fund that invests in distressed urban neighborhoods. Fayde was African-American, a Loeb Fellow, and a powerful role model for Brownhill.

In 2011, Brownhill was named one of nine recipients of the prestigious Loeb Fellowship from Harvard University's Graduate School of Design. It was a gift from her second departed industrialist, John Loeb, former head of the Wall Street firm of Loeb, Rhoades & Company (a predecessor of Shearson Lehman/American Express) and a benefactor of

Harvard. Brownhill was given the opportunity to engage for a year with other accomplished practitioners to find positive ways to influence the built and natural environments.

The move to Cambridge meant a busy schedule of classes, but it was there that her start-up, Sweeten, came to life. "I was at Harvard, I had this Warren Buffett letter wind at my back, and I'd tried starting other companies." But Brownhill seemed to drift continually back to her roots in architecture and construction. "How could I use the Internet to serve a customer who was more like me?" she says. "I had done a lot of high-end residential work—a house in the Hamptons and fancy apartments in New York—but this type of retail customer wasn't a customer I wanted to serve."

In remembering this time, she says, "The idea for Sweeten began in 2007. I had bought a house in Bedford-Stuyvesant, Brooklyn. I had hired a general contractor." Yet, even though she was a trained architect with a background in construction, "it was really crazy, hard, scary, and so much money." She began thinking about how to use the Internet to make construction more accessible to more people. "I'm sure a lot of the housing inequities that I saw in New London affected this goal," she says.

In June 2011, Brownhill founded Sweeten, a technology platform that solves the problem she had faced: helping homeowners with renovation needs find the best general contractors for their projects. The name for the free service was inspired by "home, sweet home," meaning that renovation helps to "sweeten" a home. "We have a list of carefully vetted general contractors. Once we match a homeowner to one of these contractors, we stay with the project all the way to the end." It's the mix of the high-tech digital world and the high-touch personal that Brownhill was seeking. And when it launched, she says, "It worked immediately. Its value proposition to contractors and homeowners was really clear."

Brownhill has used Sweeten to create a true sense of community. "Some of our general contractors have been with me for years, since day one. We go to their Christmas parties. We know their families. Most of them are first- or second-generation immigrants," she explains. "With homeowners, we have a different relationship, but it is just as meaningful. I'm going to the housewarming party of a woman on the Upper West Side whose apartment flooded a year ago in August. We did her gut renovation, and now I'm going to her party. It is absolutely a community."

Brownhill's reading in economics encouraged her to look at markets from a technical perspective. "But I had this breakthrough and realized that it's all based on *trust*. Any of the ways in which we exchange value over time are all just trust. What I saw in the construction industry," she says, "is that there are lots of technical problems, but at its core, neither side trusted each other. All the technical tools existed already, but we needed to establish that trust."

Sweeten has raised nearly $20 million and has more than $1 billion of construction in the pipeline. The company now serves homeowners and business owners in the New York City and Philadelphia areas and is expanding to more cities. "We have helped thousands of people create a space that they love," Brownhill says.

She is one of the few African-American female entrepreneurs in the US to raise more than $1 million in venture capital and has been named "The Contractor Whisperer" by *New York Magazine*. In 2018 she was awarded a Henry Crown Fellowship from the Aspen Institute, a program intended to inspire and equip the next generation of community-spirited leaders to meet the challenges of the twenty-first century. It is a treasured gift, Brownhill says, from the third industrialist whose legacy has changed the course of her life.

BACK AT THE BAR

"It doesn't seem so terrifying when your smart 'magic' helps people like that," one of the older entrepreneurs decided, thinking about the Luddites who smashed textile machinery in England to protect their jobs. "I suppose in my day we had the same fears about machines taking over the world," he added, "and I *did* read *Frankenstein*, back in 1818!"

"You have your *Frankenstein*," a younger voice answered, "but we have our *Terminator*, *Blade Runner*, and *Ex Machina*. All pretty scary. And truthfully, we're all still trying to make sense of the opportunities and implications ourselves. Nobody really knows what a digital world looks like."

"Buzzwords like mobile, digital, social, and data barely existed ten years ago." Brent Grinna, the CEO of EverTrue, rose from his barstool, adding, "The technology landscape has radically evolved." Just as Brenna Berman had applied these new digital tools to the urban landscape and Jean Brownhill to the construction industry, Grinna had found the opportunity to disrupt and improve a profession responsible for raising billions of dollars annually. And while his tools are modern, his community is traditional; not unlike Eli Whitney and Yale, Grinna's alma maters are at the center of his extensive network.

"Last call!" a weary but still cheerful waiter announced. Hands went up across the barroom. Maybe, more than one entrepreneur thought, he could nurse this final drink and wring a few more stories out of the evening before having to call it a night.

Chapter 19

BRENT GRINNA: QUIETLY BUILDING AN AMAZING NETWORK

L
ike most start-up entrepreneurs, Brent Grinna (b. 1981) often needs to sell himself first before he's able to pitch his company. And he's good at it, because he's authentic and because his personal story fits well with his business model. Grinna's company, EverTrue, named after the Brown University fight song "Ever True to Brown," delivers the tools of mobility and digital engagement to higher-education institutions responsible for raising $50 billion annually from their alumni.

Brown and the Harvard Business School are Grinna's alma maters, both essential to his professional network. But he has a gift for building community that sometimes feels like luck—yet is anything but.

FROM FARM TO IVY LEAGUE

"I grew up in northeast Iowa," Grinna says, on the same 160-acre farm where his father was raised. Neither of his parents had attended college, but they were determined that Brent and his two younger brothers would be given that advantage. Grinna was a good student and a good athlete, becoming captain and helping lead his high school football team to the state playoffs. This success attracted the interest of colleges.

"I remember when I first got the call from the football coach at Brown University. I didn't know there was a Brown University." Grinna laughs. Dartmouth, Cornell, and Princeton were also interested. "I didn't know anyone who'd even applied to any of those places," he recalls. Intrigued by the opportunity, though, Grinna hopped a plane with his father and headed for the East Coast.

When Brent and his father sat down with Coach Phil Estes, who had just led Brown to its first Ivy League championship in more than twenty years, Coach Estes shared that he had been born in Cedar Rapids, Iowa. "Honestly," Grinna says, "I felt like I really connected with him." Not long after, Brent was reporting for his freshman season in Providence, Rhode Island.

One attraction of Brown was the school's open curriculum, which gave Grinna the opportunity to study several foreign languages. "My town in Iowa, Postville, had experienced a tremendous amount of immigration. We had a group of Hasidic Jews from Brooklyn and beyond who had bought a defunct meatpacking plant when I was in middle school and ended up creating the largest kosher meatpacking plant in the country. I don't think I probably knew what kosher meat was, growing up, but what I did know is that we had kids showing up to school from Eastern Europe, Central America, and Mexico. And we ended up being one of the fastest-growing towns in Iowa in the '90s."

Grinna embraced this experience. "When a new classmate showed up from Russia and couldn't speak any English, I wanted to be his first friend. I also ended up spending a tremendous amount of time in the Mexican community, in part through my church, and was able to develop pretty strong Spanish-language skills. And all of that was shaping my interests in academic pursuits at Brown."

At six feet two inches and 240 pounds, Grinna felt good about his chances on the football field—until he discovered he was one of eight fullbacks vying for the position, including two others in his class who were also six feet two and 240. Grinna persevered, however, making the travel team his first year, starting as a junior, and being selected one of the team's captains his senior year. "We had a lot of people quit the team," Grinna remembers, "but I was never going to do that. And I was not the star player. I was really trying to show great work ethic and dedication. I was pretty intimidated early on, being from a small town in Iowa . . . but you quickly realized that football is a good equalizer. You work hard and don't quit."

While Grinna was succeeding on the field, he was also building his first important network. "Training camp was tough, but I got to meet a great group of guys, people from all over the country. By the time school started, I had a hundred people I already knew, and I had a network of people I could turn to." This network would begin to pay off for Grinna in his junior year as he worked his way through language classes in Spanish, Italian, and Portuguese, and began to focus on a career in international relations.

FROM IVY TO PRIVATE EQUITY

"The football program had a mentoring program to pair up players with alumni to help navigate the career-search process," Grinna explains. "One night my junior year I attended a player-alumni event, and I met a guy named Jon Skinner [Brown '90], an investment banker in Boston. I gave him my background, and for whatever reason, we just connected."

Grinna interned that summer with another former Brown football player at a commercial real estate firm. But he stayed in touch with Skinner, who encouraged him to consider investment banking. "I had not taken a finance class. I was not particularly good at math," Grinna admits. But Skinner was persistent and went out of his way to help, recognizing Grinna's work ethic, leadership abilities, and intelligence. And the Brown football community was at work.

"Jon introduced me to another former Brown football player, Mike Glascott [Brown '93], who was at William Blair & Company in Chicago."

Grinna visited Chicago and felt an immediate Midwest connection. He liked William Blair, and they liked him, so after graduation he moved to Chicago. "I didn't know anybody and didn't really know what investment banking was. Two weeks later I'm on a flight to help with this underwriting for a follow-on offering for a medical device company in Century City, Los Angeles—and I didn't know what any of that meant," Grinna recalls, with a smile. But his office mate was a finance whiz who took Grinna under his wing. Grinna enjoyed the work, and in his second year joined the mergers and acquisitions group.

New in town, Grinna attended a meeting of the Brown Club of Chicago, told everyone there how much he loved Brown, and left the meeting as the organization's young alumni coordinator. "I went back to Brown and asked if they could get me a list of the people who were in Chicago," he says. "They sent me a PDF, and I just started emailing people, inviting them to lunch or to get together at an event. It was just amazing the responses I got."

Brent became a vice president in the club and initiated more industry-oriented programming. He contacted the heads of William Blair and Madison Dearborn—both Brown grads—and put together programming. "In doing all that volunteer work, I was kind of quietly building this amazing network. So, when it came time to explore my next opportunity after William Blair, I reached out to Sam Mencoff (Brown '78, HBS '81) at Madison Dearborn [a marquee private equity firm]. We had lunch; he asked me some tough questions and then invited me in to interview. I ultimately got an offer [for a two-year position] from Madison Dearborn, and it wasn't because I was better at Excel than the other kids they were interviewing," Grinna says. "It came largely from my network and leading with my own goal of trying to help out."

Grinna's two-year stint (2006–2008) at the giant Chicago private equity firm was scheduled to end in July, just as the subprime mortgage crisis grew and a few months before Lehman Brothers declared bankruptcy. "I decided to throw my hat in the ring for business school applications. I still had this really deep passion for global business, relationships, and languages." One application went to Harvard, who liked what they saw. In the summer of 2008, Grinna married his high school sweetheart, Katie, and together, they headed for Boston.

"CAN YOU DO THIS? SURE WE CAN"

At Harvard, Grinna again sought out the right mentor. In this case, he met Professor Michael Chu (HBS '76), a partner in a venture capital fund in Monterrey, Mexico. Chu also led a program called "Business at the Base of the Pyramid," focused on the billions of people who live on tiny or no incomes but, combined, represent a massive market opportunity. "If you design businesses around that, like microfinance," Grinna says, "you can lift people up from poverty and create good businesses. So, I was fired up about that."

Chu sent Grinna off to work for the venture fund in Monterrey during the summer between his first and second year of business school. "I spent time with a farmer who was trying to create an organic produce business. It was an example where I really got into a business, and I really got to know the entrepreneur." It was another of what might be seen now as tipping points for Grinna, where he thought, *Maybe I can do that someday*. "And I knew that that was way more exciting to me than being the person selling the business or running the numbers," he adds. "I wanted to be the person leading the business."

As Grinna became more focused on international business and began to think about possibilities as an entrepreneur, his fifth reunion from Brown rolled around. The school asked if he would be willing to lead the gift campaign effort for his class. He agreed, but he remembers it as a challenging process.

"I was given a spreadsheet of inaccurate information about my class-mates. This was a time when the financial crisis was in full swing, so people are switching jobs, they're moving—there's just a lot of activity. And it's clear that there's this huge disconnect between who these people were in real life and who Brown thought they were in its database. This was also a time when the iPhone had just been released, Facebook was maturing, LinkedIn was growing very, very quickly—and those same people in that spreadsheet, who were my classmates, were increasingly sharing their information on social platforms rather than feeling compelled to let the school know every time they switched jobs."

Grinna sensed a seismic shift, where schools that had once facilitated alumni relationships were now seeing that activity shift to social platforms. And he concluded that there was a lack of innovation in the underlying software systems used not just at Brown but in educational development departments in general.

"Brown had ninety thousand alumni that were really, in a certain sense, 'leads,'" he explains. "It's a sales and marketing business that has a set of leads that it needs to nurture over the next fifty, sixty, and seventy years after graduation. They've got to segment that population, they've got to create experiences along that journey, and hopefully alumni will feel enough of a connection that they will support Brown consistently throughout." Grinna saw that university development professionals were not taking advantage of digital tools. "When I looked at innovation happening at companies like Facebook, Zillow, and LinkedIn, there was a disconnect."

So Grinna set about mocking up concepts, all while getting through his second year of business school and pursuing investor career opportunities in Brazil or Mexico. In December 2009, partnering with a friend, Grinna visited Brown and presented his vision of what mobile technology and social media could do if integrated with Brown's existing alumni operations. "Todd Andrews [Brown '83] was the VP of the alumni association at the time. I didn't know him at all at the time, but he was willing to take a meeting, and I took him through this presentation," recalls Grinna. This meeting was Grinna's Eli Whitney–musket moment. So when Andrews asked, "Can you do this?" Grinna answered, "Sure we can do it."

"The mock-up was very rough," he admits. "It was wireframes and some basic designs. But it was also clear that people like Todd weren't being presented with a lot of new, innovative ideas trying to harness these trends. So Todd said, 'If you can build a basic application, we will pilot it. How much do you need? Come back to me with a proposal.' We were just making it up, but we settled on a price and milestones, with a checkpoint in February of 2010. We hired some contract developers. We moved toward launch in May, which was exactly aligned with my graduation from Harvard."

With Brown's interest, Grinna shared his idea with a friend involved with the Virginia Military Institute. VMI signed up. Grinna thought, "Wait a second, now we've got two customers. We didn't really have a product, but we had two customers. So I decided to enter the business plan contest in April [2010] while I'm continuing to pursue full-time job opportunities." Grinna had one foot in a start-up and another in a traditional finance career. That's when things got interesting.

ACCESSING THE ECOSYSTEM

"At the Harvard Business School New Venture Competition," Grinna continues, "I shared the key stats with the judges—partners from Google Ventures, Highland Capital, Polaris Partners, and all these fancy venture capital firms. I said, 'Look, $50 billion is raised every year by higher-ed institutions. They're doing it with out-of-date spreadsheets and legacy database technologies. There's a huge opportunity to harness social and mobile trends to better streamline those efforts. And I've got Brown University as my first customer and the Virginia Military Institute as my second, and here's my sales pipeline.'"

Grinna had few expectations, but one of the judges expressed interest in investing in the company. "I thought—invest? On the basis of the PowerPoint presentation I just did? I'm used to the private equity world and doing discounted cash flows over five years and ten years of history, and I do this five-minute presentation and this guy says he'd invest! That's crazy." Grinna went on to make the semifinals and, feeling the idea was at least partially validated, got more energized about building a business.

"Remember the backdrop," Grinna says. "While I'm in business school, the financial crisis is happening. We're on the sidelines watching, hanging out—and it just felt like the opportunity cost to do something like this was lower than it had ever been, given all of the turmoil in a traditional private equity or investment banking career path." Grinna's classmates who had taken jobs at Lehman Brothers and at Bear Stearns had seen those companies collapse. "And there were other firms where offers were being rescinded. You've got consulting firms saying, 'Hey, take a year off *before* you come back.' That had just never happened before. And I think it just caused people to explore new directions."

For talented individuals like Grinna, a down economy made entrepreneurship more attractive.

"We bought a domain [Web IP address] and had a friend help us with initial designs, and we established a basic marketing website. And then I graduated in May 2010. My wife and I were in Boston. We had probably not ever planned on living in Boston, but I wanted to stay and keep pursuing the opportunity."

"WHAT'S YOUR STORY?"

At this point Grinna had an idea, a mock-up, interest, an apartment, and a skeptical but supportive wife. That's when he heard about an event called the Venture Summit East, a very large gathering of leading venture capitalists and entrepreneurs. "I'm living across the Charles River at the time," he says, "and I see that the ticket is going to be $2,000 to go to that event. There's no way I'm paying $2,000, but I reach out to the organizer, explain my situation—I'm an aspiring entrepreneur, just graduated from Harvard, I'm living right across the river—and asked if he needed any volunteers. He said sure, come work the registration desk."

By helping with registration, Grinna could attend some of the sessions and the luncheon presentation. He found as he handed out name tags that he knew almost nobody except for local venture capitalist Jeff Bussgang (HBS '95) from Flybridge Capital Partners. "He'd been an entrepreneur-in-residence at Harvard Business School during my time there, and I'd been bouncing ideas off him along the way. So I see Jeff at lunch and I go and sit down. And Jeff says, 'Brent, I'm so glad that you're here. I've got to introduce you to these guys. This is Walt Doyle; he's got a very cool company called WHERE doing some interesting work around mobile. You guys should definitely meet. I want you to hear his story and tell him your story. And I want you to meet Scott here, as well.'"

Grinna explains, "Walt is this super-high-energy guy, and he says, 'Tell me about what you're doing! What's your story?' I start telling him about the Brown experience and the reunion, and he says, 'I totally get it. I'm really involved with Middlesex, which is where I went to high school. I see the challenges. Where are you working out of?' I tell him my apartment in Cambridge (and my wife is questioning that!)—but that's where I am." Doyle tells Grinna that he's just moved into new space and invites him to visit.

As Grinna and Doyle are talking, Brent notices that Scott is taking notes. Grinna decides, "That's probably OK; we're at a conference, and I guess you take notes. So I shoot these guys thank-you emails that night, and Scott writes back with this whole set of questions. It seemed cool he was so interested in my business, so I replied with all these answers. I wake up the next day, and I find out that Scott [Kirsner] is the technology reporter for *The Boston Globe*. And he writes an article, 'New Start-up EverTrue Revolutionizing Alumni Development.' And he has all these quotes. I don't think I even knew he was a reporter—and I'm so oblivious I'm confirming comments and quotes in an email exchange. So this article hits," Grinna adds. "It's got screen shots, it's got my story, and all of a sudden, all day, I'm getting emails from people wanting jobs—my inbox is flooded. EverTrue is not a real company, but now *The Boston Globe* thinks it's a real company. So, it's a real company."

JUMPING ON THE FAST TRACK

From there, Grinna's community fully engaged. Walt Doyle would become yet another high-profile mentor, offering him space in his office. Doyle was running a hot company that had just raised money. "Every day these

VCs would come in and they'd be hearing Walt's story and his update, and then Walt would say, 'But you've got to meet Brent next door!' So now I'm meeting all these VCs in town, and I'm not running to them; they're coming to me because I'm sitting next to Walt."

The venture capitalists Grinna met were consistent in their feedback. They loved his passion and story but said he needed a cofounder, a technologist who could build the things Grinna could only envision. It was a classic chicken and egg: "I can't get a cofounder because I don't have any money, but I can't get any money because I don't have a cofounder." And that's when the larger entrepreneurial ecosystem kicked in.

Grinna attended a meet-up at a pub in Cambridge. "It was an iOS developer meet-up, so I stood up and gave my elevator pitch, and this guy came up to me and said, 'Hey, I went to Harvard, graduated in 1996. I totally get the pain you're trying to address. I'm a developer, but I'm busy working on a project right now, but I want you to meet my friend Erik Carlstrom.' So he introduces me to this guy on the other side of the room who was working as a director of product, was an engineer, had gone to the Rochester Institute of Technology, was the president of the Boston University entrepreneurship program and was getting his MBA there—and we kind of hit it off."

Grinna and Carlstrom spent the next month getting to know each other and visiting customers before negotiating their partnership. Then the two applied to Techstars, a leading accelerator. "And for the first time," Grinna says, "when we went into that pitch, people weren't concerned about my lack of a cofounder. At the same time, people like Walt Doyle and Jeff Bussgang supported our application to Techstars, calling the director and saying, 'You've got to let these guys in.' And they did. That was just a big moment. It was hard to get into, lots and lots of applications. Only ten or eleven accepted. We started there in March of 2011."

Grinna and Carlstrom built their prototype, signed another ten or twenty schools, and brought it all to five hundred investors at Techstars' Demo Day. "We ended up raising a million dollars that summer [2011]," Grinna says, "and that was really when things got going. We went from three or four people to a core team of eleven or twelve people, continued to do sales, building the product and creating an assembly line that is a company. We split roles as we went. We weren't burning a lot of money, but it became clear that we should be talking with investors about something bigger." A meeting with Bain Capital Ventures led to a $5 million investment in March 2013.

"This investment allowed us to take things to the next level," Grinna says. "We've created a solution that is so far from our first version, with a vision to introduce a new approach to CRM [customer relationship management] for higher education fund-raising, and perhaps the philanthropic world more broadly." In 2014, EverTrue raised another $8 million. Grinna assembled a strong team with experience at companies such as Brightcove, Microsoft, and HubSpot.

EverTrue soon counted more than three hundred educational institutions relying on its data insights to help generate billions of dollars in giving. "When you look at the same trends that are impacting the real estate world, and companies like Zillow and Redfin have invented that category—we want to be the Zillow of fund-raising. We think we can be that company. We're using the same kind of technology for mission-critical work that's happening at schools around the world."

"If it weren't for Brown's financial aid and donor contributions, I wouldn't be where I am now," Grinna says. "And there's nothing I'd rather be doing. It's just such a great intersection of exciting technology and a mission."

BACK AT THE BAR

Some of the younger entrepreneurs were trying to explain Microsoft, Zillow, and Redfin to their older friends, though the going was slow. The idea that language and concepts could be turned into "ones and zeros" and then manipulated across vast distances to create new products and services—even build community, as Brenna Berman, Jean Brownhill, and

Brent Grinna had done—was still a mystifying concept to the very oldest entrepreneurs.

One younger guest was using the telegraph as an analogy to explain digitization, all while hoping that one of the upcoming stories did not involve 3D printing or cryptocurrencies—in which case he might give up and just order another beer.

"How about using the digital tools of 'social and mobile' to build a community of runners?" The voice came from a small group seated near the Budweiser sign.

"Runners? What do you mean, runners?" Ames, Whitney, Downing, Grimes, and Forten all had turned, with quizzical looks on their faces. Digitization was difficult enough for some of the them to grasp—but were there really *people who ran on purpose? For fun!*

Chapter 20

JASON JACOBS:
A CHEERLEADER FOR COMMUNITY

I t took Jason Jacobs (b. 1976) more than twenty years to discover his inspiration and another ten to make it real. It was a kind of entrepreneurial marathon, often grueling, but in the process, he created an online running community with which he could share his inspiration with athletes around the world.

"I didn't grow up with a lot of entrepreneurial influences," Jacobs says, "and I was a mediocre high school student. But my standardized test scores were good, and I ended up going to a good college, Wesleyan." It wasn't a lack of motivation, he says, "but I was passionless. It wasn't really until I graduated in 1998 that I discovered business, which I'd always associated with someplace you go to die. I just didn't have a lot of those role models who were pursuing things they were passionate about."

After a brief stint as a recruiter placing engineers in high-growth start-ups, Jacobs joined Storage Networks in 1999. "I wanted to be part of the dot-com wave," he says, and he was able to ride the company as it grew from 180 to more than six hundred employees and a public offering. "Even though I was in human resources, which isn't always thought of or treated as the most strategic function—though it should be!—it was great. I could spend time with all the VPs across all the different business units, getting walked through their strategy. I really got to see a lot, at age twenty-three or twenty-four, across many functions."

After helping to build the company's sales organization, Jacobs fought his way into an inside sales position. "Sales had the bias that HR wasn't aggressive enough, but I came to them wild-eyed and was just relentless. It seemed to me that sales and recruiting had all of the same skill sets, but sales was far more lucrative." Jacobs had also caught a case of the entrepreneurial bug. "I knew by then that entrepreneurship was what I wanted, so my move to sales was about personal growth. At the time," he says, "the sales path was a common path to CEO."

A DETOUR TO BUSINESS SCHOOL

Unfortunately, the bubble that lifted Storage Networks burst in the dot-com crash of 2000. Jacobs was caught in the first layoff, with management ultimately electing to liquidate the company. "I was totally freaked out," he says.

Jacobs jumped to a small, e-learning software company as a sales rep, but that organization was acquired two months later by Skillsoft, a big, publicly traded e-learning company. "This was good," Jacobs says, "in the sense that I became an add-on to that company's sales force, and they were selling to about 80 percent of the Fortune 1000. It was not an overly stressful job, and it wasn't that hard to be effective. I was all about growth, and I wanted to be drinking from a fire hose, but after awhile I just felt kind of stale."

By then, Jacobs had already begun to envision his own entrepreneurial future. Sales didn't seem exactly right. "I'd looked at the people already established in sales, and some of the better ones were making upward of $800,000 a year. But it seemed like they were only using one side of their brain, and it seemed boring." With the digital economy continuing to crater, he took the GMATs and applied to business school, electing to attend Babson College in Massachusetts.

"At Babson, I was also a mediocre student but better." Jacobs laughs.

"And relative to where I'd been working, many of the people at Babson aspired to be entrepreneurs." Jacobs earned his MBA in 2005 and took a position with a company with which he had interned in his second year, but that company was already struggling. And that's when he really started to get frustrated.

JUMP OFF A CLIFF

"I needed to start a company, but I didn't have a team of people, and my skill set was incomplete. I thought, 'Where can I park for a few years and watch a bunch of different companies get built, while I'm figuring out what I want to do?'" That's when Jacobs discovered "headhunting for CEOs of venture-backed companies, which meant working with the boards of these start-up companies and getting a behind-the-scenes look." It was an opportunity for Jacobs to build his network and expand his community. "I thought I'd do that for three to five years and find something entrepreneurial."

Jacobs joined a search firm, learned the ropes, and was working toward taking more of the lead on searches, but he wasn't happy. "They were good people, but I was miserable, meeting with all these entrepreneurs and thinking, 'They're not smarter than I am. But they did it, and I'm just wishing I did.'"

A colleague of Jacobs's had issued a challenge, saying, "'If you want to do it so badly, go do it.' I was just turning thirty, and all I could think was: *I gotta go*. It's not *if*, it's *when*." Jacobs found himself sitting in coffee shops nights and weekends, trying to figure out his future but not getting anywhere. His next insight on community building was pivotal: "In hindsight," he says, "it's clear that my creative process is a social process, and if I don't put myself out where I can talk to people, I'm not going to make it very far."

He began laying the groundwork to make his next leap, paring down personal expenses and squirreling away a couple of years of income. "My plan was to take a jump off the cliff and start building a parachute on the way down," Jacobs says. "But I still didn't know doing *what*. So I was working all the time, and working at night and on the weekends to figure this out, and I was driving myself crazy. It was consuming me. I was going to internally combust."

To clear his head and maybe jog his creativity, Jacobs decided to train for his first marathon.

"THIS WAS MY EPIPHANY"

Jacobs had run a 5K race and had also completed a couple of half marathons. A longtime hockey player and fitness nut, he enjoyed running. So, he signed up for his first marathon and found an eighteen-week training program online. "I took it really seriously, and I was getting to know the tools that were out there—like Nike+. At a certain point in my training," Jacobs says, "my two worlds collided. I thought the Nike tool was pretty cool, but it wasn't just about data—there was this whole experience layer to help motivate people. Those who need the help most are not the super athletes, but just regular people. And there was nothing for them until Nike+."

When Jacobs investigated, he found that nobody else was doing anything like Nike. "The competitors out there weren't very good. There weren't many, and they were loaded with ads, but their growth metrics weren't very good." He imagined a product similar to Nike+ but focused in an open way across all the new sensors and mobility tools in the market. "That got me excited." For the first time, Jacobs had a way to apply his entrepreneurial longing to something that inspired him.

"That was my epiphany," he says. "I had never pursued any of a zillion ideas I had had to date because I always focused on areas that I knew instead of areas I was passionate about. Fitness is a huge part of my life. It's embedded in who I am. Now, I'm thinking: I can build a big fitness and health company, and I have two or three years to figure out what that company is going to do. I have a starting point. And even if I fail, I'll be a failed entrepreneur, and I'll have learned more in those two or three years than I would have in any other pursuit."

Jacobs began growing his community by attending hackathons and start-up meet-ups, and by talking with runners, coaches, and the big fitness brands. All the while, he was refining the idea, creating something that he liked and that he could sell to others.

LAUNCHING THE RUNKEEPER COMMUNITY

In May 2008, Jacobs began working full time on Runkeeper. "I set out to build a platform that would integrate with existing running and fitness devices," he said, but he soon came to realize that the founding of Runkeeper would coincide with one of the great innovations of the twenty-first century. "I discovered this little two-person software shop that was looking to move from desktop applications and build its first iPhone app—and it had an Apple developer license, and Apple had only authorized ten thousand of them in the world. I hadn't thought about building an iPhone app, but it made so much sense. I ran with my iPod already. And, it wasn't announced yet, but of course all these smartphones were going to have GPS. And devices would keep getting smaller and be easier to run with. It felt like the beginning of a good cycle."

Jacobs and Runkeeper had, coincidentally, arrived at the dawn of the smartphone era. "We started building the app before the Apple App Store was launched," Jacobs says. "I started working with three moonlighters to help build the Web platform. Within a few weeks of quitting my job, I had five people I could meet with every week. It felt like a team."

When Runkeeper was launched in August 2008, it became one of the first two hundred apps in the App Store. "In a few months we sold more than $50,000 worth of apps, and that began to accelerate. We added two more moonlighters, and in June of 2009 the first person from the moonlighting group came in as a cofounder. Within a few more months, two more moonlighters followed. In November we raised the first $400,000." Eighteen months after launch, Jacobs had a hot product, an operating team, and a handful of accomplished angel investors funding and mentoring the company.

"Early on," Jacobs says, "it became clear that there was a community forming. Runners wanted to know that they weren't on an island, that they were part of this greater ecosystem. They wanted to be able to interact with each other and get encouragement." In fact, running was experiencing its own rapid ascent in the United States, with nearly eleven million runners crossing a finish line in 2008, up from just five million in 1990. Jacobs had apparently caught not one but two tigers by the tail.

"A strong community formed around the Runkeeper product," Jacobs says. "We were accessible and supportive, and we highlighted stories of people overcoming adversity." The sweet spot for the product was "people just trying to get off the couch and stay off the couch." As the app and its fans evolved, Runkeeper posted "community-fueled" motivational playlists from Spotify, fitness advice, running-product suggestions, group-run opportunities, fitness safety, and other messages designed to motivate and bind the Runkeeper community.

Eventually, Runkeeper would drop its "hyper-fit dude icon" because half of its new users were women. "As we grew," Jacobs says, "we cultivated our voice as a supportive, collaborative, approachable brand that helps people of all fitness levels get out and experience the magic of running."

From the start, Jacobs was lead cheerleader for this community. "The fact that I was the only full-timer at first, and I don't write code, and I needed something to do—I ended up just immersing myself in the community. It was very personal in the beginning, especially with the most enthusiastic runners. Nobody was writing in to customer support; they were writing in to 'Jason.' We had a support forum that I was very active in. I started blogging," he says. "And we started seeing runners talking about us on Twitter, so we were one of the first corporate brands to set up a Twitter account—not just to push press releases out, but actually engaging like a human."

Runkeeper's business model, combining running with an iPhone app to build a viral community, required no marketing dollars to acquire new customers, and still saw its growth accelerate. Apple ran full-page ads in the backs of major newspapers, a picture of an iPhone with apps, "and we were one of the apps on the screen, with a paragraph saying what we do. *The New York Times*; *The Wall Street Journal*; *The Boston Globe*. Old-fashioned word-of-mouth was strong," Jacobs says, "but so was the new kind that came from social sharing."

THROUGH THE STORM: THE HEALTH GRAPH

Runkeeper's first three years were a success. It was a media darling with six million users across iOS, expanding to Android and Windows platforms. It was focused exclusively on runners and their needs. The company had raised $400,000 as a rainy-day fund but never touched it. Then, with inexpensive capital available, it raised another $1.1 million reserve—but hadn't used that, either.

By 2011, the venture capital world had emerged from the Great Recession of 2008 and markets were frenzied. The entrepreneurial ecosystem had also become infatuated with scale and pedigree. "The tech media really cared about sizes of [funding] rounds," Jacobs says, "and who they were from. If you wanted to get the credibility and the megaphone of the media—when it came to things like hiring the best people or getting strategic partners interested—there was no better way to do it than to raise a big round. Whoever raised the biggest round was perceived as winning."

It was silly, he acknowledges in hindsight, but that was the nature of the entrepreneurial ecosystem in 2011. "If you could create a lot of froth and heat and start running down a path before the world really knew if you had figured it out or not," Jacobs says, "you could get scooped up for a ridiculous multiple." And Runkeeper was one of the hottest companies in its market segment. "We thought we could raise a big round and cement our position as the king."

Such a plan required a big idea, and in 2011, Runkeeper launched the Health Graph. It was a strategic direction that would nearly sink the company. "Imagine a system that can identify correlations between a user's eating habits, workout schedule, social interactions, and more," Jacobs announced, "to deliver an ecosystem of health and fitness apps, websites, and sensor devices that really work, based on a user's own historical health and fitness data. The Health Graph has the potential to completely alter the health and fitness landscape."

This was Runkeeper's big vision, not unlike Facebook's Social Graph, and it was consistent with Jacobs's goal to "build the biggest, most impactful thing I possibly could. I was prepared to shoot for the moon. But," he admits, "we didn't have a clear vision of what we were building."

Runkeeper's Health Graph began by integrating third-party devices, such as sleep monitors and Fitbits. It seemed an impressive idea; there were so many health and fitness devices coming to market, and nobody was emerging as a hub. Google Health had just shut down, Microsoft HealthVault was struggling, and bottom-up, direct-to-consumer relationships were the future. "There was a moment in time when nobody owned this space," Jacobs says, "and here we were with the biggest audience. We had momentum and a passionate community. Why not us?"

When Jacobs went out to raise his big round, however, there was pushback. "How big could running really be?" investors asked. He was determined to prove the doubters wrong. "If you take some narcissistic twenty-something with a megaphone, all hopped up on energy drinks, with a big audience, and the press talking about him all day long," Jacobs says, smiling, "in this emergent field that nobody knows anything about, but everyone thinks is the next big wave, and he just lays it out there with fervor—in that moment of heat maybe you can make a lot of things happen that couldn't otherwise. So, with fourteen employees, we raised $10 million from new investors Spark Capital and Steve Case's Revolution Ventures—with participation from existing investors—on this big health vision."

Behind the scenes, however, operations were wobbly. The company had essentially stopped working on its mobile app, focusing instead on a new Web interface to help third parties integrate with the Health Graph. And while the tech press ate up each new integration partner, Runkeeper's running community felt abandoned. "We went from being customer-obsessed to being customer-allergic," Jacobs says. Meanwhile, new, higher-quality, laser-focused competitors had entered their space.

The original Runkeeper management team was also having trouble scaling to the new vision. When Jacobs's partner exited the business, Runkeeper had a gaping hole in its management structure. "I had been the storyteller and done hiring, strategic partnerships, customer development, rallying the community, and vision—but my partner ran the product road map. Over the next year or two we grew to fifty-one people. We hired all of these individual contributors, and somebody needed to keep all of the trains running on time, and we didn't have anyone who had done this before," Jacobs says. "It had to be me, which was bad for two reasons. I was terrible at it. And I wasn't doing any of the things I was good at, which was our secret sauce in the early days."

SCALING BACK TO WIN

By July 2013, Runkeeper had 19 million users, and by July 2014, some 30 million. But success continued to mask performance issues. Jacobs says, "We were burning a lot of money because we thought we had to become this health app, and we were executing in an uninspired way on the running app with no clear vision—so we were doing everything in an uninspired way. Our revenue was great for a ten-person company but small for a fifty-person company. We still looked like a running app. So, when it came time to raise a growth round—what story are we telling?

"In a year," he adds, "we had gone from a $6 million valuation to a $40 million valuation, and we weren't going to get a step-up with a running story, and we couldn't really tell a health story. This was the time we needed the $25 million round at the $100 million valuation."

Jacobs found that raising this new round was impossible, and he was having second thoughts as well. "I was bone tired. The landscape was getting more competitive." A Runkeeper competitor had just been acquired. And most of all, the company felt misaligned. "So I went to the board and said I think we should prepare the company for sale. It might not be ideal, but we were six months from being out of cash." Runkeeper investors agreed, but as they investigated more closely, they collectively determined the market conditions weren't right to do so. They instead put together an inside round to support Jacobs's plan to scale the vision back and focus again on a runner-centric business model.

"I hired a real VP of marketing and a key number two as COO—so while I was talking about vision, he was talking about cash flows and profits. With this new leadership, we were able to rebuild as a smaller but profitable company." Runkeeper cut some eighteen people in the summer of 2015, returning to breakeven and moving from less than a year of cash to "years of runway." Jacobs says of this retrenchment, "We were leaner, back to our scrappy roots. It was like our arteries were unclogged. We were nimble again, moving faster, getting more done, putting soul and personality into what we were doing."

In March 2016, ASICS Corporation acquired Runkeeper, a sprint across the finish line for management and a win for investors. The experience hasn't changed Jacobs's enthusiasm, however. "Even with a win under my belt, I'm not any less ambitious." Jacobs has also learned an important entrepreneurial lesson: to be aware of his own talents—what he's really good at and what gets him motivated in the morning. "I don't apply myself to things I don't feel passionate about," he says. "And I don't lack for aptitude or confidence, but I know my strengths and weaknesses. I'm not a framework and structure guy. I don't feel like I'm very analytical. But when it comes to writing, storytelling, speaking, hiring, big vision, creativity—I can be just relentless," he laughs. "Everyone's got their stuff; they just need to be self-aware, find things that make good use of those skills, and put the right people around them."

BACK AT THE BAR

While digitization remained a fuzzy concept to many of the barroom's older entrepreneurs, it seemed obvious—from smart cities and home construction to fund-raising and now sports—that there was no product, no service, no business model that it could not improve in some way.

"It's like mechanization was, in my time," Eli Whitney explained. "Everything we mechanized got better—so we mechanized everything! It practically ate the world," he chuckled.

"And much of the investment in finding better ways to mechanize came from the federal government," Oliver Ames added, "which took a risk on Mr. Whitney's musket contracts and funded the new tools my brother and others developed at the Springfield Armory."

Whitney agreed. "Without the government shouldering so much risk, I'm not sure how successful we would have been." He paused. "As our beloved Constitution says, Washington must 'provide for the common defense.' And come to think of it," he turned to Ames, "it's hard to find five words that have created more innovation than those."

Which turned out to be the perfect introduction to the next story.

Chapter 21

GUY FILIPPELLI:
FROM BATTLEFIELD
TO CYBERSECURITY

D igitization has several children, but none more important than Big Data, a concept that emerged in the early twenty-first century to describe the flood of digital information being generated by sensors and Internet-connected devices. Big Data is growing so quickly, Lt. Gen. David A. Deptula of the United States Air Force mused in 2010, that the world will eventually be "swimming in sensors and drowning in data." By 2020 the number of Internet-connected devices in the world could exceed 24 billion.

This tsunami of information has focused government and industry on machine learning, another offspring of digitization, one that enables systems to automatically improve from experience without being explicitly programmed. Machine learning offers the ability to find patterns in large data sets that yield new, sometimes unexpected insights.

The United States military was among the first to see the advantages of Big Data. Guy Filippelli (b. 1975) was an early leader in these efforts, first through his career in the military, and now in commercial entrepreneurship.

JUST A PLAN THAT WENT AWRY

"I was born in Cleveland, Ohio, in a little neighborhood on the west side," Filippelli begins. "My family included mechanics, barbers, truck drivers—but nobody was entrepreneurial." Guy's father, the first person in his family to attend college, worked at Conrail. "My father was an incredible builder of things, incredible with his hands. He could draw, paint, work in cement, construct buildings. Saturdays were spent going to lumber and hardware stores. It was project after project," Filippelli says, "and I *hated it*. I was always the kid holding the flashlight. My father started to realize this when I was about eleven years old, and he was at a bit of a loss. I was a smart kid, very mathematical, so what was he going to do with me?"

It was 1986, and Filippelli's parents were raising three kids. "My dad probably made forty thousand dollars that year, and he bought me a computer. He spent more than two thousand for an Epson for his eleven-year-old son. It was an amazing thing," Filippelli says. "And I became obsessed with this computer and began to write software. For the next six years, through high school, I became, for a kid, a very good programmer."

When Filippelli was fourteen, he tried his hand at some early hacking on "those old modems and bulletin boards" and ended up with a thousand-dollar phone bill. "It was just a plan that went awry," he laughs. Less amused, his father got his son a job stocking shelves and busing tables. "And that started to instill a lot of discipline in me," Filippelli says. "I also began making some money licensing this BBS [bulletin board system] software I'd taken over. I was sixteen years old, probably spending twenty or more hours a week writing software, with checks coming to my house for fifty dollars and a hundred dollars per week. We'd moved to Detroit, I had a car, and I was taking my girlfriend out to these nice restaurants."

Filippelli did well in school, aced his college boards, and began receiving letters from colleges. Most of these recruitment pitches ended up in a pile. But when one arrived from West Point, Filippelli found his father "beaming about it." Guy recalls, "The school was giving a talk at the Ford auditorium on Friday, and my dad offered to take off work and go down with me if I was interested. So we went, and I don't think I've ever seen my dad more excited in my life, and he looked at me and said, 'Boy, this place is for you, buddy.' And that was it. That's where I was going to go to school because I knew that was important to him, and I trusted him."

At the time, Filippelli was certain that he would be walking away from software programming. "What were the odds that I'd get out of the army in a decade and get into computer software?" Nevertheless, he matriculated at West Point and committed to four years of college and six as an officer. "That's just the way it was going to be," he thought. Filippelli received his BS in economics in 1997 and did well enough to earn a Marshall Scholarship. He studied at Oxford University for two years, 1997 to 1999, receiving his master's in politics, philosophy, and economics (PPE). At the same time, he began his service to the army.

THEN CAME 9/11

"I was in Germany," Filippelli says, "a young army intelligence officer. My job was less like the CIA and more like a financial analyst on Wall Street. The job was to aggregate and present information to my boss, give him the tools he needed to make decisions." That might mean terrain, weather, or order-of-battle analysis. "We were trying to understand the strength of the enemy force in an area and how we could counter them," Filippelli adds. "We had a whole suite of software and computer systems to help us do those things."

Then came 9/11, and the US entered Afghanistan. "We were suddenly going into a fight that looked a whole lot more like a counterdrug fight," Filippelli says. "There were no tanks, no antiaircraft systems. There were a bunch of dudes living in houses and caves. We had zero tools to counter that."

In response, the head of army intelligence decided to rebuild the entire set of software tools used to fight these battles. A message came down seeking military intelligence officers with any kind of background in software. All of that early programming and that first Epson computer in 1986 was about to pay off. "I remember thinking that maybe I have the background," Filippelli says. "So, I volunteered, and sure enough, I fit the profile. Around November 2001, I started running a team of software engineers in Germany as part of this major effort to build a whole new set of software tools. At twenty-six years old, this is my new job. I'm what you might call a product manager of a software suite."

For the next five years, Filippelli ran teams of software engineers "doing all sorts of cool stuff—building new interfaces for teams to report data into, building geospatial visualizations, a whole bunch of different things." In his book *The Finish,* author Mark Bowden describes one of those tools in a visit Filippelli was asked to make to a walled-off facility in Afghanistan. It was a place used to hold and interrogate war prisoners.

Filippelli had built a database for detainees and had also mapped the facility's population by tribal affiliation, background, kinship, and other factors. Putting a detainee in the wrong place, for instance, with a group from his own village, meant that his comrades would rapidly coach him. Filippelli could show how those poorly placed were significantly less useful afterward in interrogation.

Filippelli was a software guy speaking with soldiers "whose adrenaline rush came from . . . free-falling from high altitudes or getting shot at." But he was respectful, and he knew to be efficient. He explained how simply holding a detainee in the right part of the prison could have a meaningful impact on the quality of information gathered. Then he closed his computer screen and got ready to go, wondering if his visit had been worthwhile. "Wait," the men protested, "tell us a little more about this." Filippelli's work with the task force grew in the kinds of applications he and his team created.

Meanwhile, Filippelli was soaking up lessons in management and team building. "My work force was 95 percent government contractors, which is a pretty simple software staffing model. I started forming opinions of how I might run one of these contracting businesses," Filippelli says. "I sensed when quality was inconsistent or leadership was lacking. I began to understand how the government bought things and some of the gaps in the process."

Toward the end of his hitch in the army, Filippelli found himself commanding an intelligence detachment in Italy. He was thirty-one and knew he had to get serious about planning his future. "I lived in a northern Italian town called Vincenza, about thirty minutes outside of Venice in an industrial, very entrepreneurial part of Italy. I met a guy who ran an amazing advertising agency, and the guys who sold all the ovens to McDonalds, and guys who ran prefabricated construction plants. My best friend was a Persian-Italian whose family distributed gold in Italy, Dubai, and France. Just amazing," Filippelli says. "I got a taste of that world and how successful people could be, and it was very inspiring to me. I started to think about how I could play in this world. My first thought was to figure out how I could stay in Europe and do something entrepreneurial."

Still enlisted, Filippelli got back in touch with one of his best friends at West Point, Nick Hallam, who was planning his postmilitary career in Washington, DC. The two tried putting together a deal between an Italian architect and an Afghani construction company. The experience turned out to be more educational than lucrative. In the middle of negotiations, Filippelli was deployed to Afghanistan to lead an intelligence production organization. But he'd found his partner. "Nick and I realized that we were very good working together," Filippelli says, "even when there were only little windows of communications available. We just had something very special—complete trust in each other, maybe given where we'd come from. But we could spend ten seconds on the phone together and accomplish something. And we generally agreed on how we would do things. We had different perspectives, but we were very aligned as a team."

When Filippelli returned from Afghanistan, where he was awarded the Bronze Star, his former boss had become director of the National Security Agency (NSA). "Nick and I were still thinking about doing something internationally," Filippelli says, "but I got put on a project at NSA, and it was the most exciting thing I'd ever worked on in my life—trying to figure out how to track the massive amount of data we were collecting about people all over the country in Iraq and subsequently Afghanistan. How do you leverage all the real-time data you're collecting?"

For Filippelli, who was serving as special assistant to the director of the NSA, it was a dream project. "But it was only a short-term tour, and I was getting out of the army—my time is up, I'm done. And they said, 'Maybe you could do some consulting.'"

BERICO LAUNCHES

In September 2006, civilians Filippelli and Hallam founded Berico Technologies in Arlington, Virginia, to serve the defense and intelligence sectors. Within a month, Filippelli was back in Baghdad writing code, and shortly after that he had assembled a small team to work with him. Within five years, Berico had eighty employees and was named a finalist in the Northern Virginia Technology Council's Hot Ticket Awards.

"We probably built four software platforms that made massively significant impacts on the battlefield," Filippelli says of his work at Berico. The first one he led resulted in Filippelli receiving the National Intelligence Medallion, the highest award given to nongovernment personnel in support of the US intelligence community. "The software that we designed in Afghanistan compressed the amount of time it took people to make decisions about who to target and who to detain—reduced some of these time cycles from days to seconds."

NSA Deputy Director Rick Ledgett described these "big data" software programs as having the ability to integrate "hundreds of pieces of information," drawing connections, and then creating graphical displays so that analysts could make rapid decisions. Filippelli and his team were building tools that brigade commanders had never had before, providing capabilities that allowed them to "get in front of our adversaries" and reduce the casualties caused by ambushes and improvised explosive devices.

Filippelli's skills are partly technical. "I like to reinvent the entire system," he says, "part of which is the data; part of it's how we figure out how to get the data into the system; part of it's the user interface; part of it's how we change the incentives of the user to interact with this thing. I innovate at the system level." But Filippelli is also focused on the softer side of leadership, especially team building. "Every single company I've been actively a part of—everyone who worked there will tell you it was the greatest group of people they've ever worked with. You can do something with that, the ability to form great teams."

While the Great Recession of 2008 brought the American economy to a near halt, defense funding was untouched. "The 2008 financial meltdown had zero impact. The military—my market—was totally shielded from that."

In 2011, CEO Filippelli formed OxPoint Holdings. "We decided to split Berico into four pieces and sell off two of the pieces. That was a life-changing set of events for us. We had to negotiate and restructure and set up boards. And we started to do a little investing in some early-stage companies, and in some funds, and that's when we turned over the reins of Berico to a new team," Filippelli says. "Nick and I have been fifty/fifty ever since the beginning. And we brought his brother Matt on the team, so it's the three of us."

Despite a wealth of military- and defense-oriented work, Filippelli says, "The one thing I'd never done is run a product company and never taken any venture capital, and I was drawn to that. I was about to get married. I decided to move and do something new—scratch an itch and create new value."

Filippelli's idea for his next business came as a result of a large internal investigation Berico had been forced to conduct. "We had a couple of people in the company nearly get into some trouble—there was potential misconduct. I had to bring in a law firm and do discovery. And I realized, in a 130-person company, the lawyers are charging me a gazillion bucks to look through all my data." Filippelli realized that he had always prided himself on being a data-and-analytics guy, but when it came to the information-analytics of his own people, there was a critical gap. "I could walk out onto the floor and see all these people working really hard," he says, "and they could be doing bad things. So, I started thinking hard about cybersecurity and risk—and just what corporations face. I took the perspective of internal cybersecurity. I wondered, 'What if we could build a more responsible way to monitor for potentially high-risk employee activity?' And that," he says about the resulting business model, "was the nexus for thinking about RedOwl."

REDOWL AND BEYOND

In April 2012, Filippelli and his partners founded RedOwl Analytics, a cloud-based behavioral analytics software company that specializes—just as Filippelli did in Afghanistan—in bringing together disparate streams of data within an organization to mitigate risk. But this time the task was not about soldiers, but corporations. "I wanted to move out of DC to a new city," Filippelli says. "I'd always thought DC was antithetical to a true software start-up; the culture was government contract-y. I moved to Baltimore, which was only an hour away but felt grittier. We pooled our money from one of our sales, and we launched RedOwl. I didn't know exactly what I was getting myself into," he confesses. "I knew I had to raise a couple of million dollars. And then learn to build, fund, run, and eventually sell a commercial software company—which was hard, but super interesting, and I loved every second of it."

RedOwl raised $30 million in venture capital and saw demand for its services jump when whistleblower Edward Snowden leaked NSA internal documents in 2013. The company captured the Most Innovative Company award at the 2014 RSA Conference, a major information security conference. And in August 2017, global cybersecurity company Forcepoint announced its acquisition of RedOwl.

Filippelli retains his partnership with the Hallams. "Nick and Matt were originally on my board. We are all still equal partners in all this stuff; we got a check for RedOwl and split it three ways. I've been with Nick for eleven years, and we've never, ever gotten into an argument. There's just nobody that I respect and trust more."

How have the partners worked so well together? "When we were growing Berico Technologies, both Nick and I were running a hundred miles an hour, working eighteen hours a day. But the interesting thing was, if I had an hour free and Nick had an hour free, I would call somebody into my office and drill them on something technical. What are we doing? How's this project going? If Nick had an hour free, he'd start calling people in the company and ask about their families. Nobody ever doubted that we cared," Filippelli says, "but we cared in very different ways about people. Nick was just happy with a different part of the limelight; he liked dealing with the lawyers, bankers, and real estate people. And I liked growing the business side. And we just fundamentally trusted each other."

Filippelli is midway through his career. "The military gave me tools to do some of the things I'm doing now, but delayed some lessons," he says. "The last ten years have been amazing. And now I feel like, for the first time in my life, I have a base. Forget about whether we've made any money. The real value-creation phase of my life starts now. Just now do I have the team, confidence, internal judgment, and experience. I've never been more excited about the future because I know things now.

"I'm very much midstream," he reflects. "The next twenty years are going to be constructed with extreme deliberation and execution. And it's going to be done with a great team."

BACK AT THE BAR

"It's interesting," Alfred Sloan was saying to the small group gathered around him by the door, "that we've been talking all night about the importance of building community, but for someone like Mr. Filippelli, the army provided 'instant' community." Sloan cleared his throat. "It's the way I always felt at General Motors. When a young engineer joined our organization, he had access to our expertise, R&D labs, and test track. It was 'instant community.' And after the 1920s, it was nearly impossible to start an automobile company without huge amounts of capital and technical resources—so big companies were the only way to go."

One of the younger entrepreneurs standing nearby responded. "That debate still goes on, Mr. Sloan. Today, we often need lots of capital and people to innovate a 'big idea,' which can give large companies an edge. But large companies can be so caught up in their own success that they aren't able to innovate. Corporate culture is just as important as capital and resources. At least in that way, start-ups have the edge."

The barroom bouncer was edging over toward Sloan and his friends. This was a debate he found especially intriguing.

"Maybe," another entrepreneur wondered aloud, "the point is that success comes from accessing community effectively—whether it's the army, a large company like GM, or the entrepreneurial ecosystem."

"With all of the talented people in this tavern," Sloan said, looking around, "maybe there's another story that can explain how this works."

Chapter 22

MEGHAN WINEGRAD: INTRAPRENEUR TO ENTREPRENEUR

When economist (and bouncer) Joseph Schumpeter defined "entrepreneur" in 1911, he concluded that the ideal was an *individual* who "seeks out difficulties, changes in order to change, [and] delights in ventures." Thirty years later, with massive corporations dominating the business world, Schumpeter discarded his youthful notion of the daring solo entrepreneur to conclude that "the large-scale establishment" was the most effective innovator. Global brand and distribution, manufacturing muscle, and the R&D resources of corporations—in a world transformed by mass production and consumerism— were essential, the economist believed, to undertake creative destruction on the scale necessary to have genuine economic impact.

What is now called the *Schumpeterian hypothesis* says two things: Big firms have more incentive to spend on innovation than small firms because they can sell more rapidly to more people, and big firms have more market power and can more readily defend their innovations.

Neither of Schumpeter's theories, from 1911 or 1942, is fully satisfying. Despite advantages in size and brand, for example, large firms can be so fearful of disrupting their own successful business models that they avoid innovating. Likewise, established public companies need to be predictable to their shareholders, and disruptive innovation is anything but predictable. This encourages organizations to place many bets and quickly walk away from those that seem too small, erratic, or risky. Sometimes, too, large firms are happy to let smaller firms innovate risky ideas, confident that those start-ups can be acquired when the idea is proven.

In short, the giant organization is an enigma when it comes to entrepreneurship, having the resources to innovate but sometimes lacking the will. The *Harvard Business Review* may have captured the essence of this paradox when it published "Why Big Companies Can't Innovate" in 2012, followed four years later by the equally convincing article, "Stop Saying Big Companies Can't Innovate." 3M is used to prove that large companies can; Kodak to prove that large companies cannot. Apple, first as a start-up and later as a technology giant, can be used to support either side of the argument.

Pitting start-up entrepreneurship against big-company "intrapreneurship" may be the wrong debate, however. Innovation is successful when delivered as part of a compelling business model, and when its sponsoring entrepreneurs have the support of a robust community. These qualities can be found in start-up ecosystems, but they also exist in large, well-run organizations. The story of Meghan O'Meara Winegrad (b. 1978) is one good example.

GENERAL MILLS:
BECOMING AN INTRAPRENEUR

Graduating from Duke University in 2000 with concentrations in political science and Spanish, Winegrad concluded that a career in business made sense. "I come from several generations of entrepreneurs," she says, though she also admits that she wasn't quite ready to launch a business. "It's fair to say entrepreneurship was a lifelong dream, but I felt more comfortable getting some formal experience before taking that plunge."

Over the next four years, Winegrad held positions at two global public relations agencies, where she had the opportunity to work with clients doing business in beauty, health care, aviation, and government. Eventually, Winegrad says, "I wanted to have my clients' jobs. I wanted to be able to make the decisions." With that in mind, she and her fiancé returned to Winegrad's hometown of St. Louis to earn their MBAs at Washington University, graduating in 2006.

In the spring of that year, fate intervened. "I happened to be at a recruiting conference, and I agreed to meet with General Mills, the giant consumer foods company. It was a safety interview, a warm-up for interviews in the beauty and fashion industry, where I thought I wanted to be. General Mills knows that now." She laughs. "I popped in, really liked the people that I met, and not long after found myself visiting the company in their hometown of Minneapolis, a city which just surprised every ounce of me."

Headquarters to seventeen Fortune 500 companies, including UnitedHealth Group, Target, Best Buy, 3M, U.S. Bancorp, and SuperValu, "Minneapolis has an incredibly thriving ecosystem of really smart, really innovative people," Winegrad says. "There are lots of alumni who come out of those giant companies who are a great inspiration. These are people formally trained through intensive, rotational programs who then use those skills to form their own companies."

Minneapolis was only part of the pleasant surprise for Winegrad, however, who joined General Mills in June 2006. "What really struck me about the company was its progressive nature. Quite honestly, that wasn't expected." With $11 billion in 2006 revenue, twenty-eight thousand employees, and operations in more than one hundred countries, General Mills had roots that reached back before the Civil War. The firm was the steward of revered brands, including Cheerios, Pillsbury, and Betty Crocker. "I didn't think that General Mills and the word *innovative* could really go together," Winegrad says, "and there's probably a lot of people who don't think that a company that's so large and been around for so long could be on the leading edge of things." In 2006, however, General Mills had invested $178 million in research and development, and that commitment was just the tip of what Winegrad would find to be a culture designed to nurture innovation.

"Joining General Mills was the first time I could use the word *intra-preneur* in a legitimate way," Winegrad explains. She found the company's focus on developing world-class marketers to be determined and comprehensive. "We had First Thursdays, for example, a monthly gathering where the company brought together innovators across industries—authors, experts, and anybody who they believed could instill some great, outside-of-the-box, non-industry thinking. There might be an expert on teams," she recalls, "an expert on kids, or someone who was watching up-and-coming trends." Winegrad compared this to a "high-energy school" that constantly challenged managers to apply new concepts to existing brands.

New marketers at General Mills spent about eighteen months in any given job rotation before moving on, a way to cross-pollinate people and ideas and build community. "You might do a rotation focused on a particular customer, like Target, and you would try to figure out what types of things General Mills could be doing to help move the dial for their particular business. How can I bring them insights," Winegrad recalls, "or how can we evolve new products? How can we unlock explosive growth at a place like Target by bringing things that nobody else has?"

A marketing rotation might also focus on a traditional brand, such as Fruit Roll-Ups. No matter how established the product, marketers were responsible for bringing fresh ideas and new growth. "That doesn't mean just launching another flavor or form of essentially the same product," Winegrad explains. "You can't just bring Mini Fruit Roll-Ups, and then Berry Blast. You've got to identify the dial-moving things that will keep the snacks portfolio afloat long term. In my days," she adds, "it was all about reduced sugar. Now it's about real ingredients, putting 'real food' back into packaged goods." In traditional marketing terms, Winegrad was saying, flavor and line extensions were welcome at General Mills, but brand extensions were essential to growth and part of every intrapreneur's job.

One of Winegrad's projects involved Hamburger Helper, a Betty Crocker packaged good introduced in 1971 that included pasta and seasonings designed to help consumers stretch a pound of hamburger into a meal for five. Invented for convenience and to meet the rising price of meat, Hamburger Helper was listed by the Food Network as one of the top five food trends of the 1970s. By 2007, with more than forty Helper flavors, the brand still commanded some 61 percent of sales of dinner mixes in the US. However, as a new generation of consumers moved away from packaged goods to fresh, natural, and microwaveable options, traditional packaged brands needed to take steps to remain attractive and relevant.

In 2009, Winegrad and her colleagues put together an improbable partnership—a true "novel combination" in Schumpeterian terms—between Hamburger Helper and singer Beyoncé to support the hunger relief organization Feeding America in delivering more than 3.5 million meals to local food banks. Professor and author Mara Einstein, while understandably skeptical of Beyoncé preparing Hamburger Helper and concerned that such partnerships can shift attention from causes to celebrities and corporate interests, understood the value to General Mills. The company, she wrote, hopes "to increase its significance for a younger, hipper audience. By requiring consumers to input special codes to generate a donation to Feeding America, the brand company also captures personal data about consumers." General Mills and its product also generated free publicity and an aura of goodwill in a demographic that might have previously overlooked the entire brand category.

Another way in which the company supports intrapreneurship, Winegrad says, is a more formal innovation job. "That's when you have to figure out how to extend brands into particular spaces, or acquire brands through merger and acquisition activity, or develop new brands to fill white space [unmet market opportunities]." Whether embedded inside a division or as part of a specialized group like the "Innovation Squad" or the "New Ventures" team, the General Mills innovation teams shared many features of a traditional start-up, especially the need to identify a compelling idea. Unlike a start-up, however, these groups had ready access to funding, research, production expertise, distribution channels, and global reach—instant community. "We're talking about a big company with big resources," Winegrad adds, "that was progressive in all 360 degrees of how they do business."

BUILDING A ROCKET SHIP

Fiber One bars are one example of innovative product development at General Mills that leveraged established resources. "It was one of those magical accidents," explains Winegrad, who was working in the company's snack unit at the time. Fiber One cereal had been something of a sensation when it debuted in July 1985, but by 2006 the product was floundering. "It was perceived as your grandmother's cereal and was doing almost nothing. But there was data coming in that talked about the growing importance of fiber in the American diet. The part of our team that worked on brand extensions developed a snack bar that could deliver a high amount of fiber intake. So," Winegrad says, "Fiber One bars positioned themselves as a convenient and delicious way to get your fiber. In a world where the only convenient options to get fiber at that point was Metamucil—kind of disgusting—Fiber One was able to extend its equity into snack bars. Consumers really responded, and the product became a rocket ship."

Fiber One bars was one of just three products featured on the cover of General Mills' 2008 annual report. The product's success was highlighted in the chairman's letter to shareholders.

This story illustrates the art and science of intrapreneurship in a giant corporation. In the case of Fiber One bars, it was General Mills' marketers who had access to rich data sets and were able to sense a change in perception among consumers. "By latching on to a trend and existing equity and using their automatic distribution, big brands can go from zero to hero overnight," Winegrad says. "Speed to market, shelf space, and giant resources to scale very quickly are the big wins for corporate America. If you wanted to launch a start-up fiber bar, you would not have a brand, credibility with retailers, or selling and distribution, and you'd run into all kinds of production problems. In the meantime, General Mills would blow by you."

Despite these advantages, intrapreneurs in large corporations face their own set of obstacles. "Big companies cannot easily build businesses from scratch. When you talk about entrepreneurship in its purest sense, it's really, really hard," Winegrad says. One issue is scale. A large company such as General Mills can identify an almost endless number of opportunities, but for one to have impact on revenue, profits, or share price, it must be able to scale substantially. For some large companies, that means a new product must have the potential of reaching one billion dollars in revenue before the firm is willing to invest the first dollar in research or development.

That threshold leaves countless interesting and still sizable opportunities for start-ups, many of whom would be delighted to build a hundred-million-dollar business. "When a giant corporation sees a new trend in the market but no existing equity to slap on it," Winegrad says, "it will just be a stumble every time. This problem is true in all the large companies where I've worked, and in the feedback I get from my colleagues."

This market dynamic suggests that most of the innovation coming from large companies will arise from leveraging existing brands, a kind of new combination with less risk and more immediate upside. The made-from-scratch product can always be acquired by a large organization once the start-up proves its market potential. Examples of this phenomenon include Facebook's acquisition of WhatsApp, Google's acquisitions of Android and YouTube, and General Mills' 2018 venture into pet food with the $8 billion acquisition of Blue Buffalo pet products.

SERIAL INTRAPRENEURSHIP

Winegrad was happy at General Mills, but circumstances changed when she gave birth to her first child. She and her husband elected to return to St. Louis to be closer to their extended family. She went to work as a merchandising director for a family-owned regional grocer, immersed in some of the tactical pressures of retail. She then moved to a second intrapreneurial position inside a large corporate environment, taking a position in product management with Express Scripts in 2013, a company seven times the size of General Mills.

With $100 billion in revenue and nearly thirty thousand employees worldwide, Express Scripts is the largest pharmacy benefits company in America, administering prescription drug programs for business and government. The company has grown both organically and through an aggressive program of acquisitions. "I worked in the innovation cell," Winegrad says, "where we had the freedom to do lots of great work on really cutting-edge things." Some of this work involved Big Data, using the wealth of information Express Scripts generated each day to create new services that could improve the lives of patients. Other initiatives involved more subtle innovations that, given the company's size, could still carry enormous impact.

"There was an operations project that laser-printed messages on the tops of pill bottles in our mail-order pharmacy," Winegrad says. "You could just add a message that said, 'No Refills Left—Call Your Doctor.' Our research proved that something as simple as printing that message on top of a pill bottle cap could have a measurable outcome on the health of patients. Other projects focused on combining high-tech products, like smart asthma inhalers or smart diabetes monitors, with specialist pharmacist interventions, looking at how we could improve patient outcomes and drive down the cost of care. It was something that only a company with massive scale could execute in a meaningful way."

The innovation group at Express Scripts was lean and effective, leveraging resources throughout the company. Much like General Mills, however, Winegrad found the same obstacle to innovation. "Anything that looks like a true start-up will have very little impact on the bottom line or share price," she says. "It's hard to measure and will never show up in the annual report. Everyone wrestles with this issue."

READY FOR START-UP

In March 2018, Winegrad took the leap from intrapreneurship to start-up, founding a company called Generopolis. Her vision, keying off a longtime interest in nonprofits, is to create an online marketplace where users can sell nearly anything, but instead of pocketing the proceeds, they select their favorite charity to receive the money. It's designed to appeal to millennials, who are, Winegrad says, "making 20 percent less than their parents. They are deeply connected to causes, though, and we've got to find a way that allows them to contribute."

What gives Winegrad an advantage over many recently graduated start-up entrepreneurs is classic training and deep skills as a marketer, along with nearly twenty years working as an intrapreneur launching innovations. Because of this, she brings a powerful network to her new challenge, one that will form the basis for the community she'll need to be successful.

BACK AT THE BAR

The waitstaff in the bar was ready to gently but firmly begin ushering the evening's patrons toward the exit. It had been a long night full of wonderful stories, and it was unclear if anyone would go home without a push.

"So, an 'intrapreneur,'" Oliver Ames said. "Maybe that's what I was at the Springfield Armory!" He chuckled. "That experience certainly introduced me to a lot of fine mechanics who were helpful later when I built my shovel business."

Willis Carrier pondered the community of engineers and sales executives at Buffalo Forge that had been transformed into the personal network he relied upon to launch his namesake air-conditioning business. Maybe he had been an intrapreneur before he became an entrepreneur, too.

"Sounds like the answer to Schumpeter's "paradox" about whether large companies or start-ups are better at innovation is—one of the young entrepreneurs paused: 'Yes!'" Even the bouncer smiled.

Seated near Carrier was Buddy Bolden, who had been quietly listening for most of the evening. "Sustainability. Digitization. Intrapreneurship. Ugh," Bolden said. "What ever happened to music? Food? Sports? What happened to the *social entrepreneurship* we talked about? Don't you ever *laissez les bons temps rouler* in the twenty-first century?" He laughed.

"I told my story about jazz. We've heard about Mr. Downing's oyster house and Mr. Rickey's professional baseball teams. Maybe there's one last story," Bolden pleaded with the other entrepreneurs in the barroom, "that's got a little music in it—and maybe a beat to boot?"

It was the perfect question because, it turns out, there was.

Conclusion

A MODEL FOR INNOVATION AND COMMUNITY: LIN-MANUEL MIRANDA AND *HAMILTON*

H*amilton* is an improbable stroke of musical genius that tells a rap-filled story of Founding Father Alexander Hamilton (1755–1804). The show arrived on Broadway in August 2015 with $32 million in advance sales. Scalpers commanded prices as high as $3,000 for a pair of tickets, topping off an average audience at 101.8 percent of capacity. Critics were effusive. One referred to the show as "the great work of art, so far, of the twenty-first century." The overnight review in *The New York Times* stated simply, "Yes, it really is that good." The following June, *Hamilton* received eleven Tony Awards.

If an entrepreneur is defined by the introduction of an innovation that disrupts an economic flow, then *Hamilton's* creator, Lin-Manuel Miranda (b. 1980), is a model success. Investors put up $12.5 million to produce the show, which is expected to gross $1 billion in less than a decade. By December 2017, investors had already earned returns exceeding 600 percent.

New sources of revenue extend far beyond Broadway. The musical's forty-six-track album was the highest-selling Broadway cast album of 2015 and reached No. 1 on Billboard's chart of rap albums. *Hamilton* is available to audiences in a variety of touring and international productions and has spawned a best-selling book about the show's creation. In 2019, a special, limited run of the production in Puerto Rico raised $14 million to revitalize the arts on an island still recovering from Hurricane Maria.

A CULTURAL PHENOMENON

Few people have the range of interests to appreciate all the historical and musical combinations found within the show. But few fail to understand instantly—as a story unfolds of the American Founding Fathers, played by people of color—that there is a "novel combination" happening onstage that is the very definition of innovation. Miranda neatly summarizes one defining theme: "Let's make the founders of our country look like what our country looks like now."

The Smithsonian Institution recognized the musical's unique contribution when it awarded its playwright a 2015 American Ingenuity Award alongside a planetary scientist and neurologists researching Alzheimer's. The MacArthur Foundation bestowed a "genius" grant on Miranda for "bringing the traditional Broadway musical into the 21st century with modern musical styles that reflect the diversity of contemporary America." The Rockefeller Foundation understood the special value of *Hamilton* when it financed an unprecedented program to bring twenty thousand New York City eleventh graders from low-income families to see the show.

And in April 2016, *Hamilton* won the Pulitzer Prize for Drama.

Ripples from the show reached the highest levels of government. President Barack Obama called the musical "brilliant" and immediately suggested his own secretary of the treasury attend. Failure to score a ticket in the competitive political worlds of New York and Washington was, one observer noted, like "the grown-up equivalent of sitting alone in the cafeteria." The Treasury Department felt the show's impact when a proposal to replace Alexander Hamilton on the ten-dollar bill was scrapped. And the global community was witness to the show's influence when America's ambassador to the United Nations invited the entire UN Security Council to a performance.

Hamilton was hailed as a unique lesson in American civics that upended traditional thinking. One fan of *Hamilton* enthused, "They should teach it like this in the schools."

Hamilton's journey from its source, historian Ron Chernow's 2004 biography of Alexander Hamilton, to a Broadway sensation, provides a textbook case in how entrepreneurs bring together novel combinations to change the present and invent the future. In some ways, the process that created *Hamilton* is easier to understand than technological innovations grounded in silicon and software code. The "things" that Miranda connected were bits and pieces of his and his audience's own experiences, along with rich veins of history, music, and theater—but combined in ways few could anticipate.

As social innovation, *Hamilton* embodies the kind of disruption narrative usually reserved for technological phenomena like the telegraph, electric grid, and iPhone: No amount of advance market research would have predicted its success, because few consumers were capable of imagining that such an innovation *could* exist.

HAMILTON: THE MAN

At the heart of *Hamilton* the musical lies Hamilton the man. As Chernow documents, Alexander Hamilton not only became the country's first secretary of the treasury, but he was a battlefield hero, congressman, abolitionist, founder of the Bank of New York, founder of the Coast Guard, member of the Constitutional Convention, lawyer, and patron saint of the *New York Evening Post*. Hamilton was instrumental in establishing the country's first political parties and was the lead player in America's first national sex scandal. He became a gunshot victim when the sitting vice president, Aaron Burr, fired on him at a dueling field in Weehawken, New Jersey.

Hamilton died before turning fifty years old, leaving his reputation to be defined by enemies that included some of the most influential and articulate politicians of the early republic, including Thomas Jefferson and John Adams. Chernow's work has helped to restore and burnish Hamilton's legacy.

Taking full measure of Hamilton's life, Chernow concluded that this man "made the greatest contribution of any immigrant in the history of the United States." This view became the launchpad for *Hamilton*'s dazzling opening number, which describes the future founding father as "a bastard, orphan, son of a whore and a Scotsman / dropped in the middle of a forgotten spot in the Caribbean." (That once-forgotten spot is the island of Nevis, today home to an active tourist trade and a five-star hotel.) Unlike Washington, Jefferson, Adams, and Madison, Alexander Hamilton arrived in America a penniless, low-born immigrant. His rise was as meteoric in political terms as immigrant Andrew Carnegie's business success was a century later.

Hamilton was driven and, it seems, simply more talented than those around him. At sixteen years old, he entered King's College, now Columbia, and by twenty, he was George Washington's top aide. When he married Elizabeth Schuyler in 1780, he also married into one of New York's most prominent families. Hamilton practiced law brilliantly, wrote two-thirds of the *Federalist Papers* (hoping to create a strong, central government, at odds with men like Jefferson), and at thirty-two years old, became the first secretary of the treasury, appointed by George Washington. "Hamilton was the supreme double threat among the founding fathers," Chernow wrote, "at once thinker and doer, sparkling theoretician and masterful executive."

Alexander Hamilton was possibly the only Founding Father who understood modern economics, and the only one of his peers who even sensed the Industrial Revolution engulfing the country. Hamilton's vision of what America could become led Chernow to describe him as "the messenger from a future that we now inhabit."

Hamilton the musical highlights its hero's growing stature but never loses sight of Hamilton the immigrant making his way in a nation of immigrants. From the days of George Washington to the time of Lin-Manuel Miranda's birth, whites of European descent never accounted for less than 80 percent of the US population. The year *Hamilton* opened on Broadway, that percentage had fallen below two-thirds. Demographers forecast that the white majority in America will vanish sometime around 2040. The show bears witness to this cultural transformation.

"By telling the story of the founding of the country through the eyes of a bastard, immigrant orphan, told entirely by people of color," the journalist Rebecca Mead noted, *Hamilton* "is saying, 'This is our country. We get to lay claim to it.'" Indeed, audiences erupt after a musical exchange between Hamilton and his soldier-friend Marquis de Lafayette when they announce together, "Immigrants / we get the job done!" This line so consistently drew applause that *Hamilton's* creators lengthened the pause before the scene continued.

LIN-MANUEL MIRANDA: THE ENTREPRENEUR

Lin-Manuel Miranda is the son of Puerto Rican immigrants, his mother a clinical psychologist and his father a political consultant. Miranda was raised in upper Manhattan, attended Hunter College High School, and participated in musical theater. "You're a Latino kid in a school that isn't Latino," he said. "You either try to blend in or you overcompensate." He was funny. He could sing a little. He could act a little. And, like Hamilton and Chernow before him, he could write a little.

Steve Jobs has observed that "creativity is just connecting things." This suggests that entrepreneurs with rich life experiences have a distinct advantage. The more time spent listening, observing, reading, experimenting, sharing, and *living*—the more "things" they ultimately have to connect, and the more opportunity they uncover.

So it was with Miranda. Raised in two cultures, he was introduced by his parents to two very different musical traditions. "I grew up in a house where cast albums were almost always playing . . . That was the music we played to clean up after parties. It was Latin music at the party, and we'd dance outside and we'd dance merengue, 'cause we're Puerto Rican, and then when we cleaned up the house after the party we'd put on the cast album—and that's what I keyed into."

His own tastes drew him to Gilbert and Sullivan, *West Side Story*, pop music, and rappers like the Notorious B.I.G. and Tupac Shakur. Daveed Diggs, who played the original role of Thomas Jefferson in *Hamilton*, said, "Lin exists at the intersection of a bunch of worlds that don't often intersect." If innovation is all about novel combinations, there is no better address for an entrepreneur.

By 2005, Miranda was a member of a hip-hop improvisation group popular for creating instant rap from words supplied by the audience. He was also working on a musical that would become *In the Heights*, a show set in his beloved Washington Heights. In the process, he had found his life's passion, though it wasn't always a comfortable passion.

> *I can't tell you how many friends I graduated with who were all going to conquer New York City. And it's not like a bad-guy ending; they found happiness somewhere else, they found stability somewhere else. While I was the roommate who stayed in the cheap rent place while other people got married, and other people moved out of town. So I understood that struggle. I understood the relationships ending because, "Well, I'm doing this. And if our relationship means you're not going to let me do this, then you gotta go. And I'm always going to choose this." And the price that comes with that.*

> *This single-minded focus paid off. In the Heights opened on Broadway in 2008 and won for Miranda, not yet thirty years old, the Tony Award for Best Musical.*

While readying for a vacation from performing in *Heights*, Miranda purchased Chernow's biography of Hamilton. As he read the opening chapters, Miranda began googling to see who had already set Hamilton's

colorful life to music. Surprising to him—but probably to no one else—
the coast was clear.

INNOVATION IN COMMUNITY

While the idea for setting the life of Hamilton to music might have struck
Miranda like lightning, it took six years of hard work and constant evolution for a final product to emerge. The source materials—Chernow's
eight-hundred-page opus and Hamilton's avalanche of papers—were
almost overwhelming. As Miranda wrestled with the project, he thought,
"I feel like a mosquito that hit an artery. There's so much here—how am
I going to get it all?"

The answer to that question, asked often by entrepreneurs who
uncover enormous opportunities, inevitably comes down to one simple
solution: *in community*. "The secret history of *Hamilton*," writes author
and producer Jeremy McCarter, "is that Lin's uniquely singlehanded
achievement (as composer, lyricist, librettist, and star) required the art-
istry of dozens of very gifted people to be realized. A bunch of people
from a bunch of backgrounds had to come together to make it work."
And in Miranda's case—as is so often true—the most effective innovation
community was one that already spoke the same language, had a shared
history of struggle and success, offered complementary strengths, and was
grounded in trust.

To begin, there was Tommy Kail, the director of *In the Heights*. A
Wesleyan alumnus like Miranda, Kail remembers, "I met Lin in May of
2002 and we basically never stopped talking. It's basically been a thirteen-year conversation." The alchemy between the two resides in the fact
that Kail provides structure around Miranda's creativity. Miranda says:

> *Tommy is someone who likes to come in and work no matter*
> *what the outside world wants of us. So, when In the Heights*
> *happened and we were both broke and had day jobs, he would*
> *say, "Well, bring in a song on Friday and we'll talk about it." He*

kind of created deadlines for me even when we had no appara-
tus, or even knowing if the show was going to be anything. And
it created somewhere for me to go, and something for me to do,
and something for me to work towards.

Kail sees the flip side of that coin, adding:

What Lin is able to do is take very complex ideas and—not
show you how smart he is, but—make them accessible to all
of us. One of the great gifts that he's given us with this show is
he doesn't stand up there and say, "Look where I am—you're
down there." He builds a ladder, and he says, "Come up here,
and be up here with me." And so my job was to help try to
architect that ladder, and get every single person who walks into
the Public Theater—and the Richard Rodgers on Broadway—to
participate and feel like it's also for them.

Kail's gifts are described as selflessness and having an ability to draw
out the best from every person in a production. "My job was not to have
the best idea in the room at any time but to identify the best idea," Kail
says. One proof of his impact on Miranda, and vice versa, is that the
shows each man has done separately is considered inferior to those on
which they have collaborated.

Another essential player in Miranda's innovation community is
Alex Lacamoire, an award-winning Cuban-American arranger, conductor, and musical director of *In the Heights*. Miranda says of Lacamoire, "[He] is Cuban, grew up in Miami, so he comes to all of the
Latin stuff really naturally. But he also associate-conducted *Wicked*.
He's got the Broadway and Latin chops in equal measure." Like Kail,
Lacamoire has a personal and professional connection with Miranda
that multiplies their capacity for entrepreneurial output. *Hamilton*'s
choreographer, Andy Blankenbuehler, describes the relationship
between the two by saying, "Lin will have an amazing inspiration and

put it forward in a way that you know exactly where he's driving. Alex will pave the street."

Jeff Seller is the lead producer of *Hamilton*. Seller's Broadway credentials are likewise impeccable, having coproduced *Rent*, *Avenue Q*, and *In the Heights*. His job involves overseeing the show's Broadway run while taking it worldwide, maximizing profits, and keeping everyone from the audience, investors, and the cast happy. Like Kail and Lacamoire, Seller was involved for five years in the development of *Hamilton*, working with Miranda and becoming an integral part of the larger creative team. At rehearsal, Kail said, Seller has "the intense focus of a twelve-year-old building with Legos."

Miranda bolstered this brilliant innovation community of ladders, paved streets, and Legos with world-class inspiration and mentoring from the outside. One source of inspiration was renowned librettist John Weidman, who wrote *Assassins* and *Pacific Overtures*, and, Miranda said, "has wrestled history to the stage about as well as anyone who's ever done it . . . And I emailed Weidman and said, 'I'm getting really daunted by this prospect.' And he said, 'Just keep your head down and write.'"

Miranda also called on Broadway legend Stephen Sondheim. Miranda says:

> *If something I feel like is really ready—I know how valuable that guy's time is. So when I email him . . . I'm asking really specific questions. I'm not here to be like, "Hey, pat me on the back and tell me how good this is." I'm like: "I need help. I have this, this, this, and this." So I go to him—it's like climbing the mountain to go to him and talk to him about the stuff that's really important, stuff that he would get—because he's done the work. He's gone up the hill and gotten the tablets so many times, and it's a lonely road."*

Hamilton was a step process, a groundbreaking innovation that started as anything but. Miranda read the biography in 2004 and first thought "mixtape." He did not start writing for another four years. It was in May 2009 that he performed what would become the musical's opening number before an audience that included President Obama and the First Lady—a full six years before its Broadway debut. In 2012, he staged a concert production of the songs for Lincoln Center's American Songbook series, presenting as "The Hamilton Mixtape."

Meanwhile, the composer-lyricist waded into Chernow's source materials, reading Hamilton's letters and published works as he continued to develop the language and tempo of a longer musical. He visited sites all over New York City where events took place, and even composed some of the musical in the mansion where Aaron Burr once lived and Washington had held some of his first cabinet meetings.

Only gradually did it begin to morph into a Broadway show, first in workshops and then at the Public Theater—all before becoming an "overnight success" on Broadway.

The process of creation throughout involved a circular feedback process, one where Miranda could test ideas and reshape them based on his team's, performers', and audience reactions. But within this collaborative process, Miranda carefully reserved personal creative time. "What I'd do is write at the piano until I had something I like," he said. "I'd make a loop of it and put it in my headphones and then walk around until I had the lyrics." Neighbors could not know it at the time, of course, but the guy with the headphones walking the dog and talking to himself—that was an entrepreneur at work.

Manuel also relied on his wife, Vanessa, to create the "white spaces" so essential to his creative process. "*Hamilton* was written in Mexico, Spain, Nevis, Sagaponack, St. Croix, Puerto Rico, the Dominican Republic—long trips where Vanessa would take me there and then leave me alone to write while she explored."

Always, however, Miranda would return for group feedback, validation, and new ideas. "I'm fine with sitting alone," he says. "Writing *Hamilton* was six years of sitting alone. But—the payoff is I get to go into a room with Tommy Kail, and I get to play it for him, and then he's got three ideas on how to make it even better. And then Alex has three more ideas on how to make it better. And then Andy's going to know how to stage it. So there's this 'show and tell.'"

In the end, Miranda's *Hamilton* is a testament to community. "Working with other people makes you smarter," he said. "We elevate each other."

INNOVATION: CONNECTING THE DOTS

One of the great entrepreneurial ambiguities is that innovation—the really *new* stuff—honors, borrows from, and sometimes sits squarely in the midst of tradition—the really old stuff. In the case of *Hamilton*, Miranda was able to "disrupt" and galvanize the American musical because he was so conversant in its history. "Lin knows where musical theatre comes from," Sondheim says, "and he cares about where it comes from."

The connected dots leading to *Hamilton*'s brilliance are too numerous to describe completely, but Miranda and his team have noted the following:

- The musical *Rent*, itself a show that upended Broadway, gave Miranda permission to write musical theater about the present, about what he knew. He called it "the starter pistol" for his career.

- A show about Alexander Hamilton is written, ironically, from Aaron Burr's perspective—a technique pioneered in several Broadway shows: Judas narrates *Jesus Christ, Superstar*, for example, and Che narrates *Evita*.

- Miranda studied 1980's *Les Misérables* to determine how best to reintroduce themes in Hamilton. Theatergoers sometimes hear the closing number in Act I of *Les Misérables* in its *Hamilton* counterpart.

The music is also full of "connected dots" to the past. "You'll Be Back," thanks to Lacamoire's talent, pays homage to the Beatles." A kinetic Hamilton tends to be associated musically with the drums, while George Washington performs with the Wurlitzer; "It's an electric piano. Ray Charles used it a lot," Lacamoire says. "It has a vintage feel to it, an older feel, which is Washington—that earthy, organic stature." Hamilton's "My Shot" has parallels with Tony's *West Side Story* edition of "Something's Coming." Aaron Burr advises Hamilton with a piece reflective of 1949's *South Pacific*. The concluding song from Hamilton's wife, Eliza, was inspired by Caroline's last moment in the Broadway show *Caroline, or Change*. The Schuyler sisters' "Helpless" plays off Beyoncé, and their harmonies off the female R&B group that she fronted, Destiny's Child. The "Duel Commandments" riffs off the "Ten Crack Commandments" of deceased rapper Notorious B.I.G.

In fact, Miranda saw connections between Alexander Hamilton and rappers Notorious B.I.G. and Tupac Shakur in a way few others could. All three men were brilliant with words. All three were pugnacious and battle-ready. And all three were tragically shot to death. "The idea of hip-hop being the music of the revolution appealed to me immensely," Miranda said. "It felt right."

Hamilton's innovations transcend the purely musical, however. Having America's first black president experience a show where a person of color plays George Washington takes a satisfying swipe at the nineteenth-century minstrel show, where white performers played racist stereotypes in blackface. This thoroughly modern twist, alongside Hamilton's featured immigrant roots, were just two elements that suggest to *Hamilton's* audience that there might be more than one history of America worth remembering.

The entrepreneurial lesson is that Miranda innovates radically, but with a steady grasp of traditional artistic forms. His ability to draw from both musical theater and pop music, one friend noted, "is inseparable from the fact that he loves both forms—he's not being a tourist when he visits one or the other, but he's deeply embedded in both of them." His ability to connect things, Steve Jobs might agree, is not a function of market research or due diligence but of life experience.

DELIVERING GENIUS

Hamilton's opening night on Broadway was a sensation. But then—after the reviews were clipped and the parties over—the show had to be repeated. Night after night. Dance after dance. Rap after rap. Even when performers and musicians were tired, bored, or not feeling a hundred percent. And the stakes were high, because each performance brought a new audience with overflowing expectations about the show's brilliance.

Delivering innovation can resemble an assembly line, the reliable yet inspired delivery of an experience that can feel at odds with the highly creative process that precedes it. Success at this stage involves excellence in organization—building habits and consistent process, obsessing about quality, and inspiring people to do the same thing virtually the same way, day after day. It has become a recognized theme in today's entrepreneurial world, the idea that delivering a product to scale is every bit as important as conceiving and launching that product. It sometimes explains why dazzling inventors fail to become successful entrepreneurs. To pit management against entrepreneurship, Peter Drucker once wrote, is "like saying that the fingering hand and the bow hand of the violinist are 'adversaries' or 'mutually exclusive.' Both are always needed and at the same time. And both have to be coordinated and work together."

Miranda views performance as a craft that requires focused attention. It is not unlike the way McDonald's feels about every single meal it serves, or Amazon about each order it fulfills. When asked during the show's first year what he worried about most, it was clear that Miranda's role as a creative disrupter had shifted. "The most important thing for me," the composer said, "is meeting those expectations every night." Costar Leslie Odom Jr., the show's original Aaron Burr, says, "I want to know that I'm gonna knock 'em dead every night . . . When you came on Wednesday, you didn't care that we were great on Tuesday . . . You want to see your Wednesday night show as good as we did it for the president and Oprah and Beyoncé and Jay Z."

This attention to performance is perhaps best summed up by Chris Jackson, who played George Washington in the original Broadway musical.

When Jackson addressed the prayer circle every night before the show, he said to his fellow performers something like, "Let's agree that for the next two and a half hours, this is the most important thing we'll do in our lives." For a member of the audience who might have waited years for a ticket and whose expectations could not be any higher, this commitment is the way a community of entrepreneurs ultimately translates a decade of innovation and unrelenting work into an evening of unsurpassed delight.

LEAVING THE BAR

Half the chairs were already neatly stacked on tables. A bucket and mop had been rolled out to the middle of the barroom. It was very late, and there was not going to be "one more story" if the waitstaff could help it.

"I was thinking about what I would tell my team tomorrow, what lessons I learned from tonight's stories," said one of the entrepreneurs, chatting with a group headed to the exit. "One giant takeaway for me," he decided, "is that it's great if you have transcendent technology, but sometimes you just need to get the Founding Fathers rapping." He smiled. "I think that's a good reminder of what Schumpeter meant: The novel combination of two *existing* ideas can change the world."

The bouncer seemed pleased by that comment as he held the door for patrons.

"And innovation is everywhere," another guest said. "It might mean a new technology for building shovels or automobiles, or new data applied to finding a trusted building contractor, or," he chuckled, "knowing where to locate rat infestations in a city. But it might also mean bringing insurance products to underserved communities," remembering John Merrick, "or combining three or four musical styles into something brand new, like King Bolden did in New Orleans."

"Agreed," added another, thinking about Alfred Sloan's focus on consumer credit, brand architecture, and his concept of GM's annual model change. "If we only think about entrepreneurship as the latest technology start-up, we're completely missing some of the most powerful 'novel combinations' going on around us."

The group was quiet, thinking about all the stories they had heard that evening. "I guess I learned that innovation is a good start," a young entrepreneur added, "but there's no surviving a flawed or broken business model." Several thought back to Eli Whitney's marvelous cotton gin and the abject misery it had caused its inventor, and the difficulty Jason Jacobs had faced pivoting from a runners' community to a "health graph."

"I wonder," another said as he tried to get the opening song from *Hamilton* out of his head, "if there's any other important lesson I should share tomorrow with my leadership team?"

The bouncer began to reply but then thought better of it, saying his good-byes as the last of the entrepreneurs headed into the night. This was a remarkable group, he thought. They'd figure it out.

* * *

There will probably never be a barroom of entrepreneurs as enchanted as the one we've just departed. The magic comes, in part, from the creation of a shared history of American innovation across personalities, industries, and eras that can both teach and inspire. The magic also derives from the grand themes that emerged during the evening—mechanization, mass production, consumerism, sustainability, and digitization—that build upon one another and unite eras. And always running alongside, social entrepreneurs in America work their own special magic in creating innovations just as powerful as those of their commercial and technology peers.

The barroom conversation also teaches that no single story is as powerful as the sum of all the stories. There is a fable, a funny reminder, about a scientist who published an astonishing study concerning the behavior of rats. When a colleague challenged his conclusions, the scientist dragged out his voluminous and impressive records, saying, "Here they are!" And then, pointing to a tiny cage in the corner, he beamed, "And there's *the rat!*" For living entrepreneurs, the astonishing "study" inevitably appears in the guise of the latest best seller about a brilliant entrepreneur and his or her unique formula for achieving success.

The guests in our virtual barroom would undoubtedly agree that there is no single formula, no one entrepreneur with a lock on genius. The reason, economist and bouncer Joseph Schumpeter reminds us, is that innovation is a "leap-like change of the norm" with "no strictly continuous path." In other words, it's *disruptive*, and that makes it erratic and unpredictable. Sensible entrepreneurs understand that exposure to a broad sweep of business history is the best preparation to launch (and survive) their own leap-like change. Knowledge comes from perspective, wisdom from synthesis. There is no one "rat" we can rely on for all the answers, no matter how brilliant his or her story.

Thinking back to my evening in Boston, armed now with twenty-five stories of disposable razor blades and company towns, rooftop gardens and cybersecurity, I would reinforce the three principles synthesized from our barroom stories. First, successful entrepreneurs never stop building and cultivating community. Second, they focus obsessively on the health of their business model. And third, they are unafraid to think expansively about innovation, looking well beyond the day's dominant narrative.

It is the first principle that is the most important lesson, however, and the ironclad takeaway.

Bill James was once asked what he learned about success from his work consulting in Major League Baseball. "The most surprising thing," he said, "was an understanding of how many people contribute to a championship. And it literally is impossible to explain to an outsider how many people it requires doing how many different jobs at a high level in order for a baseball team to win a World Championship and the number of little streams that feed into that river," he concluded is "almost incalculable."

Likewise, our stories suggest that each river of entrepreneurial success is fed by an incalculable number of little streams. These streams flow from the talent, resources, wisdom, and luck generated by the community each entrepreneur works to assemble. Our virtual barroom of entrepreneurs, encompassing three centuries and delivering innovations as different as the cotton gin and *Hamilton*, would undoubtedly endorse this truth: the stronger the community, the greater the chances for success.

ACKNOWLEDGMENTS

T his book was made possible by the entrepreneurs willing to share their stories with me, including Brenna Berman, Jean Brownhill, David Bruemmer, Kate Cincotta, Guy Filippelli, Brent Grinna, Will Housh, Jason Jacobs, Kevin Ness, Viraj Puri, Emily Rochon, Blake Sabatinelli, Holly Schmidt, Micah Tindor, Marius Ursache, and Meghan Winegrad. Early conversations with start-up CEO Jessica Angell were especially helpful in shaping the book's narrative. This is a group of talented business leaders that understands what it means to build community.

Two of my business school professors at Harvard, Richard S. Tedlow, the Class of 1949 Professor of Business Administration, Emeritus, and Daniel Isenberg, currently adjunct professor at Columbia Business School and author of *Worthless, Impossible, and Stupid: How Contrarian Entrepreneurs Create and Capture Extraordinary Value*, were both encouraging and generous with their time and in sharing materials. Mike Roberts, my section-mate from HBS '83, went on to serve as the executive director of the Arthur Rock Center for Entrepreneurship. He reviewed a draft of this manuscript and made several insightful suggestions.

I also shared an early version of the material on Willis Carrier and air-conditioning with Bernard Nagengast, who is a technical historian, author, HVAC&R engineer, and member of the Historical Committee, American Society of Heating, Refrigerating and Air-Conditioning Engineers, and Jon Shaw, director of global communications and sustainability at Carrier Transicold and Refrigeration Systems. Both have an impressive knowledge of the history and technology of the air-conditioning industry, and both were gracious and helpful with their ideas. None of these friends and scholars bears any responsibility for my conclusions or for shortcomings in the text.

Freelance editor Martha Bustin was a supportive and encouraging partner, often turning my first drafts into English. Thanks also to family and friends willing to read and offer suggestions, including my talented sister, Elizabeth Ransley, fellow WBRU director and Zildjian advisor Jerry Hubeny, friends Pembroke and Bill Kyle (to whom we also owe eternal thanks for securing our *Hamilton* tickets), and HBS classmate Bud Rockhill. Special thanks to Alexandria Dolph for her research assistance on the history of the US patent office.

Gregg Tripoli, executive director of the Onondaga Historical Association, gave me my first taste of Mary Elizabeth chocolate and introduced me to Mary Elizabeth Sharpe's son, Henry D. Sharpe Jr., and his wife, Peggy. They were gracious in hosting me one afternoon in their home, where I was able to peruse Mary Elizabeth's personal photo book. Both the Sharpes and Gregg provided helpful comments and suggestions on the draft. Thanks also to the Schlesinger Library at Radcliffe for the use of the incredible interview conducted with Mary Elizabeth in 1979, when she was a sprightly ninety-five years old.

Henry Ames, Bill Ames, and Nicole Tourangeau Casper, director of archives and historical collections, encouraged and guided my visits to the Industrial Archives of Stonehill College, which contain the Arnold B. Tofias Industrial Archives (Ames Shovels), including 783 shovels, and the Ames Family Archives of more than 1,500 linear feet of manuscript material. It was a treat to present Oliver's early years at the Springfield Armory at the Ames annual family dinner in May 2015. Henry is a longtime friend and business colleague.

Dr. Greg Galer, executive director of the Boston Preservation Alliance (and former curator of the Stonehill Industrial History Center), also helped me understand the Ames material and guided me in tackling the issues surrounding Eli Whitney. He and I attended a steam-engine convention a few years ago just to see the old stuff in action. Greg and I have carried on what he describes as "a decades-long, multifaceted engagement of disparate technology topics," which, in the spirit of this book, sometimes involved beer. Greg's reading of several sections of early drafts was especially helpful to me.

The late Elaine Varley, town historian for Dighton, Massachusetts, spent several sessions with me, reviewing documents related to Mount Hope Finishing Company, where her father worked for more than forty years as the head of the cotton dye house. Two houses away from Elaine, Patrick Menges provided detail and color about the 1951 strike, when his father was appointed chief of police for Dighton. Patrick is a true gentleman and possesses encyclopedic knowledge about our beloved hometown.

Thanks to Chris Beneke, professor of history at Bentley University, who was supportive throughout, and whose suggestion that I pursue Branch Rickey turned out to be an inspired choice.

Thanks to Luca Bertuccelli, Gordon Beittenmiller, Andy Brownell, Lance Bultena, Tom Chase, Chuck Christensen, Ed Clark, Jeffrey Clopeck, Neil Collins, Tony Dolph, Ash Egan, Matt Fates, Steve Finn, Jon Geggatt, Laura Goldin (and her "Greening the Ivory Tower" class at Brandeis University), Jim Hanni, David and Sean Hartman, Mike Hurton (and our many lunch conversations), Cheryl Johnson, Jon Klein, Jim Knutsen, Elle Lamboy, Jeff Leshuk, John Mandyck, Allen McGonagill, Frank Meninno, Mary Milmoe, Mike Milsom, Matthew Moen, Meredith Nelson, Amy Rappaport, (the late, sorely missed) Jon Resnick, Sandy Santin, Andrew Schultz (brother and steady source of useful, relevant links), Rupert Schmidtberg, Bill Shreffler, Brenton Simons, Mark Strickland, Gayle Sudit, Mike Tougias, Clark Wangaard, Beth Welch, Baiyin Zhou Murphy, and Craigie Zildjian, all of whom made introductions to entrepreneurs, led me to new sources, forwarded relevant articles, provided much needed moral support, or just said smart things along the way that helped to improve the final product. Some may have forgotten how they contributed, but, as anyone who has worked with me knows, I take notes.

Thanks to the incredible team at Greenleaf Book Group, including Karen Cakebread, Jen Glynn, Carrie Jones, Olivia McCoy, April Jo Murphy, Pam Nordberg, Kristine Peyre-Ferry, Chase Quarterman,

Danny Sandoval, and Nathan True. They helped me to gracefully "put ten pounds in a five-pound sack," which an old mentor once advised was impossible. It's not.

While we were preparing this book for publication, the world lost Steven Dodge. Steve hired me out of business school and showed me—a fledgling general manager at American Cablesystems—how a great company puts people first. He invited me to cofound Atlantic Ventures and to join his board at Windover, and he was a valued director at Sensitech. Shortly after my promotion there, I asked Steve if he had any advice for a new CEO. "Make your numbers," he said. "Anything else?" I asked. "No." He smiled. "Just make your numbers." That was Steve, a guy who thought "doing what you said you would do" was fundamental to success, a brilliant builder of companies, and the most important influence on the careers of hundreds of entrepreneurs, mine included. His talented wife, Anne, was an essential part of that positive influence. Steve's spirit runs throughout this book.

Finally, thanks and love to Ned, Abbey, and Emily, who somehow graduated from high school and college while I was researching and writing this book. And most of all, thanks and love to Susan. I would detail her many contributions to my life and work—including the hours and years of beautiful bell choir music she practiced in the dining room while I hammered out paragraphs in the study—but hopefully she already knows.

NOTES

INTRODUCTION

1 **My first company barely:** Unless otherwise noted, all barroom conversations are invented by the author and intended to emphasize themes in the book.

2 **In 1911, the:** In Schumpeter's words, this kind of economic development is the "carrying out of new combinations" that lead to "spontaneous and discontinuous change in the channels of the flow, disturbance of equilibrium, which forever alters and displaces the equilibrium state previously existing . . . The individuals whose function it is to carry them out we call 'entrepreneurs.'" Joseph A. Schumpeter, *The Theory of Economic Development*, New Brunswick, New Jersey: Transaction, 2010 (Rpt: 1934), 64–66, 74.

2 **Whatever their shape:** Schumpeter did not use the term "creative destruction" until 1942. Thomas K. McCraw, Prophet of Innovation: Joseph Schumpeter and Creative Destruction, Cambridge, MA: The Belknap Press of Harvard University Press, 2007, 3.

2 **Capitalism's belief in:** Yuval Noah Harari, *Sapiens: A Brief History of Humankind* (New York: HarperCollins, 2015), 315.

3 **Schumpeter's definition is:** Scott Shane's research suggests that, globally, most people are so bad at launching growth oriented, innovative businesses that the number of business starts is *negatively* associated with economic growth. See Scott Shane, "Why Encouraging More People to Become Entrepreneurs Is Bad Public Policy," World Entrepreneurship Forum, 2008, 2.

3 **To paraphrase a:** Schumpeter's actual quote is "Add successively as many mail coaches as you please, you will never get a railway thereby." See Joseph A. Schumpeter, *The Theory of Economic Development* (New Brunswick, NJ: Transaction, 2010; Rpt: 1934), xix.

4 **There is not:** Brooke Hindle, *Emulation and Invention* (New York: W. W. Norton, 1981), 140.

5 **This vast nation:** Mark Sullivan, *Our Times, The United States 1900–1925: The Turn of the Century* (New York: Charles Scribner's Sons, 1926), volume 1, 34. Alfred D. Chandler Jr., *The Visible Hand: The Managerial Revolution in American Business* (Cambridge, MA: Belknap Press of Harvard University Press, 1977), 240.

6 **By the Civil:** Brooke Hindle and Steven Lubar, *Engines of Change: The American*

Industrial Revolution 1790–1860 (Washington, DC: Smithsonian Books, 1986), 218–226.

7 **The journalist Samuel:** Samuel Strauss, "Things Are in the Saddle," *The Atlantic Monthly*, November 1924, pp. 577–588.

8 **Three of our:** "Elizabeth Arden Is Dead at 81; Made Beauty a Global Business," *The New York Times*, October 19, 1966.

8 **The giant of:** Thomas K. McCraw, *Prophet of Innovation: Joseph Schumpeter and Creative Destruction* (Cambridge, MA: Belknap Press of Harvard University Press, 2007), 267.

8 **A GM executive:** R. H. Grant, "Motors Bring Progress," *The New York Times*, January 6, 1929.

8 **When Sloan retired:** "Alfred P. Sloan Jr. Dead at 90; G.M. Leader and Philanthropist," *The New York Times*, February 18, 1966.

9 **For some, sustainability:** "Expo '74 World's Fair Full Color Official Souvenir Book" (Miami: Seville Enterprises, 1974).

9 **Maurice Strong, executive:** Dawn Bowers, *Expo '74 World's Fair Spokane* (Spokane, WA: Expo '74 Corporation, 1974), 89.

10 **Four years later:** Otto Friedrich, "The Computer Moves In," *Time*, January 3, 1983, Web March 31, 2019, http://www.time.com/time/subscriber/article/0,33009,953632,00.html (subscriber only).

11 **In the earliest period:** John H. Hewitt, "Mr. Downing and His Oyster House: The Life and Good Works of an African-American Entrepreneur," *American Visions*, Heritage Information Holdings, June–July 1994, 22+, Web March 31, 2019, http://www.questia.com/read/1G1-15495012/mr-downing-and-his-oyster-house-the-life-and-good.

PART ONE: MECHANIZATION

CHAPTER 1: ELI WHITNEY: ACCIDENTAL ENTREPRENEUR

17 **At twelve years:** Denison Olmsted, *Memoir of Eli Whitney* (London: Forgotten Books, www.forgottenbooks.org, 2012; rpt: Durrie & Peck: New Haven, 1846), 7.

17 **Friends were perplexed:** Ibid., 11.

18 **The climate is:** Jeannette Mirsky and Allan Nevins, *The World of Eli Whitney* (New York: Macmillan, 1952), 44. Italics by the author.

18 **While attending Yale:** Constance M. Green, *Eli Whitney and the Birth of American Technology* (Glenview, IL: Scott, Foresman/Little, Brown Higher Education, 1956), 27.

19 **A roller gin:** D. A. Tompkins, *The Cotton Gin: The History of Its Invention* (Charlotte, NC: Published by the Author, 1901), 5.

20   **Common wisdom held:** Ibid.

20   **The colonial records:** Carroll Pursell, *The Machine in America: A Social History of Technology* (Baltimore: Johns Hopkins University Press, 1995), 16.

20   **In 1792, two:** "Correspondence of Eli Whitney Relative to the Invention of the Cotton Gin," *The American Historical Review*, Vol. 3, No. 1, Oxford University Press on behalf of the American Historical Association, October 1897, Web April 2, 2019, http://www.jstor.org/stable/1832812.

20   **Raising a crop:** "In 1793, many actually raised short-staple cotton in the hope that someone would invent an effective gin . . . in time for the crop." See Joseph and Frances Gies, *Those Ingenious Yankees: The Men, Ideas, and Machines That Transformed a Nation, 1776–1876* (New York: Thomas Y. Crowell, 1976), 29.

20   **Whitney denied any:** Olmsted, *Eli Whitney*, 14.

20   **However, he also:** Mirsky and Nevins, *Eli Whitney*, 59.

21   **Charles Morris concluded:** Charles R. Morris, *The Dawn of Innovation* (New York: Public Affairs, 2012, Amazon Digital Services, Loc. 5105).

22   **Talbot also offered:** "Introduction of the Cotton Gin—A Southern Patriarch," *The New York Times*, October 20, 1852. Author's italics.

22   **The Hollander was:** T. Barrett, "European Papermaking Techniques 1300–1800," *Paper through Time: Nondestructive Analysis of 14th- through 19th-Century Papers*, University of Iowa, last modified January 18, 2012, Web April 1, 2019, http://paper.lib.uiowa.edu /european.php.

23   **In one study:** Karim R. Lakhani and Lars Bo Jeppesen, "Getting Unusual Suspects to Solve R&D Puzzles," *Harvard Business Review*, May 2007, Web March 31, 2019, http://hbr.org/2007/05/getting-unusual-suspects-to-solve-rd-puzzles/ar/pr.

23   **In another modern:** Derek Thompson, "Finding the Next Edison," *The Atlantic*, December 19, 2013, Web March 31, 2019, http://www.theatlantic.com/magazine/archive/2014/01/finding-the-next-edison/355747/.

23   **Tis generally said:** Mirsky and Nevins, *Eli Whitney*, 66.

24   **He confided to:** Larry E. Tise, *The American Counterrevolution: A Retreat from Liberty, 1783–1800* (Mechanicsburg, PA: Stackpole Books, 1998), 199.

24   **There could have:** Miller has been all but lost to history despite his extraordinary contribution to the development of the cotton gin and America's textile industry. He rests in an unmarked grave somewhere on the old plantation at Catharine Greene's Dungeness home in Georgia. See John F. Stegeman and Janet A. Stegeman, *Caty: A Biography of Catharine Littlefield Greene* (Athens, GA: University of Georgia Press, 1977), 181.

24   **The happy inventor:** Mirsky and Nevins, *Eli Whitney*, 79. This falls under Section 8, the "Enumerated Powers" of Congress, Web March 31, 2019, http://en.wikipedia.org/wiki/Article_One_of_the_United_States_Constitution#Enumerated_powers.

25   **From 1790 to:** Kenneth L. Sokoloff, "Inventive Activity in Early Industrial America: Evidence from Patent Records, 1790–1846," NBER Working Paper

Series (1988), Working Paper No. 2707 (Cambridge, MA: National Bureau of Economic Research), 7.

26   **Change of material:** "Graham v. John Deere Co. – 383 U.S. 1 (1966), *Justia.com*, 2013, Web March 31, 2019, http://supreme.justia.com/cases/federal/us/383/1/case.html.

26   **Short on time:** B. Zorina Khan, *The Democratization of Invention: Patents and Copyrights in American Economic Development, 1790–1920* (Cambridge: Cambridge University Press, 2005), 78.

27   **Do not let:** Olmsted, *Eli Whitney*, 20.

28   **Lyon's gins even:** Angela Lakwete, *Inventing the Cotton Gin: Machine and Myth in Antebellum America* (Baltimore: Johns Hopkins Publishing, 2003), 61.

28   **Toil anxiety and:** "Correspondence of Eli Whitney . . . ," *The American Historical Review*, 111

28   **I think with:** Olmsted, *Eli Whitney*, 21–22.

30   **Thanks to Whitney:** Ibid., 40.

30   **The whole interior:** Ibid.

30   **Finally, the judge:** Ibid., 41.

31   **We cannot express:** Ibid.

31   **George Washington had:** Mirsky and Nevins, *Eli Whitney*, 143.

32   **I have a:** Edwin A. Battison, "Eli Whitney and the Milling Machine," *The Smithsonian Journal of History*, Smithsonian Institution, Summer 1966, Vol. 1, Issue 2, 20.

32   **Whitney later admitted:** Mirsky and Nevins, *Eli Whitney*, 146.

32   **Tench Coxe (1755:** Robert S. Woodbury, "The Legend of Eli Whitney and Interchangeable Parts," Johns Hopkins University Press on behalf of the Society for the History of Technology, Summer 1960, Vol. 1, No. 3, Web April 2, 2019, https://www.jstor.org/stable/3101392?seq=1#page_scan_tab_contents, Document6237.

32   **A good musket:** "Arms Production at the Whitney Armory," Eli Whitney Museum, Web. March 31, 2019, http://www.eliwhitney.org/museum/eli-whitney/arms-production.

33   **Whitney was suddenly:** Olmsted, *Eli Whitney*, 49.

34   **His congressman was:** Morris, *Innovation*, Loc. 2031.

34   **Likewise, Thomas Jefferson:** Joseph and Frances Gies, *Those Ingenious Yankees: The Men, Ideas, and Machines That Transformed a Nation, 1776–1876* (New York: Thomas Y. Crowell, 1976), 78.

34   **He then asked:** Mirsky and Nevins, *Eli Whitney*, 210.

35   **The long-term significance:** Green, *Eli Whitney*, 143.

35   **Whitney fathered the:** Mirsky and Nevins, *Eli Whitney*, 177. Woodbury, "Eli Whitney," 247. See also Battison, "Milling Machine," 23, 239.

35   **Edward Battison, curator:** Battison, "Milling Machine," 9–34.

35   **The revisionist articles:** Carolyn C. Cooper, *Myth, Rumor, and History: The Yankee*

Whittling Boy as Hero and Villain, 2003, Web March 31, 2019, http://www. infoamerica.org/teoria_articulos/rumor.htm.

36   **As late as:** Donald Hoke, "Ingenious Yankees: The Rise of the American System of Manufactures in the Private Sector," *Business and Economic History*, University of Illinois, Second Series, Vol. 14, 1985, 223–235.

36   **Even Woodbury struck:** Robert S. Woodbury, review of "Eli Whitney Armory Survey (CT-2) by Historic American Engineering Record," *Technology and Culture*, Johns Hopkins University Press and the Society for the History of Technology, Vol. 18., No. 1, January 1977, Web March 31, 2019, http://www.jstor.org/stable/3103244.

36   **This controversy was:** Obituary for Eli Whitney, Esq., *Niles' Weekly Register*, Third Series, No. 22, Vol. IIII, Baltimore, MD; Published Materials Division, South Caroliniana Library.

37   **And he ran:** Woodbury, "Eli Whitney," 245.

CHAPTER 2: OLIVER AMES: RIDING THE PERFECT STORM

38   **Forty years later:** Gregory Galer, *Forging Ahead: The Ames Family of Easton, Massachusetts and Two Centuries of Industrial Enterprise, 1635–1861*, Unpublished, Copyright Gregory J. Galer (2001), Submitted to the Doctoral Program in the History and Society Study of Science and Technology in Partial Fulfillment of the Requirements for the Degree of Doctor of Philosophy in the History of Technology at the Massachusetts Institute of Technology, February 2002, 168.

39   **President Thomas Jefferson's:** Henry Adams, *History of the United States of America During the Administrations of Thomas Jefferson* (New York: Library of America, 1986; rpt: 1921), 13. [[boats or bridges]]

39   **A trip from:** Daniel Walker Howe, *What Hath God Wrought: The Transformation of America, 1815–1848* (Oxford: Oxford University Press, 2007), 41.

39   **A letter posted:** Adams, *History of the United States,* 14.

39   **Where a manufacturer:** Howe, *What Hath God Wrought,* 40.

39   **By 1816, an:** George Rogers Taylor, *The Transportation Revolution 1815–1860,* The Economic History of the United States, Vol. 4 (Armonk, NY: M. E. Sharpe, 1976), 17.

39   **By 1820, Oliver:** Galer, *Forging Ahead,* 70–72.

39   **Historian George Rogers:** Taylor, *Transportation Revolution,* 33.

39   **Opened in stages:** Taylor, *Transportation Revolution,* 34.

40   **Digging a ditch:** Peter L. Bernstein, *Wedding of the Waters* (New York: W.W. Norton, 2005), 204.

40   **Exasperated with an:** Wm. Russ McClelland and H. J. Popowski, *Pards: A Novel of the Civil War* (Bloomington, IN: AuthorHouse, 2012), 1–2.

40   **The economics were:** Jean-Paul Rodrigue, "Transportation in the Pre-Industrial Era," *The Geography of Transport Systems*, Dept. of Global Studies and

Geography, Hofstra University, New York, 1998–2014, Web March 31, 2019, https://transportgeography.org/?page_id=995.

40   **By 1840, the:** "Inflation Calculator," Alioth LLC, 2019, Web March 29, 2019, https://www.officialdata.org/1840-dollars-in-2018?amount=1.

40   **By 1840, the:** Taylor, *Transportation Revolution*, 32–55.

40   **Buffalo went from:** Bernstein, *Wedding of the Waters*, 348–349.

41   **The business writer:** John Steele Gordon, *An Empire of Wealth: The Epic History of American Economic Power* (New York: Harper Perennial, 2005), 108.

41   **In 1836, Pittsburgh:** *Agriculture of the United States in 1860 Compiled from the Original Returns of the Eighth Census* (Washington, DC: Government Printing Office, 1864).

41   **Meanwhile, Niles' Weekly:** *Niles' Weekly Register*, from *Portland Daily Courier*, Vol. XLVIII, Whole No. 1,224, March 7, 1835, 77.

41   **In 1828, it:** "Historic Easton Welcomes You: Easton, Massachusetts," The Easton Historical Society, 2013.

42   **By 1860, Americans:** Taylor, *Transportation Revolution*, 79.

42   **The fortunes of:** Winthrop Ames, *The Ames Family of Easton, Massachusetts*, printed privately (rpt: Higginson Book Company, Salem, MA, 1938), 103.

42   **Coupled with the:** Leo Marx, *The Machine in the Garden: Technology and the Pastoral Ideal in America* (New York: Oxford Press, 1964), Kindle edition, Loc 1906.

42   **By the late:** Gregory J. Galer, "Showing Landscape Architects from Around the Nation the Many Tools of Preservation," *Alliance Views*, Boston Preservation Alliance, November 17, 2013.

42   **Likewise, Oliver's brother:** Ames, *Ames Family*, 72.

43   **Established by an:** Derwent Stainthorpe Whittlesey, *The Springfield Armory: A Study in Institutional Development* (Dissertation Submitted to the Faculty of the Graduate School of Arts and Literature in Candidacy for the Degree of Doctor of Philosophy), The University of Chicago Department of History, Chicago, IL, December 1920, Transcribed and edited 2006 by John McCabe, Objects Curator and Richard Colton, Historian Springfield Armory NHS, One Armory Sq., Suite 2, Springfield, MA, 44.

43   **Established by an:** Michael S. Raber et al., "Conservative Innovators and Military Small Arms: An Industrial History of the Springfield Armory, 1794–1968," prepared for the U.S. Department of the Interior, National Park Service, Richard Colton, ed., (Springfield, MA: 1989), Web February 13, 2017, https://www.nps.gov/parkhistory/online_books/spar/spfld_armory_history.pdf, 14.

43   **With improvements over:** Thomas A. Moore and William P. Goss, "The Springfield Armory" (Springfield, MA: 1980), 2.

43   **Once these firing:** Raber, "Conservative Innovators," 15.

43   **Gun stocking required:** Whittlesey, *Springfield Armory*, 173.

44   **The next you:** Ibid., 166.

44   As archaeologist Michael: Raber, "Conservative Innovators," 2.

44   The Springfield Armory: David A. Hounshell, From the American System to Mass Production, 1800–1932: The Development of Manufacturing Technology in the United States (Baltimore: Johns Hopkins Press, 1984), 349.

44   With constant pressure: In 1907, the Connecticut Valley Historical Society dedicated a plaque to David and his sons, "First Paper Manufacturers in the Connecticut Valley," Web March 31, 2019, https://archive.org/stream/exercisesinconne02conn#page/n1/mode/2up.

45   Historian Greg Galer: Galer, Forging Ahead, 3–4.

45   The May 1796: Papers of the War Department 1784–1800, Web March 31, 2019, http://wardepartmentpapers.org/document.php?id=17390.

45   In any case: Bishop, J. Leander, A History of American Manufactures from 1608–1860, Philadelphia: Edward Young & Co., 1861, 487.

45   One aged shovel-maker: Ames, Ames Family, 115.

46   There are lots: Greg Galer, correspondence with the author, January 7, 2017.

46   In 1817, Ames: Ames, Ames Family, 94.

46   By 1820, Galer: Galer, Forging Ahead, 76.

46   By 1837, the: Ibid., 113.

46   In California during: Ames, Ames Family, 105.

46   In 1870, when: "A Day with the Shovel-Makers," The Atlantic Monthly, Vol. 26, Issue 155, September 1870, 367.

47   This brand equity: Dvarecka, Springfield Armory, "Forward."

47   Another time the: Ames, Ames Family, 116.

47   After that, Oliver: Ibid., 117. Also, "A Day with the Shovel-Makers," 374.

47   He was a: William L. Chaffin, History of the Town of Easton, Massachusetts (Cambridge, MA: John Wilson and Son, 1886), 649–650.

48   He also invented: This and all subsequent quotes in this section from Oliver Ames Sr., Diaries of Oliver Ames Sr. (2 volumes, unpublished) covering 1803–1864, written 1839–1863 (with entries 1863–64 by Oliver Ames Jr.), Easton, MA: Arnold B. Tofias Industrial Archives, Stonehill College.

CHAPTER 3: AGAINST THE ODDS:
SOCIAL ENTREPRENEURSHIP IN THE EARLY REPUBLIC

51   By 1815, more: Daniel Walker Howe, What Hath God Wrought: The Transformation of America, 1815–1848, Oxford: Oxford University Press, 52.

51   In 1839, Kentucky: Ibid.

51   When the Frenchman: Michael Chevalier, Society, Manners, and Politics in the United States [1839], John William Ward, ed. (Ithaca, NY: Cornell University Press, 1961), 361.

52   A field and: Lois E. Horton and James Oliver Horton, "Power and Social Responsibility:

Entrepreneurs and the Black Community in Antebellum Boston," *Entrepreneurs: The Boston Business Community, 1700–1850*, Conrad Edick Wright and Katheryn P. Viens, eds. (Boston: Massachusetts Historical Society, 1997), 325–341.

52   **At another time:** William Grimes, *Life of William Grimes, the Runaway Slave*, William L. Andrews and Regina E. Mason, eds. (Oxford: Oxford University Press, 2008; rpt: 1825), 82.

53   **This I found:** Grimes, *Life*, 85.

53   **I found it:** Ibid., 86.

54   **Old Grimes is:** Ibid., 91.

54   **In 1817, William:** Ibid., 97.

54   **Living as a:** Ibid., 101–102.

54   **I "have always:** Ibid., 112.

55   **We get a:** John H. Hewitt, "Mr. Downing and His Oyster House: The Life and Good Works of an African-American Entrepreneur," *American Visions*, Heritage Information Holdings, June–July 1994, 22+, Web March 31, 2019, http://www. questia.com/read/1G1-15495012/mr-downing-and-his-oyster-house-the-life-and-good.

55   **The lower half:** Carmen Nigro, "History of the Half-Shell: The Story of New York City and Its Oysters," *NYC Neighborhoods*, June 2, 2011, Web March 31, 2019, http://www.nypl.org/blog/2011/06/01/history-half-shell-intertwined-story-new-york-city-and-its-oysters.

56   **Downing's "cellar" earned:** Hewitt, "Mr. Downing."

56   **Industry sales in:** Hewitt, "Mr. Downing."

56   **Few knew that:** Michael Batterberry and Ariane Batterberry, *On The Town in New York: The Landmark History of Eating, Drinking, and Entertainments from the American Revolution to the Food Revolution* (Abingdon-on-Thames: Routledge, 1998), 99.

57   **When Thomas Downing:** "Obituary: Thomas Downing," *The New York Times*, April 12, 1866.

57   **Ironically, his grandson:** "Anatomy of a Restaurant Family: The Downings," *Restaurant-ing Through History*, 2009, Web March 31, 2019, https://restaurant-ingthroughhistory.com/2009/02/28/anatomy-of-a-restaurant-family-the-downings/.

57   **By 1910, 600:** Michael Kane, "Why New York Should Become the City of Oysters Again," *New York Post*, June 21, 2014, Web March 31, 2019, http://nypost.com/2014/06/21/why-new-york-should-become-the-city-of-oysters-again/.

57   **By 2019, this:** Jackie Wattles, "Cleaning New York's Filthy Harbor with One Billion Oysters," *CNN Business*, January 17, 2019. Web February 24, 2019, https://www.cnn.com/2019/01/16/tech/billion-oyster-project/index.html.

58   **By age thirty-two:** Julie Winch, *A Gentleman of Color: The Life of James Forten* (Oxford: Oxford University Press, 2002), 75.

58   **Around 1800, Forten:** L. Maria Child, "James Forten," *The Freedmen's Book* (Boston: Tricknor and Fields, 1865), 102.

58   **Forten might have:** Ibid., 103.

59   **He was also:** Richard Newman, "Not the Only Story in 'Amistad': The Fictional Joadson and the Real James Forten," *Pennsylvania History: A Journal of Mid-Atlantic Studies*, Vol. 67, No. 2 (Spring 2000), 225.

59   **Forten was able:** Emma J. Lapansky-Werner, "Teamed Up with the PAS: Images of Black Philadelphia," *Pennsylvania Legacies*, November 2005, 12.

59   **There was scarcely:** Winch, *A Gentleman of Color,* 6–7.

59   **By 1832, Forten:** "Inflation Calculator," Alioth LLC, 2018, Web March 29, 2019, https://www.officialdata.org/1832-dollars-in-2018?amount=1.

59   **He was, as:** Winch, *Gentleman of Color,* 77.

PART TWO: MASS PRODUCTION

CHAPTER 4: KING GILLETTE:
MASS PRODUCTION IN AN AGE OF ANXIETY

62   **Gillette warned his:** King C. Gillette, *The Human Drift* (Boston: New Era Publishing, 1894), 3, 6–9, 42–44.

63   **The introduction of:** David A. Hounshell, *From the American System to Mass Production, 1800–1932: The Development of Manufacturing Technology in the United States* (Baltimore: Johns Hopkins Press, 1984), 1.

63   **By focusing on:** Hounshell, *American System*, 106–107 (Singer), chapter 4 (McCormick).

63   **A generation later:** Allan Nevins and Frank Ernest Hill, *Ford: The Times, the Man, the Company* (New York: Charles Scribner's Sons, 1954), 447.

63   **Where America's farmers:** Sean Dennis Cashman, "Industrial Spring: America in the Gilded Age." Print. Rpt. in *Major Problems in the Gilded Age and the Progressive Era* by Leon Fink, 2nd. ed. (Belmont, CA: Wadsworth, 2011), 6.

64   **Some of America's:** Naomi R. Lamoreaux, *The Great Merger Movement in American Business, 1895–1904* (Cambridge: Cambridge University Press, 1988) 1–13, 45, 107.

64   **Could these enormous:** Frederick Lewis Allen, *The Big Change: America Transforms Itself, 1900–1950*, (eStar Books, 2014; rpt: 1952), loc. 364.

64   **Gillette's plan was:** Gillette, *Human Drift*, xii–xv.

64   **While King Gillette:** Russell R. Adams, *King C. Gillette* (Boston: Little, Brown, 1978), 5.

65   **Gillette himself had:** King Camp Gillette, "Origin of the Gillette Razor," *The Gillette Blade*, Vol. I, No. 4, February 1918, 3.

65   "King," he asked: Ibid., 4.

65   I saw it: Ibid., 6.

65   I could not: Ibid.

66   In 1895, Americans: Randel C. Picker, "The Razors-and-Blades Myth(s)," *Chicago Unbound* (Chicago: University of Chicago Law School, 2011), 230.

66   Others relied instead: George B. Baldwin, "The Invention of the Modern Safety Razor: A Case Study of Industrial Innovation," Explorations in Industrial History, December 15, 1951, 75.

66   From a consumer: Adams, *Gillette*, 22.

66   His biographer, Russell: Ibid., 13, 14.

66   Gillette was both: Baldwin, "Invention," 79.

67   If I had: Gillette, "Origin," 7.

68   He later wrote: Baldwin, "Invention," 95.

68   I am as: Ibid., 82.

69   But those in: Gillette, "Origin," 7.

69   Six months later: Ibid.

69   It was a: Baldwin, "Invention," 92.

69   The plan was: "Wants Roosevelt to Head His Trust," *The New York Times*, September 25, 1910, 9.

69   A simple explanation: Ibid.

70   One associate said: Baldwin, "Invention," 94.

70   The employees working: Anne Bezanson, "The Invention of the Safety Razor: Further Comments," *Explorations in Entrepreneurial History*, May 15, 1952, 198.

70   By 1918, he: Gillette, "Origin," 10.

71   We talk of: Ibid, 12.

71   By the 1930s: "K.C. Gillette Dead: Made Safety Razor," *The New York Times,* July 11, 1932, 13.

71   The median wage: "Average Salary Information for US Workers," Dotdash Publishing, Web December 11, 2018, https://www.thebalancecareers.com/average-salary-information-for-us-workers-2060808.

71   However, Gillette wrote: Baldwin, "Invention," 90.

71   The promise of: Gillette, "Origin," 12.

72   Those who purchase: Ibid.

72   Gillette's promise of: "K.C. Gillette Dead," *The New York Times*.

72   Despite their different: Gillette, "Origin," 10.

72   Nickerson, who had: Baldwin, "Invention," 98.

72   Their Innovative Spirit: Kaitlyn Tiffany, "The Absurd Quest to Make the 'Best' Razor," Vox.com, December 11, 2018, Web December 12, 2018, https://www.vox.com/the-goods/2018/12/11/18134456/best-razor-gillette-harrys-dollar-shave-club.

CHAPTER 5: MARY ELIZABETH EVANS SHARPE: THE INSTINCT *TO DO*

74   **In the early:** Alice Kessler-Harris, *Out to Work* (Oxford: Oxford University Press, 2003), 4.

74   **The wholesale employment:** Alexander Lewis, "Manhood Making, Studies in the Elemental Principles of Success," print. rpt. in *Major Problems in the Gilded Age and the Progressive Era* by Leon Fink, 2nd. ed. (Belmont, CA: Wadsworth, 2011), 26.

75   **From 1890 to:** Mansel G. Blackford and K. Austin Kerr, *Business Enterprise in American History* (Boston: Houghton Mifflin, 1994), 156–165.

75   **By 1910, women:** *Leon Fink, Major Problems in the Gilded Age and the Progressive Era*, 2nd. ed. (Belmont, CA: Wadsworth, 2011), 225–226.

75   **By 1910, women:** William Strauss and Neil Howe, *Generations: The History of America's Future, 1584–2069* (New York: William Morrow, 1991), 239.

75   **Quality was excellent:** *The New Position of Women in American Industry*, U.S. Department of Labor, Bulletin of the Women's Bureau, No. 12 (Washington, DC: Government Printing Office, 1920), 18.

75   **By 1930, the:** James R. McGovern, "The American Woman's Pre–World War I Freedom in Manners and Morals," *Women and Womanhood in America*, Ronald W. Hogeland, ed. (Lexington, MA: D. C. Heath, 1973), 153–162.

75   **This "home in:** McGovern, "American Woman's," 153–162.

76   **Born in Syracuse:** For clarity, I use Evans in the period that Mary Elizabeth is single, and Sharpe after her marriage.

76   **I think I'm:** Unless otherwise noted, all quotes from Evans are taken from transcripts of oral interviews conducted with Mary Elizabeth Evans Sharpe, 1979, by Jeanette Cheek for the Schlesinger Library, Radcliffe College, Cambridge, Massachusetts, provided to the author by Henry D. and Peggy Sharpe, 2012.

77   **At the turn:** "Great Candy Consumers," *The New York Times*, January 25, 1899.

77   **A British newspaper:** "No Poisonous Candy Nowadays," *The New York Times*, March 31, 1896.

77   **A British newspaper:** "No More 'Brandy Drops' for Children," *The New York Times*, May 15, 1894.

77   **Other manufacturers added:** "Adulterations of Food," *The New York Times*, March 4, 1900.

77   **In 1899, the:** "Great Candy Consumers," *The New York Times*, January 25, 1899.

79   **Less a stroke:** "Mary Elizabeth Made Good Candy; Now She's Worth Half a Million," *The Pittsburgh Press*, September 20, 1912.

79   **In the fall:** "Mary Elizabeth—Her Plan," *Printer's Ink*, New York, June 5, 1907, 28.

79   **Everybody warned us:** Ibid., 19.

79   **Open these doors:** Ibid., 28.

80   **The Evans sisters:** "Confidence in Honesty of Buffalo's Citizens," *The Buffalo*

Review, October 30, 1903. From Mary Elizabeth Evans Sharpe's personal scrapbook, provided to the author by Henry D. and Peggy Sharpe, 2012.

80   **By March 1902:** *Union Springs NY Advertiser*, March 6, 1902.

80   **In 1903, Grocery:** "The Most Famous Candy Business in the United States," *Grocery World*, 1903.

80   **With this success:** "Mary Elizabeth—Her Plan," 28.

81   **Trade was strong:** Ibid.

81   **The business was:** *The Story of Mary Elizabeth*, Onondaga Historical Association, 2012.

81   **Mary Elizabeth, the:** Ibid.

82   **The kitchen presented:** Ibid.

83   **In fact, the:** "Mary Elizabeth—Her Plan," 28.

83   **And yet, as:** Elbert Green Hubbard, *Note Book of Elbert Hubbard* (Wm. H. Wise, 1927), 170.

83   **An article in:** "Mary Elizabeth Made Good Candy."

85   **By that time:** Hugh R. Covington, *Financing an Enterprise* (New York: Ronald Press, 1921), 22.

85   **At its peak:** "Mary Elizabeth Tells of Career," *Syracuse Post-Standard*, August 9, 1916.

85   **Sharpe's operations and:** "Mary Elizabeth—Her Plan," 28.

85   **When interviewed by:** "Do Women Keep Their Word?" *Forbes Magazine*, after 1912 but date unknown, Mary Elizabeth Evans Sharpe's personal scrapbook, provided to the author by Henry D. and Peggy Sharpe, 2012.

86   **With a husband:** Correspondence with Gregg Tripoli, executive director, Onondaga Historical Association, November 10, 2012.

CHAPTER 6: JOHN MERRICK:
BUILDING A GREAT INSTITUTION

88   **African-Americans, who:** Herbert S. Klein, *A Population History of the United States* (Cambridge: Cambridge University Press, 2004), 120.

88   **The black American:** Robert H. Wiebe, *The Search for Order 1877–1920* (New York: Hill and Wang, 1967), 58.

88   **Reformer and statesman:** Sean Dennis Cashman, "Frederick Douglass Describes a Legacy of Race Hatred, 1883," print. rpt. in *Major Problems in the Gilded Age and the Progressive Era* by Leon Fink, 2nd. ed. (Belmont, CA: Wadsworth, 2011), 93.

89   **We got into:** Unless otherwise noted, all quotes from R. McCants Andrews, *John Merrick* (Durham: Seeman Printery, 1920), 32–40, 73–74, 84, 88–89, 98, 103–104, 125, 150.

90   **These informal meetings:** Ray Oldenburg, *The Great Good Place* (New York, Marlowe, 1989), 22.

90   There must be: Ibid., 22.

95   Merrick's gift was: R. McCants Andrews, *John Merrick* (Durham: Seeman Printery, 1920), 150.

96   "In 1918," Gillette: Margaret Ingels, *Willis Haviland Carrier: Father of Air Conditioning* (Garden City, NJ: Country Life Press, 1952), 40.

CHAPTER 7: WILLIS CARRIER: MASS PRODUCTION MEETS CONSUMERISM

98   He described to: "New York Chapter Discusses Control of Atmospheric Conditions in Printing Establishments," *The Heating and Ventilating Magazine*, December 1914, 49.

100   Henry Wendt seemed: Newcomen address dealing with Buffalo Forge Company delivered at the "1952 Niagara Dinner" of The Newcomen Society of England, held at Buffalo, NY, on May 6, 1952, Web March 30, 2019, http://wiki.vintagemachinery. org/Buffalo%20Forge%20Company%20History.ashx

100   He encouraged his: "Henry W. Wendt," *The Heating and Ventilating Magazine*, Vol. 26, July 1929 and letter from C. A. Booth, Buffalo Forge Company to Margaret Ingels, July 15, 1950, Carrier Archives, box 92662, 1.

100   Henry would consistently: Newcomen address dealing with Buffalo Forge Company delivered at the "1952 Niagara Dinner" of The Newcomen Society of England, held at Buffalo, NY, on May 6, 1952, Web March 30, 2019, http://wiki.vintagemachinery. org/Buffalo%20Forge%20Company%20History.ashx

101   This system of: Margaret Ingels, *Father of Air Conditioning* (Garden City, NY: Country Life Press, 1952), 18.

101   The installation had: "New York Chapter Discusses Control of Atmospheric Conditions in Printing Establishments," *The Heating and Ventilating Magazine*, December 1914, 49.

101   Carrier himself put: W. H. Carrier, "Air Conditioning—Its Phenomenal Development," *The Heating and Ventilating Magazine*, June 1929, 116. Logan Lewis, *The Romance of Air Conditioning* (Syracuse, NY: Carrier Corporation, 1955).

102   Architectural critic Reyner: Reyner Banham, *The Architecture of the Well-Tempered Environment* (Chicago: University of Chicago Press, 1984; 1st ed. 1969), 295.

102   Carrier, Lyle, and: Architectural critic Reyner: Logan Lewis, memo dated, January 25, 1957, Carrier archives.

104   Meanwhile, the Carrier: Ingels, *Father*, 42.

104   The elder Wendt: Ingels, *Father*, 192.

105   I saw that: Ibid.

105   Both felt wounded: Ibid. [[they could make a go of it]]

105   His secretary recalled: Ibid., 198. [[swiped them from a tavern]]

105   This was certainly: Willis Carrier, "Seven Men Grasped Opportunity," delivered to the Carrier Business Institute, February 1944.

106   The fourth job: Ingels, *Father,* 203.

106   In December 1918: J. Irvine Lyle, "Refrigeration in Relation to Air Conditioning in War Industries," ASRE Annual Meeting, December 2–4, 1918, 376.

106   Looking back at: Logan Lewis, "Fate," a verbatim transcription of an interview with Willis Carrier, done sometime during World War II, where he reminisces about the start of the company in 1915. Lewis placed a cover memo dated June 18, 1964, in which he takes issue with some of the facts and casts doubt as to the authenticity of Carrier's words, Carrier archives, 1964, 1.

106   In fact, a: Ibid.

106   In retrospect, Willis: Margaret Ingels, a memo to the files after clarifying with Willis Carrier certain facts related to the founding of Carrier Engineering Corporation in 1915, Carrier archives, 1950.

107   By the 1920s: *The Weather Vein,* Vol. 3, 1930, 29.

108   This "place is: *Transactions of The American Society of Heating and Ventilating Engineers,* Vol. XIX, Nineteenth Annual Meeting, New York, January 21–23, 1913, Summer Meeting, Buffalo, NY, July 17–19, 1913, 1914, 172.

108   Prior to a: "Cooling the Crowd," *Variety,* August 7, 1935, 23.

109   Unveiled in May: Called "Dilene," it was a transitional step between traditional ammonia and carbon dioxide refrigerants and Thomas Midgely's pioneering Freon, released in 1930.

109   Described as "the: Bernard A. Nagengast, "The 1920s: The First Realization of Public Air Conditioning," *ASHRAE Journal's Official Product and Show Guide,* January 1993, S49–S56.

109   Described as "the: *The Weather Vein,* Vol. 4, 1923, 36.

109   The owner of: *Theatre Cooling: A Restful Refuge, Summer & Winter,* Carrier Marketing, Carrier archives, box 92675, 1925, 10.

109   Long before the: Ingels, original *Father,* 11.

110   In July came: Rivoli Times, 1925.

110   By 1929, 95: David E. Kyvig, Daily Life in the United States: How Americans Lived Through the "Roaring Twenties" and the Great Depression (Chicago: Ivan R. Dee, 2002), 91.

110   Carrier's marketing team: *The Weather Vein,* Vol. 4, 1925, 48.

110   By 1957, an: *Carrier Courier,* July 1957, 1.

110   The 1970 Federal: "The Air-Conditioned Census," *The New York Times,* September 6, 1970.

111   The magazine added: *U.S. News & World Report,* December 27, 1999.

CHAPTER 8: CHARLES "BUDDY" BOLDEN:
THE SOUND OF INNOVATION

113   Jelly Roll Morton: Alan Lomax, *Mister Jelly Roll* (Berkeley, CA: University of California Press, 1950), 68.

113   Frank Walker, the: Samuel Charters, *A Trumpet Around the Corner: The Story of New Orleans Jazz* (Jackson, MS: University of Mississippi, 2008), 238.

114   During the carnival: Nat Shapiro and Nat Hentoff, *Hear Me Talkin' to Ya* (New York: Dover Publications, 1955), 3, 4.

114   As one participant: Ibid., 25.

115   At age seventeen: Donald M. Marquis, *In Search of Buddy Bolden: First Man of Jazz* (Baton Rouge: Louisiana State University Press, 1978), 125. Marquis's work is careful, thoughtful, and the definitive account of the Bolden myth.

115   He was described: Shapiro and Hentoff, *Hear Me*, 36.

115   When Buddy and: Marquis, *In Search*, 44.

115   I remember we'd: Marshall W. Stearns, *The Story of Jazz* (USA: Oxford University Press, Kindle edition), Loc. 696–715.

116   When you come: Shapiro and Hentoff, *Hear Me*, 35.

116   Another contemporary trumpeter: Ibid., 36.

116   Without a word: Frederic Ramsey and Charles Edward Smith (Ed.), *Jazzmen* (New York: Harcourt, Brace, 1939), 5.

116   Jazz historian Charles: Ibid., 4.

116   Another wrote that: Ibid., 14.

116   Yet another referred: Samuel Charters, *A Trumpet Around the Corner* (Jackson: University Press of Mississippi, 2008), 89.

116   From the start: Marquis, *In Search*, 39.

117   In 1925, Bolden: Stearns, *Jazz*, Loc. 680–83.

117   Don Marquis resolved: Marquis, *In Search*, xv.

117   Another shining product: Shapiro and Hentoff, *Hear Me*, 39.

118   Bolden "did not: Marquis, *In Search*, xviii.

PART THREE: CONSUMERISM

CHAPTER 9: ELIZABETH ARDEN:
A RIGHT TO BE BEAUTIFUL

121   A journalist traveling: "The Spectator," *The Outlook*, New York, September 7, 1901, Vol. 69, No. 1, 15.

122   The problem before: Samuel Strauss, "Things Are in the Saddle," *The Atlantic Monthly*, November 1924, pp. 577–588.

122   **To find markets:** Arch Wilkinson Shaw, *An Approach to Business Problems*, Cambridge: Harvard University Press, 1916, xv.

122   **People purchase new:** Earnest Elmo Calkins, "Beauty the New Business Tool," *The Atlantic Monthly*, August 1927.

122   **This is our:** Strauss, "Saddle," 577–588.

123   **The journalist Mark:** Mark Sullivan, *Our Times, United States 1900–1925: I: The Turn of the Century* (New York: Charles Scribner's Sons, 1926), 411.

123   **When Robert and:** Robert S. Lynd and Helen Merrell Lynd, *Middletown: A Study in American Culture, 1929*, "The Twenties in Contemporary Commentary: Consumerism," National Humanities Center, America in Class, 2012, Web April 2, 2019, http://americainclass.org/sources/becomingmodern/prosperity/text3/colcomconsumerism.pdf.

123   **We are urged:** Stuart Chase, *Prosperity: Fact or Myth, 1929*, "The Twenties in Contemporary Commentary: Consumerism," National Humanities Center, America in Class, 2012, Web April 2, 2019, http://americainclass.org/sources/becomingmodern/prosperity/text3/colcomconsumerism.pdf.

123   **Elizabeth Arden was:** "Elizabeth Arden Is Dead at 81; Made Beauty a Global Business," *The New York Times*, October 19, 1966.

124   **From there her:** Virginia G. Drachman, *Enterprising Women: 250 Years of American Business*, Chapel Hill and London: University of North Carolina Press, 2002, 88.

125   **Nearly one-third of:** David E. Kyvig, *Daily Life in the United States: How Americans Lived Through the "Roaring Twenties" and the Great Depression* (Chicago: Ivan R. Dee, 2002), 128.

125   **If loyal and:** Virginia G. Drachman, *Enterprising Women: 250 Years of American Business* (Chapel Hill and London: University of North Carolina Press, 2002), 91.

125   **She is tyrannical:** Margaret Case Harriman, "Glamour, Inc.," *The New Yorker*, April 6, 1935, 27.

126   **She created cosmetics:** Drachman, *Enterprising Women*.

126   **For example, a:** Harriman, "Glamour, Inc.," 28.

126   **In one day:** Harriman, "Glamour, Inc.," 24.

127   **Although she stood:** "Elizabeth Arden Is Dead at 81."

127   **If you read:** Ibid.

127   **In a final:** Douglas Robinson, "Elizabeth Arden's Will Is Filed; Her Bequests Total $11-Million," *The New York Times*, October 28, 1966.

CHAPTER 10: J. K. MILLIKEN:
COMMUNITY IN A MODEL VILLAGE

130   **Knowles had advised:** Burke Davis, *A Fierce Personal Pride*, Butner, North Carolina: Mount Hope Finishing Company, 1981, 23.

131   **By 1916, Mount:** To Establish the Manufacture of Dyestuff Hearing Before the

Committee on Ways and Means, House of Representatives, Sixty-Fourth Congress, First Session on H.R. 702, Washington: Government Printing Office, 1916. At this hearing, the National Association of Cotton Finishers listed 37 companies doing $35 million in revenue (1.25 billion yards of cloth), employing 22 thousand people for a total payroll of $13 million.

131   **Over the next:** Harriet E. O'Brien, *From Grey to Beauty* (Boston: Privately Printed, 1927), 77.

131   **All houses were:** "North Dighton a Modern Village," *Mount Hope News,* Vol. 2, No. 2, July 1922, 10–11.

131   **If the worker:** O'Brien, *From Grey to Beauty,* 77.

132   **Milliken himself lived:** William S. Dwyer, all quotes in this paragraph from "North Dighton a Bee-hive of Industry," *The Fall River Globe,* May 17, 1924.

133   **One feature highlighted:** *Mount Hope News,* Number 2, Volume 4, March 1920.

133   **In 1922, New:** Robert W. Dunne and Jack Hardy, *Labor and Textiles* (New York: International Publishers, 1931), 217–226. Web April 1, 2019, http://archive.org/details/laborandtextiles00dunnrich.

133   **Six years later:** Ibid.

133   **The convoy was:** "Death and Violence Occur in Mill Strike," *Taunton Daily Gazette,* Vol. 158, No. 56, September 6, 1934, 1.

134   **A virtual state:** Ibid.

134   **Dighton resident Patrick:** Personal correspondence with Patrick W. Menges, February 2013.

134   **As resident Harry:** Davis, *Personal Pride,* 44.

134   **One of the:** "Heavy Guard Placed Around No. Dighton," *Taunton Daily Gazette,* Vol. 158, No. 57, September 7, 1934, 3.

135   **One person, for:** Davis, *Personal Pride,* 55.

136   **Residents recall the:** Patrick W. Menges, personal correspondence with the author, January 13, 1987.

136   **One cotton producer:** Dunne and Hardy, *Labor and Textiles,* 46. Web April 1, 2019, http://archive.org/details/laborandtextiles00dunnrich.

136   **By 1931, for:** Ibid.

137   **A crowd of:** Richard H. Daly, "2,300 at Mt. Hope Half-Century Fete," *Taunton Daily Gazette,* June 13, 1951.

137   **He made a:** "Text of Milliken Talk to Strikers," *Taunton Daily Gazette,* August 21, 1951, 3.

137   **Some saw duplicity:** Kelsey Murphy, "The Politics of Paternalism: New England's Textile Industry from Corporate Capitalism to the Second Red Scare," In BSU Honors Program Theses and Projects, Item 215, Kelsey Murphy, 2017, 37.

138   **Milliken made a:** Letter from J.K. Milliken, President and Treasurer, Mount Hope Finishing Company, North Dighton, Mass. to "Our Employees," September 13, 1951.

138   One worried resident: Davis, *Personal Pride*, 88–89.

138   When we located: Ibid., 93.

CHAPTER 11: ALFRED SLOAN:
AMERICA'S MOST SUCCESSFUL ENTREPRENEUR?

141   I was thin: Alfred P. Sloan Jr., *Adventures of a White-Collar Man* (New York: Doubleday, 1940), 3, 4.

141   It is astonishing: Ibid, 18. GM purchased Frigidaire in 1919, scratching Sloan's itch to be in the refrigerator business.

142   I looked upon: Ibid., 43.

142   Ford "had the: Ibid., 74, 75.

142   Right there lies: Ibid., 42.

142   Humanity never had: Ibid., 53, 57.

143   By 1920, Detroit: John Steele Gordon, *An Empire of Wealth* (New York: HarperCollins, 2004), 299–300.

143   In 1895, 125: George S. May, *A Most Unique Machine* (USA: William B. Eerdmans Publishing Company, 1975), 9.

145   Spin-offs tend: Steven Klepper, "The Origin and Growth of Industry Clusters: The Making of Silicon Valley and Detroit," Carnegie Mellon University, Pittsburg, PA, April 2009, Web December 26, 2018, https://conference.nber.org/conferences/2009/CEs09/Klepper.pdf, 8, 17–18.

145   This phenomenon is: Ibid., 8, 42.

145   From 1895 to: Ibid., 7, 8.

145   By 1909 there: *Financing Innovation in the United States*, Naomi R. Lamoreaux and Kenneth L. Sokoloff, eds., Cambridge: MIT Press, 2007, 87.

145   And he recognized: Sloan, *White-Collar Man*, 64.

146   Often the search: Ibid., 80.

146   It was the: George S. May, *A Most Unique Machine* (USA: William B. Eerdmans Publishing Company, 1975), 345.

147   Despite all these: Sloan, *White-Collar Man*, 106.

147   If General Motors: Ibid., 107.

147   The founder was: Alfred P. Sloan Jr., *My Years at General Motors* (New York: Doubleday, 1963), 39.

147   The founder was: Ibid., 42.

147   A giant of: Alfred D. Chandler, Jr. and Stephen Salsbury, *Pierre S. Du Pont and the Making of the Modern Corporation* (Washington, D.C.: BeardBooks, 2000) [rpt: 1971], 434.

148   I believe it: Sloan, *White-Collar Man*, 133.

148   Associates described him: "Alfred P. Sloan Jr. Dead at 90; G.M. Leader and Philanthropist," *The New York Times*, February 18, 1966.

148   I never give: Ibid.

148   Sloan once described: Sloan, *White-Collar Man*, 50.

149   It was a paradox: Sloan, *General Motors*, 47.

149   He would soon: Sloan, *White-Collar Man*, 135.

149   Between 1920 and: Ibid., 171.

150   The hard fact: Sloan, *General Motors*, 56.

150   Middle-income buyers: Ibid., 163.

151   No conceivable amount: Ibid., 69.

151   Sloan wrote of: Ibid., 162.

152   One of the: Daniel J. Boorstin, *The Americans: The Democratic Experience* (New York: Vintage, 1974), Loc. 10572.

152   GM and its elite: Thomas K. McCraw, "Schumpeter's *Business Cycles* as Business History," *Business History Review* 80 (Summer 2006), Boston: The President and Fellows of Harvard College, 2006, 231–261, 267.

152   In 1927 Cadillac: Sloan, *White-Collar Man*, 183.

152   One GM executive: R. H. Grant, "Motors Bring Progress," *The New York Times*, January 6, 1929.

152   In 1918, he: Sloan, *General Motors*, 59. Statistics also taken from appendices in Chandler's *Pierre S. Du Pont and the Making of the Modern Corporation*.

152   By 1929, when: Ibid., 59. Statistics also taken from appendices in Chandler's *Pierre S. Du Pont and the Making of the Modern Corporation*.

152   When Sloan retired: "Alfred P. Sloan Jr. Dead at 90; G.M. Leader and Philanthropist," *The New York Times*, February 18, 1966.

153   Sloan is credited: William Perley, *Billy, Alfred, and General Motors* (New York: AMACOM, 2006), 1.

153   Historian Daniel Boorstin: Daniel J. Boorstin, *The Americans: The Democratic Experience* (New York: Vintage, 1974), 555.

153   GM, in its: Sloan, *General Motors*, vii.

CHAPTER 12: BRANCH RICKEY:
PROPHET OR PROFIT

156   This new "farm: United Press International, "Branch Rickey, 83, Dies in Missouri, *The New York Times on the Web*, December 10, 1965, Web March 31, 2019, http://www.nytimes.com/learning/general/onthisday/bday/1220.html.

156   Rickey's innovation altered: Bill James, *The New Bill James Historical Baseball Abstract* (New York: The Free Press, 2001), 160.

157   One fan described: Lee Lowenfish, *Branch Rickey: Baseball's Ferocious Gentleman* (Lincoln & London: University of Nebraska, 2007), 324.

157   The Rickey brain: J. Roy Stockton, "A Brain Comes to Brooklyn," *The Saturday Evening Post*, February 13, 1943, 24.

157   **He was perhaps:** *Moneyball: The Art of Winning an Unfair Game* is a 2003 book by Michael Lewis about the Oakland Athletics baseball team. Lewis described management's focus on analytics to identify the hidden value of players and assemble a competitive baseball team at bargain prices.

157   **"Theoretically," one sportswriter:** Stockton, "A Brain Comes to Brooklyn," 57.

157   **In St. Louis:** James, *The New Bill James*, 485–486.

157   **What Rickey understood:** Lowenfish, *Branch Rickey*, 354.

158   **All but one:** United Press International, "Branch Rickey, 83, Dies."

158   **One sportswriter suggested:** Lowenfish, *Branch Rickey*, 320.

158   **From its beginnings:** James, *The New Bill James*, 57, 166.

158   **A black newspaper:** Donn Rogosin, *Invisible Men: Life in Baseball's Negro Leagues* (Lincoln and London: University of Nebraska Press, 2007) [rpt: 1983], Kindle edition, Loc. 1760.

158   **In 1941, the:** Michael Stevens, "Leo Durocher: The All American Contradiction," *Front Porch Republic*, October 22, 2018, Web January 2, 2019, Web April 1, 2019, https://www.frontporchrepublic.com/2018/10/leo-durocher-the-all-american-contradiction/.

158   **With black Americans:** Mitchell Nathanson, *A People's History of Baseball*, (Champagne-Urbana, IL: University of Illinois Press, 2012) 78, 79.

159   **Controlling the game:** David Kaiser, "A Troubling Myth About Jackie Robinson Endures," *Time*, April 5, 2016, Web February 12, 2019, http://time.com/4294175/jackie-robinson-burns-landis-myth/. Kaiser argues that it was the owners, not Landis, who banned blacks from baseball.

159   **When asked about:** Larry Schwartz, "Jackie Changed Face of Sports," *ESPN.com Sport Century*, Web February 1, 2019, https://www.espn.com/sportscentury/features/00016431.html.

159   **When it came:** Rogosin, *Invisible Men*, Loc. 1943.

160   **Only when Rickey:** Chris Lamb, "Catcher's Tears Were a Likely Inspiration for Rickey," *The New York Times*, April 14, 2012, Web April 1, 2019, http://www.nytimes.com/2012/04/15/sports/baseball/branch-rickey-found-inspiration-in-catchers-tears.html.

160   **Rickey remained positive:** Ibid.

160   **Rickey himself said:** Arthur Mann, *Branch Rickey: American in Action* (Boston: Houghton Mifflin Company, 1957), 215–217.

160   **This was the:** Lowenfish, *Branch Rickey*, 7.

160   **I'd play an:** John Chamberlain, "Brains, Baseball and Branch Rickey," *Harper's Magazine*, April 1948, 347.

160   **Bill James Agreed:** James, *The New Bill James*, 57, 195.

160   **However, Jackie Robinson:** Rogosin, *Invisible Men*, Loc. 1987.

160   **And at certain:** Ibid., Loc. 1994.

PART FOUR: SUSTAINABILITY

CHAPTER 13: STEPHEN MATHER: MACHINE IN THE GARDEN

164   **As the twentieth:** Allan Nevins, "The Audacious Americans," *Life*, Chicago: Time Inc., Vol. 28, No. 1, January 2, 1950, 83.

164   **The journalist Edwin:** Edwin E. Slosson, "Back to Nature? Never! Forward to the Machine," *The Independent* (New York: Independent Corporation, January 3, 1920), Volume 10, Number 3703, 5–6, 37–40.

164   **Likewise, common wisdom:** Mark Sullivan, *Our Times, United States 1900-1925: I: The Turn of the Century* (New York: Charles Scribner's Sons, 1926), 40.

165   **Senator George Graham:** Robert Shankland, *Steve Mather of the National Parks* (New York: Alfred A. Knopf, second edition, 1954), 4.

166   **Undeterred, Mather wrote:** Ibid., 27. [[moment in the kitchen.]]

167   **The benefits he:** Gretchen Reynolds, "How Walking in Nature Changes the Brain," *The New York Times*, July 22, 2015.

168   **Its name derived:** Adolph Rosekrans, "Hetch Hetchy: Many things to many people," Restore Hetch Hetchy 2014, January 9, 2016, Web January 5, 2019, https://www. hetchhetchy.org/hetch_hetchy_many_things_to_many_people.

168   **A plan to:** "History of the Valley," Restore Hetch Hetchy, 2014, Web November 5, 2016, Web April 1, 2019, http://www.hetchhetchy.org/history_of_the_valley.

168   **The battle over:** The terms can be confusing in modern use, however. See "Nature Without Nurture: Progressives Confront Environmental Destruction," *Major Problems in the Gilded Age and the Progressive Era*, Leon Fink, ed., Wadsworth, Cengage Learning, Belmont, CA, 2nd edition, 2001, 412.

168   **To provide for:** "The Pros and Cons of the Great Hetch Hetchy Dam Debate, 1913," *Major Problems in the Gilded Age and the Progressive Era*, Leon Fink, ed., Wadsworth, Cengage Learning, Belmont, CA, 2nd edition, 2001, 422–423.

169   **We hold that:** Ibid.

169   **He witnessed a:** Paul Sutter, *Driven Wild: How the Fight Against Automobiles Launched the Modern Wilderness Movement* (Seattle: University of Washington Press, 2005), Loc. 1278.

169   **The conscience of:** "History of the Valley," Restore Hetch Hetchy, 2014, Web November 5, 2016, Web April 1, 2019, http://www.hetchhetchy.org/history_of_the_ valley.

170   **With both the:** Shankland, *Steve Mather*, 3.

170   **I have never:** Horace M. Albright and Marian Albright Schenck, *Creating the National Park Service: The Missing Years* (Norman, Oklahoma: University of Oklahoma Press, 1999), 36.

170   With plans and: Ibid., 43.

171   Talking over an: Ibid., 54.

171   He was an: Ibid., 39–40.

171   In his first: Shankland, *Steve Mather*, 83.

171   I thanked my: Albright and Schenck, *Creating the National Park Service*, 46.

171   These parks and: Albright and Schenck, *Creating the National Park Service*, 35.

172   Not many knew: Herbert Corey, "Steve Mather Sells the Parks," *Collier's, The National Weekly*, June 21, 1924, 10.

172   Giving things to: Shankland, *Steve Mather*, 58.

173   Needless to say: Albright and Schenck, *Creating the National Park Service*, 49.

174   One of his signature: Shankland, *Steve Mather*, 72.

174   By July 26: Albright and Schenck, *Creating the National Park Service*, 80.

174   Grosvenor said, "His: Shankland, *Steve Mather*, vii.

174   To others, who: Ibid., 58.

174   His friend Francis: Ibid., 8.

174   From valley to: Albright and Schenck, *Creating the National Park Service*, 39.

175   He has been: Corey, "Steve Mather Sells the Parks," 10.

176   From the beginning: Albright and Schenck, *Creating the National Park Service*, 57.

176   Between 1915 and: Sutter, *Driven Wild*, Loc. 2249.

176   Yellowstone, whose amenities: Ibid.

176   Mather and his: Ibid.

177   In 1955, 56: Charlotte Simmonds et al., "Crisis in Our National Parks: How Tourists Are Loving Nature to Death," *The Guardian*, November 20, 2018.

177   Zion has twenty-five: Julie Turkewitz, "National Parks Struggle With a Mounting Crisis: Too Many Visitors," *The New York Times*, September 27, 2017.

177   An environmental assessment: "Revisiting Leopold: Resource Stewardship in the National Parks," National Park System Advisory Board, August 25, 2012, Web April 1, 2019, https://www.nps.gov/calltoaction/PDF/LeopoldReport_2012.pdf.

177   These are irreplaceable: Jim Robbins, "How A Surge in Visitors Is Overwhelming America's National Parks," *Yale Environment 360*, July 31, 2017.

178   Success will come: Simmonds et al., "Crisis in Our National Parks."

CHAPTER 14: EMILY ROCHON:
GIVING VOICE TO THE ENVIRONMENT

179   The largest enterprises: "The Fortune Directory," *Fortune*, Vol. XCIII, No. 5, May 1976, 318.

179   Of 107 million: James T. Patterson, *Restless Giant: The United States from Watergate to Bush v. Gore* (Oxford: Oxford University Press, Kindle, 2005), 356.

179   With less than: "The State of Consumption Today," Worldwatch Institute, 2013. Also, "Use It and Lose It: The Outsize Effect of U.S. Consumption on the

Environment," *Scientific American*, September 14, 2012, Web April 1, 2019, http://www.scientificamerican.com/article/american-consumption-habits/.

179   **And Americans each:** "The State of Consumption Today," Worldwatch Institute, 2013.

179   **In a fight:** Naomi Klein, *This Changes Everything: Capitalism vs. The Climate* (New York: Simon & Schuster, 2014), 22.

180   **In June 1988:** "From the Editor," *MIT Technology Review*, Vol. 119, No. 1, Jan/Feb 2016, 2.

180   **Time is not:** "High Cost of Deteriorating Environment Is Charted," *The New York Times*, February 12, 1989, Web March 27, 2017, http://www.nytimes.com/1989/02/12/world/high-cost-of-deteriorating-environment-is-charted.html.

180   **It was the:** Klein, *This Changes Everything*, 12.

181   **In 2018, the:** Robin McKie, "Portrait of a Planet on the Verge of Climate Catastrophe," *The Guardian*, December 2, 2018.

181   **It also means:** "Global Greenhouse Gas Emissions Data," US EPA, Web May 31, 2018, https://www.epa.gov/ghgemissions/global-greenhouse-gas-emissions-data. Sources 2010 and 2014 data.

181   **It was really:** "Renewable Energy," *Economist*, April 5, 2018, Web May 23, 2018, https://www.economist.com/economic-and-financial-indicators/2018/04/05/renewable-energy.

181   **It was really:** Unless otherwise noted, all quotations from Emily Rochon, Interview by Eric B. Schultz, telephone, May 16, 2018.

182   **At graduation in:** Green organizations saw the Bush years "as a concerted assault, from the administration's undermining of the science on climate change to its dismantling of environmental safeguards to its support for mining and oil interests." See Suzanne Goldenberg, "The Worst of Times: Bush's Environmental Legacy Examined," *The Guardian*, January 16, 2009, Web May 24, 2018, https://www.theguardian.com/politics/2009/jan/16/greenpolitics-georgebush.

183   **Such rhetoric, Romm:** Joe Romm, "No Bill Gates, We Don't Need 'Energy Miracles' to Solve Climate Change," *ThinkProgress*, February 23, 2016, Web May 24, 2018, https://thinkprogress.org/no-bill-gates-we-dont-need-energy-miracles-to-solve-climate-change-60ac8fbb9e2e/.

183   **Investment in CCS:** Emily Rochon et al., "False Hope: Why Carbon Capture and Storage Won't Save the Climate," Greenpeace International, Amsterdam, 2008, 5, 8.

184   **The organization's solar:** "About Us," Boston Community Capital, Web May 23, 2018, http://www.bostoncommunitycapital.org/about-us. Also, "Sustainability Initiatives," http://www.bostoncommunitycapital.org/programs-services/sustainability-initiatives.

CHAPTER 15: KATE CINCOTTA:
CREATING CLIMATE ENTREPRENEURS

188   When her week: Unless otherwise noted, all quotations from Kate Cincotta, Interview by Eric B. Schultz, Boston, March 16, 2016.

188   At eighteen, she'd: "The Road I Chose and the Car I Bought for the Ride: Kate Clopeck at TEDXMiddlebury," August 18, 2013, https://www.youtube.com/watch?v=hhdmSRcIp9E.

189   I had been back: Ibid.

189   Cincotta stuck with: "Our Founding Story," Saha Global, accessed 2016, http://sahaglobal.org/our-story/overview/.

189   After a year: "The Road I Chose."

190   During her research: "Our Founding Story," Saha Global, accessed 2016, http://sahaglobal.org/our-story/overview/. Green was Phi Beta Kappa from Dartmouth College who earned her M. Eng. Environmental Engineering from MIT in 2008 and her MBA from Sloan in 2011. She is a co-Founder of FINsix Corporation and sits on the Saha Global board.

190   Michel Jarraud, secretary-general: Tom Bawden, "Climate Change: World 'Faces Food Shortages and Mass Migration' Caused By Global Warming," The Independent, December 23, 2015, Web June 5, 2017, http://www.independent.co.uk/environment/climate-change-world-faces-food-shortages-and-mass-migration-caused-by-global-warming-a6784911.html.

190   Some 3.6 billion: Jonathan Watts, "Water Shortages Could Affect 5bn People By 2050," The Guardian, March 19, 2018, Web April 16, 2018, https://www.theguardian.com/environment/2018/mar/19/water-shortages-could-affect-5bn-people-by-2050-un-report-warns.

190   The three million: "Ghana," The World Factbook, Central Intelligence Agency, May 9, 2017, Web June 5, 2017, https://www.cia.gov/library/publications/the-world-factbook/geos/gh.html.

190   Women collected water: Kate Clopeck and Eric Angkosaala, "Empowering Women Entrepreneurs Through Access to Water in Ghana," HuffPost Impact, June 13, 2015, HuffPost Impact, Web April 1, 2019, http://www.huffingtonpost.com/kate-clopeck/empowering-women-entrepre_b_7058122.html?utm_hp_ref=tw.

191   The cofounders secured: "Our Founding Story," Saha Global.

191   The entire village: Clopeck and Angkosaala, "Empowering Women."

191   When she told: "Empower Women Takes More Than Just Money/Kate Clopeck/TEDxAccra," February 15, 2015, Web April 1, 2019, https://www.youtube.com/watch?v=ztDbQZevSiI.

192   One hundred percent: Saha Global website, Web December 28, 2018, http://sahaglobal.org/.

192   Saha's first entrepreneur: Clopeck and Angkosaala, "Empowering Women."

193   **"Our goal," Cincotta:** Kate Cincotta, personal communications, January 29, 2019.

CHAPTER 16: VIRAJ PURI: PLANTS ARE NOT WIDGETS

196   **I grew up:** Unless otherwise noted, all quotations from Viraj Puri, Interview by Eric B. Schultz, telephone, January 11, 2018.

197   **Agriculture is humankind's:** "The State of Food and Agriculture 2014 In Brief," United Nations Food and Agriculture Organization," 2014, Web January 2, 2018, http://www.fao.org/3/a-i4036e.pdf.

197   **Together, these farms:** Jonathan Foley, "A Five-Step Plan to Feed the World," *National Geographic*, National Geographic Society, 1996–2014, Web January 12, 2018, http://www.nationalgeographic.com/foodfeatures/feeding-9-billion/.

197   **In addition, some:** Roger LeB. Hooke et al., "Land Transformation by Humans: A Review," GSA Today, Vol. 22, No. 12, November 2012, Web December 29, 2017, http://www.geosociety.org/gsatoday/archive/22/12/pdf/i1052-5173-22-12-4.pdf, 7.

197   **In 2008, for:** "Food, Agriculture and Cities: Challenges of Food and Nutrition Security, Agriculture and Ecosystem Management in an Urbanizing World," FAO Food for Cities multi-disciplinary initiative position paper, Food and Agricultural Organization of the United Nations, 2011, Web December 12, 2018, http://www. fao.org/3/a-au725e.pdf, 12.

197   **In response, about:** Nancy Karanja and Mary Njenga, "Feeding the Cities," *State of the World 2011: Innovations That Nourish the Planet*, 2011, Web December 29, 2017, http://blogs.worldwatch.org/nourishingtheplanet/wp-content/uploads/2011/02/ Chapter-10-Policy-Brief_new.pdf?cda6c1.

198   **Plantagon sells its:** Adele Peters, "This Underground Urban Farm Also Heats the Building Above It," *Fast Company*, December 6, 2017, Web December 28, 2017, https://www.fastcompany.com/40503488/this-underground-urban-farm-also-heats-the-building-above-it.

198   **In France, Cycloponics:** Leena ElDeeb, "3 Cities That Are Reinventing the Urban Garden," *Progrss*, December 25, 2017, Web December 28, 2017, https://progrss. com/sustainability/20171225/3-cities-reinventing-urban-farm/.

199   **Let's create an:** Viraj Puri, "Innovations in Urban Agriculture," TEDxBrooklyn, December 31, 2011, Web December 29, 2017, https://www.youtube.com/ watch?v=ftV2mYp7Epw.

199   **We were in:** Laura Drotleff, "Gotham Greens Takes Locally Grown Produce to a Whole New Level," *Greenhouse Grower*, July 2014, Web December 29, 2017, http://www.greenhousegrower.com/varieties/vegetables/gotham-greens-takes-locally-grown-produce-to-a-whole-new-level/. [[cleantech/sustainability field,"]]

200   **But in 2011:** "Gotham Greens Reinvents Urban Agriculture," Triple Pundit, October 7, 2016, Web December 29, 2017, https://www.triplepundit.com/2016/10/ gotham-greens-urban-agriculture/.

202   **In June 2018:** Beth Kowitt, "Urban Agriculture Startup Gotham Greens Closes $29 Million Round of Funding," *Fortune*, June 20, 2018, Web July 27, 2018, http://fortune.com/2018/06/20/gotham-greens-funding-series-c-urban-agriculture/. [[development in five states]]

202   **In its opening:** "Gotham Greens Reinvents." [[basil, kale, and tomatoes]]

202   **From 2015 to:** "4 Brooklynites Make Crain's 40 Under 40," Technical.ly Brooklyn, March 30, 2017, Web December 29, 2017, https://technical.ly/brooklyn/2017/03/30/4-brooklynites-make-crains-40-40/.

203   **We use 100:** Steve Dolinsky, "Pullman Greenhouse Supplies Fresh Produce Year-Round," ABC Inc., WLS-TV Chicago, November 17, 2017, Web December 29, 2017, http://abc7chicago.com/food/pullman-greenhouse-supplies-fresh-produce-year-round/2662032/.

203   **We use 100:** "Gotham Greens Reinvents."

203   **But I believe:** Steve Schiff, "Viraj Puri Is on a Mission to Change How Families Eat," *Fatherly*, August 25, 2017, Web December 29, 2017, https://www.fatherly.com/health-science/viraj-puri-gotham-greens-urban-farming/.

PART FIVE: DIGITIZATION

CHAPTER 17: BRENNA BERMAN: BUILDING A SMARTER CITY

205   **And RCA highlighted:** *Fortune*, Vol. XCIII, No. 5, May 1976, 20, 22, 40.

205   **Three years later:** Otto Friedrich, "The Computer Moves In," *Time*, New York, January 3, 1983, Web April 1, 2019, http://www.time.com/time/subscriber/article/0,33009,953632,00.html. Subscriber only.

206   **By the close:** "World Wide Web Timeline," PewResearchCenter, Web April 1, 2019, http://www.pewinternet.org/2014/03/11/world-wide-web-timeline/.

206   **More important, science:** George Dyson, "Childhood's End," *Edge*, January 1, 2019, Web January 28, 2019, https://www.edge.org/conversation/george_dyson-childhoods-end.

206   **These same researchers:** Katja Grace et al., "When Will AI Exceed Human Performance? Evidence from AI Experts," Future of Humanity Institute, Oxford University, May 30, 3017, Web April 18, 2018, https://arxiv.org/pdf/1705.08807.pdf.

206   **When chess grandmaster:** Vivek Wadha, "Is AI the End of Jobs or a New Beginning," *The Washington Post*, May 31, 2017, Web July 20, 2017.

206   **When Ke Jie, the:** Paul Mozur, "Google's AlphaGo Defeats Chinese Go Master in Win for A.I.," *The New York Times*, May 23, 2017, Web April 18, 2018, https://www.nytimes.com/2017/05/23/business/google-deepmind-alphago-go-champion-defeat.html?_r=0.

207   **By 2050, the:** Shin-Pei Tsay and Victoria Herrmann, "Rethinking Urban Mobility: Sustainable Policies for the Century of the City," Washington, D.C.: Carnegie Endowment for International Peace, July 31, 2013, Web March 13, 2018. http:// carnegieendowment.org/2013/07/31/rethinking-urban-mobility-sustainable-policies-for-century-of-city-pub-52536. Also, *About City Science*, "Why Cities?", MIT Media Lab, October 2012, Web March 13, 2018, http://cpowerhouse.media. mit.edu/Public/City%20Science%20Brochure%20Oct%202012.pdf.

207   **Harvard economist Edward:** Edward Glaeser, *Triumph of the City: How Our Greatest Invention Makes Us Richer, Smarter, Greener, Healthier, and Happier* (New York: The Penguin Press, 2012), 6, 7.

207   **More than 80:** "Air Pollution Levels Rising in Many of the World's Poorest Cities," World Health Organization, May 12, 2016, Web March 13, 2018, http://www.who. int/mediacentre/news/releases/2016/air-pollution-rising/en/.

207   **By 2050, cities:** *About City Science*, "Why Cities?", MIT Media Lab, October 2012, Web March 13, 2018, http://cpowerhouse.media.mit.edu/Public/City%20 Science%20Brochure%20Oct%202012.pdf.

207   **The trend of:** Unless otherwise noted, all quotations from Brenna Berman, Interview by Eric B. Schultz, telephone, March 3, 2018.

208   **The Rockefeller Foundation's:** "Six Big Reasons We Focus on Cities," 100 Resilient Cities, 2018, Web March 13, 2018, http://www.100resilientcities.org/six-big-reasons-we-focus-on-cities/.

210   **This position cast:** The Internet of Things, or IoT, describes the network of interconnected physical devices embedded with electronics, software, and sensors that enable these devices to exchange data. [[Internet of Things]]

211   **By sharing this:** Stephen Goldsmith, "Predictive Analytics: Driving Improvements Using Data," Data-Smart City Solutions, November 8, 2016, Web March 13, 2018, https://datasmart.ash.harvard.edu/news/article/predictive-analytics-driving-improvements-using-data-932. [[infestation on record]]

211   **These sets support:** Linda Rosencrance, "In Chicago, Smart City Data Drives Innovation, Efficiency," Tech Target, December 4, 2017, Web March 13, 2018, http://internetofthingsagenda.techtarget.com/feature/In-Chicago-smart-city-data-drives-innovation-efficiency. [[river to elevator inspections.]]

212   **Berman's move in:** UI Labs was established in 2013 to foster collaboration between universities, industry, and civic organizations. UI Labs focused on manufacturing and urban infrastructure, the latter of which spawned City Digital, the organization Berman joined in May 2017. City Digital merged with the Smart Chicago Collaborative in December 2017 to form City Tech. For consistency, City Tech is the organization I use in the text.

213   **What if the:** "Array of Things," 2016, Web March 13, 2018, https://arrayofthings. github.io/.

CHAPTER 18: JEAN BROWNHILL: A COMMUNITY OF TRUST

217 **My parents are:** Unless otherwise noted, all quotations from Jean Brownhill, Interview by Eric B. Schultz, telephone, May 9, 2018. [[child pretty early on]]

219 **But my mom:** The Cooper Union for the Advancement of Science and Art is a private college located in New York City, open and free at the time of Brownhill's acceptance to anyone who qualified regardless of race, religion, sex, wealth, or social status.

220 **For the first:** "Jean Brownhill, "Keynote at Cooper Union Inauguration," YouTube, March 5, 2018, Web June 12, 2018, https://www.youtube.com/watch?v=hvgZhJYR9_4&feature=youtu.be.

224 **Sweeten has raised:** "Sweeten," Crunchbase, Web June 12, 2018, https://www.crunchbase.com/organization/sweeten#section-overview.

224 **We have helped:** "Jean Brownhill Inauguration," YouTube, March 5, 2018, Web June 12, 2018, https://www.youtube.com/watch?v=hvgZhJYR9_4&feature=youtu.be.

225 **Buzzwords like mobile:** Adapted from EverTrue website, Web December 30, 2018, https://www.evertrue.com/company/.

CHAPTER 19: BRENT GRINNA: QUIETLY BUILDING AN AMAZING NETWORK

227 **I remember when:** Unless otherwise noted, all quotations from Brent Grinna, Interview by Eric B. Schultz, Boston, April 12, 2017.

233 **He'd been an:** WHERE was acquired by PayPal in May 2011. Doyle was on the board of EverTrue from 2010 to 2016. [[very cool company called WHERE]]

CHAPTER 20: JASON JACOBS: A CHEERLEADER FOR COMMUNITY

238 **I didn't grow:** Unless otherwise noted, all quotations from Jason Jacobs, Interview by Eric B. Schultz, October 10, 2017.

239 **With the digital:** In the 2018 U.S. News & World Report's "Best Graduate Schools," Babson's MBA program was ranked number one in entrepreneurship for the twenty-fourth consecutive year.

241 **I took it:** Launched in 2006, Nike+iPod Sports Kit had a small transmitting device embedded in a running shoe to track distance and pace.

243 **In fact, running:** "2017 U.S. Road Race Trends," runninguse.org, March 23, 2017, Web November 13, 2017, http://www.runningusa.org/2017-us-road-race-trends.

243 **The sweet spot:** Curt Woodward, "RunKeeper's Marathon Push for Startup Success: 'We're Not in a Rush'," Xconomy, November 7, 2012, Web November 13, 2017,

https://www.xconomy.com/boston/2012/11/07/runkeepers-marathon-plan-for-startup-success-were-not-in-a-rush/.

243   **As we grew:** Harrison Weber, "RunKeeper Drops the Dude from Its Logo Because More Than Half Its New Users Are Women," Venturebeat.com, July 23, 2015, Web November 13, 2017, https://venturebeat.com/2015/07/23/runkeepers-redesigned-logo-drops-the-dude-icon-for-shoelaces/.

244   **Imagine a system:** Courtney Boyd Myers, "RunKeeper Opens Its API Allowing 3rd Parties to Tap into The Health Graph," thenextweb.com, June 7, 2011, Web November 13, 2017, https://thenextweb.com/apps/2011/06/07/runkeeper-opens-its-api-allowing-3rd-parties-to-tap-into-the-health-graph/.

246   **By July 2013:** Paul Sawers, "Data, Smartwatches and the Future of Fitness, with RunKeeper's Jason Jacobs," thenextweb.com, July 6, 2013, Web November 13, 2017, https://thenextweb.com/insider/2013/07/06/data-smartwatches-and-the-future-of-fitness-with-runkeepers-jason-jacobs/. Also, Hiawatha Bray, "Seven Things You Should Know about Jason Jacobs," bostonglobe.com, July 13, 2014, Web November 13, 2017, https://www.bostonglobe.com/business/2014/07/12/seven-things-you-should-know-about-jason-jacobs-fitnesskeeper/GRpxBmtb1jxPT7kqJc9yBM/story.html.

CHAPTER 21: GUY FILIPPELLI:
FROM BATTLEFIELD TO CYBERSECURITY

249   **Big Data is:** Kevin Morris, "Swimming in Sensors, Drowning in Data," *Electronic Engineering Journal*, February 7, 2017, Web April 30, 2018, https://www.eejournal.com/article/20170207-swimming-in-sensors/.

249   **By 2020 the:** "There Will Be 24 Billion IoT Devices Installed on Earth by 2020," *Business Insider Intelligence*, June 9, 2016, Web April 30, 2018, http://www.businessinsider.com/there-will-be-34-billion-iot-devices-installed-on-earth-by-2020-2016-5.

250   **"I was born:** Unless otherwise noted, all quotations from Guy Filippelli, Interview by Eric B. Schultz, telephone, October 3, 2017.

252   **Filippelli could show:** Mark Bowden, *The Finish: The Killing of Osama bin Laden*, Atlantic Monthly Press, 2012, 103.

254   **Within five years:** Berico Technologies, Web September 18, 2017, https://archive.is/20110707224301/http://www.bericotechnologies.com/about/history#selection-1543.2-1551.277. Also, "Get to Know the 40 Under 40 Honorees," *Washington Business Journal*, September 13, 2010, Web September 18, 2017, https://www.bizjournals.com/washington/datacenter/get_to_know_the_40_under_40_honorees.html.

254   **Filippelli and his:** Catherine Herridge, "Inside the Government's Secret NSA Program to Target Terrorists," Fox News, May 17, 2016, Web November 9, 2017, http://

www.foxnews.com/politics/2016/05/17/inside-governments-secret-nsa-program-to-target-terrorists.html.

256   **And in August:** "Forcepoint Acquires RedOwl, Extends Global Human-Centric Security Leadership," PR Newswire Association, LLC, August 28, 2017, Web September 18, 2017, http://www.prnewswire.com/news-releases/forcepoint-acquires-redowl-extends-global-human-centric-security-leadership-300510103.html?tc=eml_cleartime.

CHAPTER 22: MEGHAN WINEGRAD: INTRAPRENEUR TO ENTREPRENEUR

259   **When economist (and:** Thomas K. McCraw, *Prophet of Innovation: Joseph Schumpeter and Creative Destruction*, (Cambridge, MA: The Belknap Press of Harvard University Press, 2007) 71.

259   **Thirty years later:** Robert W. Vossen, "Combining Small and Large Firm Advantages in Innovation: Theory and Examples," University of Groningen, 1998, Web May 11, 2018, https://www.rug.nl/research/portal/files/3183201/98b21.pdf, p. 2.

259   **What is now:** Michael Mandel, "Scale and Innovation in Today's Economy," *Progressive Policy Institute*, December 2011, 1, 4.

260   **The Harvard Business:** Maxwell Wessel, "Why Big Companies Can't Innovate," *Harvard Business Review*, September 27, 2012, and Vijay Govindarajan, "Stop Saying Big Companies Can't Innovate," *Harvard Business Review*, June 6, 2016.

260   **I come from:** Unless otherwise noted, all quotations from Meghan O'Meara Winegrad, Interview by Eric B. Schultz, telephone, May 3, 2018.

261   **In 2006, however:** Form 10-K for the Fiscal Year Ended May 27, 2007, General Mills, Inc., pp. 1–3, 12.

262   **One of Winegrad's:** "Meet the 2017 Emerging Leaders," *Olin Blog*, Olin Business School, April 7, 2017, Web May 13, 2018, https://olinblog.wustl.edu/2017/04/meet-the-2017-emerging-leaders/.

263   **Invented for convenience:** Hollis Ashman and Jacqueline Beckley, "Product Spotlight: Hamburger Helper—Instantly and For One," *Food Processing*, January 4, 2007, Web May 13, 2018, https://www.foodprocessing.com/articles/2007/003/.

263   **By 2007, with:** Annie Gasparro and Saabira Chaudhuri, "So Long, Hamburger Helper: America's Venerable Food Brands Are Struggling," *The Wall Street Journal*, June 6, 2017, Web May 13, 2018, https://www.wsj.com/articles/so-long-hamburger-helper-americas-venerable-food-brands-are-struggling-1499363414.

263   **In 2009, Winegrad:** "General Mills' Hamburger Helper®, Beyoncé, and Feeding American Launch *Show Your Helping Hand* Campaign to Help Fight Hunger," *Business Wire*, April 23, 2009, Web May 13, 2018, https://www.businesswire.com/news/home/20090423005917/en/General-Mills-Hamburger-Helper%C2%AE-Beyonc%C3%A9-Feeding-America.

263   **General Mills and:** Mara Einstein, *Compassion, Inc.: How Corporate America Blurs the Line Between What We Buy, Who We Are, and Those We Help* (Berkeley, CA: University of California Press, 2012), loc. 711–728. [[entire brand category]]

CONCLUSION: A MODEL FOR INNOVATION AND COMMUNITY: LIN-MANUEL MIRANDA AND *HAMILTON*

269   **Scalpers commanded prices:** Jeremy Gerard, "*Hamilton* by the Numbers: Anatomy of a Broadway Blockbuster," Penske Business Media, LLC, September 18, 2015, Web April 3, 2019, http://deadline.com/2015/09/hamilton-by-the-numbers-anatomy-of-a-broadway-blockbuster-1201534240/. Also, Gregory Bresiger, "Big First Year For Hamilton Pays Dividends for Investors," *The New York Post*, April 2, 2016, Web April 3, 2019, http://nypost.com/2016/04/02/big-first-year-for-hamilton-pays-dividends-for-investors/.

269   **One referred to:** Adam Gopnik, "'Hamilton' and the Hip-Hop Case For Progressive Heroism," *The New Yorker*, February 5, 2016, Web April 3, 2019, http://www.newyorker.com/news/daily-comment/hamilton-and-the-hip-hop-case-for-progressive-heroism.

269   **The overnight review:** Ben Brantley, "'Hamilton,' Young Rebels Changing History and Theater," *The New York Times*, August 6, 2015, Web April 3, 2019, http://www.nytimes.com/2015/08/07/theater/review-hamilton-young-rebels-changing-history-and-theater.html?ref=theater.

269   **Investors put up:** Michael Sokolove, "The C.E.O of Hamilton Inc.," *The New York Times*, April 5, 2016, Web April 3, 2019, http://www.nytimes.com/2016/04/10/magazine/the-ceo-of-hamilton-inc.html?_r=0.

269   **By December 2017:** Keshia Hannam, "'*Hamilton*' Investors Have Seen Returns of Over 600% on the Hip Hop Musical," *Fortune*, December 21, 2017, Web January 15, 2018, http://fortune.com/2017/12/21/hamilton-investors-unprecedented-returns/.

270   **In 2019, a:** Emily Price, "*Hamilton* Helps Raise $14 Million for the Arts in Puerto Rico," *Fortune*, Fortune Media IP Limited, February 15, 2019, Web February 27, 2019, http://fortune.com/2019/02/15/hamilton-puerto-rico/.

270   **Miranda neatly summarizes:** "Hip-hop and History Blend for Broadway Hit 'Hamilton,'" *PBS NewsHour*, November 20, 2015, Web April 3, 2019, https://www.youtube.com/watch?v=HAiEVjW-GNA.

270   **The MacArthur Foundation:** Imogen Lloyd Webber, "*Hamilton*'s Lin-Manuel Miranda & More Win $625,000 MacArthur Foundation 'Genius' Grants," Broadway.com, September 29, 2015, Web April 3, 2019, http://www.broadway.com/buzz/182236/hamiltons-lin-manuel-miranda-more-win-625000-macarthur-foundation-genius-grants/.

270   **The Rockefeller Foundation:** Michael Paulson, "Students Will Get Tickets to 'Hamilton,' With Its Hip-Hop-Infused History," *The New York Times*, October 27,

2015, Web April 3, 2019, http://www.nytimes.com/2015/10/27/theater/students-will-get-tickets-to-hamilton-with-its-hip-hop-infused-history.html.

270   **President Barack Obama:** "Patriotism on Broadway," *The Economist*, December 19, 2015, http://www.economist.com/news/books-and-arts/21684118-why-everyone-wants-see-hamilton-patriotism-broadway.

270   **Failure to score:** Erica Orden, "What's Worse Than Getting Shot by Aaron Burr? Not Having Seen '*Hamilton*,'" *The Wall Street Journal*, March 6, 2016, Web April 3, 2019, http://www.wsj.com/articles/whats-worse-than-getting-shot-by-aaron-burr-not-having-seen-hamilton-1457298388.

270   **The Treasury Department:** Robert Viagas, "It's Official: Alexander Hamilton Will Stay on $10 Bill," Playbill.com, April 20, 2016, April 3, 2019, http://www.playbill.com/article/treasury-secretary-to-announce-today-that-hamilton-will-stay-on-10-bill-com-351602.

271   **One fan of:** Jeff MacGregor, "Meet Lin-Manuel Miranda, the Genius Behind 'Hamilton,'" Broadway's Newest Hit,' Smithsonian.com, November 12, 2015, Web April 3, 2019, http://www.smithsonianmag.com/arts-culture/lin-manuel-miranda-ingenuity-awards-180957234/?no-ist.

271   **As Chernow documents:** Ron Chernow, *Alexander Hamilton* (New York: Penguin Books, 2005), Kindle edition, loc. 342.

272   **Taking full measure:** "'Hamilton': A Founding Father Takes to the Stage," *CBS Sunday Morning*, March 8, 2015, Web April 3, 2019, https://www.youtube.com/watch?v=0wboCdgzLHg&app=desktop.

272   **This view became:** "Alexander Hamilton," Hamilton: An American Musical, (Original Broadway Cast Recording), Avatar, 2015.

272   **Hamilton's was the:** Chernow, *Alexander Hamilton*, location 317.

272   **Hamilton's visions of:** Ibid 2, location 359.

273   **The year Hamilton:** "Tu Casa Es Mi Casa," *The Economist*, May 13, 2015, Web April 3, 2019, http://www.economist.com/blogs/graphicdetail/2015/03/daily-chart-5.

273   **Demographers forecast that:** Eric Kayne, "Census: White Majority In U.S. Gone by 2043," *NBC News*, June 13, 2013, Web April 3, 2019, http://usnews.nbcnews.com/_news/2013/06/13/18934111-census-white-majority-in-us-gone-by-2043.

273   **By telling the:** Rebecca Mead, "All About the Hamiltons," *The New Yorker*, February 9, 2015, Web April 3, 2019, http://www.newyorker.com/magazine/2015/02/09/hamiltons.

273   **You're a Latino:** Lois Smith Brady, "Vanessa Nadal and Lin Miranda," *The New York Times*, September 10, 2010, Web April 3, 2019, http://www.nytimes.com/2010/09/12/fashion/weddings/12VOWS.html?_r=0.

273   **I grew up:** "Charlie Rose: A Conversation with Lin-Manuel Miranda," March 21, 2016, Web April 3, 2019, https://charlierose.com/videos/28051.

274   **Daveed Digs, who:** Mead, "Hamiltons."

274   **I can't tell:** "Lin-Manuel Miranda," Theater People podcast, Patrick Hinds and Mike Jensen, episode 21, October 5, 2014.

275   **As Miranda wrestled:** "Hip-hop and History Blend for Broadway Hit 'Hamilton,'" *PBS NewsHour*, November 20, 2015, Web April 3, 2019, https://www.youtube.com/watch?v=HAiEVjW-GNA.

275   **The secret history:** Lin-Manuel Miranda and Jeremy McCarter, *Hamilton: The Revolution* (New York: Grand Central Publishing, 2016), 11.

275   **A Wesleyan alumnus:** "Charlie Rose: Hamilton," May 2, 2015, April 3, 2019, https://charlierose.com/videos/28020.

276   **What Lin is:** Ibid.

276   **Miranda says of:** "Miranda," Theater People podcast.

276   **Hamilton's choreographer, Andy:** Miranda and McCarter, *Hamilton*, 53.

277   **At rehearsal, Kail:** Sokolove, "Hamilton Inc."

277   **One source of:** "Rose: A Conversation."

277   **If something I:** "Miranda," Theater People podcast.

278   **Hamilton was written:** Miranda and McCarter, *Hamilton*, 268.

278   **I'm fine with:** "Rose: A Conversation."

279   **Working with other:** Jeff MacGregor, "Meet Miranda."

279   **Lin knows where:** Mead, "Hamiltons."

279   **The musical Rent:** "Rose: A Conversation."

279   **Miranda studied 1980's:** Mead, "Hamiltons."

279   **You'll be back:** Miranda and McCarter, *Hamilton*, 55.

280   **It's an electric:** Nate Jones, "Nerding Out with 'Hamilton' Musical Director, Alex Lacamoire," Vulture.com, January 13, 2016, Web April 3, 2019, http://www.vulture.com/2016/01/hamilton-alex-lacamoire-interview.html.

280   **Hamilton's "My Shot:** Jack Viertel, *The Secret Life of the American Musical: How Broadway Shows Are Built* (New York: Sarah Crichton Books, Farrar Straus and Giroux, 2016), location 1124.

280   **Aaron Burr advises:** Mead, "Hamiltons." "I'm with you but the situation is fraught / You've got to be carefully taught."

280   **The Schuyler Sisters:** Jones, "Nerding Out"

280   **The idea of:** Jody Rosen, "The American Revolutionary," *The New York Times*, July 8, 2015, Web April 3, 2019, http://www.nytimes.com/interactive/2015/07/08/t-magazine/hamilton-lin-manuel-miranda-roots-sondheim.html.

280   **His ability to:** Michael Paulson, "Lin-Manuel Miranda, Creator and Star of 'Hamilton,' Grew Up on Hip-Hop and Show Tunes," *The New York Times*, August 12, 2015, Web April 3, 2019, http://www.nytimes.com/2015/08/16/theater/lin-manuel-miranda-creator-and-star-of-hamilton-grew-up-on-hip-hop-and-show-tunes.html.

281   **To pit management:** Peter F. Drucker, *The Essential Drucker* (New York: HarperCollins [PerfectBound Kindle edition], 2001), 8.

281   **The most important:** Hip-hop and History Blend for Broadway Hit 'Hamilton,'" *PBS NewsHour*, November 20, 2015, Web April 3, 2019, https://www.youtube.com/watch?v=HΛiEVjW-GNΛ.

281   **Costar Leslie Odom:** Louis Peitzman, "Leslie Odom Jr. Is Not Throwing Away His Shot," BuzzFeed, April 28, 2016, Web April 3, 2019, https://www.buzzfeed.com/louispeitzman/leslie-odom-jr-is-not-throwing-away-his-shot?utm_term=.hmrDxdgZVM#.eu81xQARv3.

282   **Let's agree that:** Miranda and McCarter, *Hamilton,* 59.

283   **There is a fable:** David Hackett Fischer, *Historians' Fallacies: Toward a Logic of Historical Thought* (New York: Harper Colophon, 1970), 109.

284   **The reason, economist:** Joseph Schumpeter, "Development," *Journal of Economic Literature*, Vol. XLIII, March 2005 [rpt: 1932], 115–116.

284   **The most surprising:** Russ Roberts, "Bill James on Baseball, Facts, and the Rules of the Game," EconTalk Episode with Bill James, Library Fund, Inc., January 15, 2018, Web February 4, 2018, http://www.econtalk.org/archives/2018/01/bill_james_on_b.html.

INDEX

ABOUT THE AUTHOR

Eric B. Schultz has spent his career in entrepreneurial and leadership roles, including as senior vice president of Midwest operations for American Cablesystems, cofounder and president of Atlantic Ventures, and chairman and CEO of Sensitech, a venture-backed business twice named to the Inc. 500 before being acquired by Carrier Corporation. Eric served as a CEO-partner with Ascent Ventures, as executive chairman of HubCast, on the board of advisors of the Avedis Zildjian Company and Windover LLC, and as a mentor for student start-up teams in the Brown University B-Lab. His nonprofit historical work includes chairing the Gettysburg Foundation and the New England Historic Genealogical Society.

He is co-author of *Food Foolish: The Hidden Connection Between Food Waste, Hunger, and Climate Change* and *King Philip's War: The History and Legacy of America's Forgotten Conflict*, and author of *Weathermakers to the World*. Eric has a bachelor's degree in history from Brown University and an MBA from Harvard Business School.

Eric's blog is "The Occasional CEO" at theoccasionalceo.blogspot. com where he posts updates to *Innovation on Tap*. He can also be found on Twitter at @ericebs, on LinkedIn, and on Amazon.